FOURTEEN TO EIGHTEEN

D1388359

FOURTEEN TO EIGHTEEN

The Changing Pattern of Schooling in Scotland

edited by David Raffe

Contributors:
Peter Burnhill
Andrew McPherson
David Raffe
Penelope Weston

ABERDEEN UNIVERSITY PRESS

First published 1984
Aberdeen University Press
A member of the Pergamon Group
© Centre for Educational Sociology, University of Edinburgh 1984

British Library Cataloguing in Publication Data
Fourteen to eighteen.
1. Education, Secondary—Scotland
2. Vocational education—Scotland
I. Raffe, David
373.2'38'09411   LA656

ISBN 0 08 030374 9 (flexi)

PRINTED IN GREAT BRITAIN
THE UNIVERSITY PRESS
ABERDEEN

Contents

Acknowledgements

This book uses data from the 1981 Scottish School Leavers Survey, which was conducted by the Centre for Educational Sociology (CES) at the University of Edinburgh in conjunction with the Scottish Education Department (SED). The 1981 survey was funded by the Social Science Research Council with additional funding from the Manpower Services Commission. The CES also acknowledges the continuing financial support of the SED. Like many large surveys, the School Leavers Survey depends on the co-operation and goodwill of a large number of people, including the staff of schools and officials of the SED, for their help in collecting names and addresses, and careers officers, for their help in tracing change-of-addresses. Over and above this we recognise the contribution to our own research of the hundreds of "collaborators" who have taken part in the Collaborative Research Programme, both in their use and analysis of data from previous School Leavers Surveys and in their participation in the formulation of questions for the 1981 survey. We also acknowledge and are thankful for the support given by colleagues in the CES and in the University: our survey staff, in particular Eve Scougall, who supervised the despatch, receipt and coding of the questionnaires; the data preparation staff of the Edinburgh Regional Computing Centre who processed the questionnaires; Joanne Lamb, Cathy Garner and Heather MacDuff, who provided computing expertise in the administration of the survey and the processing and storage of the survey data; and the Edinburgh Regional Computing Centre, for their general computing services. Finally we are grateful to the many thousands of school leavers who took part in the 1981 survey; we hope this book goes some way to justify their efforts.

Additional data used in chapters 3 and 5 were supplied by the SED and the Department of Education and Science; we are grateful to Jack Arrundale, David Braunholtz, Jim Cuthbert and Trevor Knight for their help in this matter. Some of the school leavers' comments quoted in this book are published in a companion volume, *The Best Years? Reflections of School Leavers in the 1980s* (ed. J.M. Hughes, Aberdeen University Press, 1984).

For comments on drafts of some of the chapters we are grateful to David Allan, Jack Arrundale, Jim Cuthbert, Peter Cuttance, Briatl Main, Charles Raab and David Walker.

For processing the almost endless flow of drafts and re-drafts of the chapters we are grateful to Carole Holliday and Kathy Rogers, and also to Margaret MacDougall whose skill in preparing computer-held chapter drafts for the phototypesetter was indispensable. We would like to thank Pamela Armstrong for her assistance, and David Stewart-Robinson (of the Edinburgh Regional Computing Centre) for the use of the phototypesetter, Sheila Edgar for preparing the tables and Chris McKinnell for preparing the figures. We are particularly grateful to Joan Hughes, the administrator of the CES, who has supervised and co-ordinated the proofing of the text, production of the master pages and the compilation of the index.

The responsibility for the views and judgements expressed in this book, and for any errors, rests with the authors.

Chapter 1

Introduction

The purpose of this book

This book is about the recent performance of comprehensive schooling for the 14-18 age group, and about the future prospects for education in the light of current policy initiatives. It describes the experiences of a sample of young people who left education authority schools in Scotland during, or at the end of, the 1979/80 academic session. In the spring of 1981 these young people were sent questionnaires which asked a range of questions about their experiences and attainments at school, their attitudes to schooling, their families, and their experiences of employment, unemployment or continuing education since leaving school. Full details of the sample, the questionnaires and other aspects of the survey are shown in Appendix 1 at the end of this book. Here it is sufficient to note that a large majority of the young people completed and returned their questionnaires. Their answers are the main source of information for this book.

In Scotland pupils transfer to secondary school at 12 and are required by law to remain there until the age of 16. Those who stay on at school do so for a further one or two years. Most of the young people in our study had therefore begun their secondary schooling between 1974 and 1976. These dates are significant. By 1974 about 95 per cent of Scottish 12 year olds entered state schools that were comprehensive in the sense of having non-selective intakes to first year. The young people in this study were among the first to pass through a secondary school system that was almost fully comprehensive.

So the first purpose of this book is to describe and analyse the recent performance of comprehensive schooling, to provide a framework for an evaluation of the system, and in places to offer our own judgements on it. With the experience of the 1979/80 school leavers in mind we ask about the

1

promise of schooling: what do those who provide it hope to achieve, and
with what expectations do pupils or students enter each stage of schooling?
We ask about the delivery: what happens during schooling, what happens
to young people as a result of schooling, and what is their own subsequent
judgement on their schooling? And we ask about the alternatives. All these
questions need to be considered in relation to each stage of schooling.
Moreover, each question may receive a different answer depending upon
which young people the schooling is provided for. "Schooling for whom?"
is an essential question in any discussion of the subject, and its ramifications
provide a major theme of this book.

However, educational change did not cease with the comprehensive
reorganisation of secondary schools. In 1977, while the young people in this
book were still at school, two major reports were published on the third and
fourth years of secondary school: the Munn Report on the curriculum and
the Dunning Report on assessment (SED, 1977b, 1977a). Since then a
feasibility study, a development programme and continuing debate have
paved the way towards the implementation of their proposals (or some of
them) in the second half of the 1980s. Also in 1977 the Holland Report
(MSC, 1977) outlined a programme of work experience and work
preparation schemes that was to become the Youth Opportunities
Programme (YOP); this was in response to a rising level of youth
unemployment, a problem which has implications for schools as well as for
other educational institutions. In 1983 YOP was replaced by a new Youth
Training Scheme (YTS) (MSC, 1982a); earlier that year the Scottish
Education Department (SED) published its own Action Plan for the 16-18s
(SED, 1983b). Schools and colleges must come to terms, not only with the
implications of YTS for their own work, but also with the demand for a more
co-ordinated pattern of post-compulsory provision and for a new approach
to vocational preparation.

The second purpose of this book is to inform the debate about these policy
initiatives. In practice this overlaps substantially with the first purpose
which is to describe and analyse the comprehensive system of recent years.
We hope to show the problems to which the policy initiatives respond, to
demonstrate the continuing dilemmas and constraints that they must
confront, and to comment on the likely consequences of these changes. In
the rest of this chapter we describe the policy changes in more detail; and
explain how we believe that a study of the recent past can inform an
understanding of the future of education.

Fourteen to sixteen

The status of the third and fourth years as a distinct stage in Scottish
education dates from the introduction in 1962 of the O-grade examination

for 16 year olds. Later, in 1965, Circular 600 set in train the reorganisation of secondary schools on comprehensive lines (SED, 1965); an indirect effect of this was to postpone the critical age for selection in Scottish education from 12 to 14 years. Finally, in 1973 the school-leaving age was raised to 16, which meant that pupils ended compulsory education at or around the end of fourth year. Partly as a result of this, the proportions taking the O-grade soared. The original intention had been that 30 per cent of the age group should have a reasonable chance of passing the examination in three or more subjects; by 1976 some 70 per cent of the age group were attempting the examination. Pass rates declined in consequence; and in 1973 the pass/ fail distinction was replaced by five bands, A to E, with the A, B and C bands corresponding to the original pass grade.

It is from this time that we can date the debate over the third and fourth years that continues today. The use of qualifications to select for higher education and employment, and the resulting pressure of competition for qualifications, produced both an excess of pupils attempting the O-grade, relative to the original intentions, and a strong bias towards the higher-status and more marketable "academic" subjects. As a result the curriculum has been too difficult for some pupils and too easy for others, with an even greater loss of motivation among that minority of pupils who are excluded after their second year from the possibility of examination presentation. A non-academic curriculum of equal status has failed to emerge.

The problems are familiar: over-presentation for examinations; high failure rates, even if the "failures" are not officially recognised as such; courses which are of unequal relevance and interest to pupils at different levels of the hierarchy of academic attainment; disproportionate emphasis on the pupils at the top of this hierarchy; and problems of poor motivation, truancy and indiscipline among pupils at the bottom. Similar problems have been diagnosed south of the border (Hargreaves, 1982).

Critics of Scottish secondary education argue that the curriculum is too "academic" for many or all pupils: that over the post-war period a curriculum that had been considered appropriate for a small minority of pupils who aspired to university entrance has gradually been extended to all 14-16 year olds in comprehensive schools (Gatherer, 1980; Gray et al., 1983). The structure of secondary education, with its progressive vertical differentiation of pupils, has created strong pressures for the curriculum to retain its academic bias (ibid., chapter 8). Within the constraints imposed by the selective function of secondary education it is difficult to effect a cure. Among those who would like less emphasis given to the academic objectives of schooling, there is an important division between those who propose a new curriculum for all pupils and those who see the answer in increased selection and differentiation, with the "able" pupils continuing to receive an academic curriculum. One of the most significant proposals for curriculum reform was the Brunton Report, published in 1963 (SED, 1963). Although this did not specifically defend selection, it took as its starting point the existing situation in which 65 per cent of each age group were not expected to take Scottish Certificate of Education (SCE) courses; the Brunton Report's recommendations were largely restricted to this group. It proposed that the "vocational impulse" should be used as "the core round which the curriculum should be organised" (*ibid.*, para.55). It acknowledged the need for safeguards – in particular that pupils should not be prematurely committed to a limited choice of occupations, and that the education should have general value to the pupil "as a person" (*ibid.*, para.63). But it felt that, from the third year, courses should "provide a broad general preparation for a group of occupations associated with a particular industry or service" (*ibid.*, para.58).

The Brunton Report offered a possible turning which Scottish education did not take. The main reason for its rejection was that it presupposed the prior differentiation of pupils. This was unacceptable to many educationists; yet the rejection of early selection meant that all pupils should follow a version of the same curriculum, and given the pressure of competition among the abler pupils this was bound to be a strongly "academic" one. This structural dilemma became more acute following comprehensive reorganisation, the raising of the school-leaving age, and the growth in the number of O-grade presentations.

In 1977 the Munn and Dunning Reports proposed reforms of the curriculum and assessment for the third and fourth years (SED, 1977b, 1977a). The Munn Report outlined a curricular framework for all pupils, based on seven core areas plus options. The Dunning Report proposed that the O-grade should be replaced by a certificate, to be attempted at one of three levels, Credit, General and Foundation. Nearly all pupils would be able to take each subject at one or other of these levels.

It was two years before the SED published its feasibility study (SED, 1979a) which "analysed the implications of the recommendations of both reports" (SED, 1982a, p.1). The study was published, along with *Proposals for Action* (SED, 1979b), before the general election which brought a change of government and some consequent delay as the new administration reviewed the proposals. In fact the effects of this change were felt more in terms of the resources that were to be made available for the reforms than in terms of their direction; and in March 1980 a new document appeared setting out details of the government's development programme (SED, 1980a). This outlined the arrangement for carrying forward detailed plans for the new curriculum and assessment structure to a point where the Secretary of State could make a decision in 1983 on the viability of the whole scheme. This programme involved curriculum development, with particular emphasis on the innovatory Foundation courses in English, maths and science which were to be piloted in some 200 schools, together with detailed discussions of the assessment and certification implications of the reforms and consideration of the in-service training provision that would be required. Research studies commissioned under this brief were mostly concerned with providing support for the development work. Before the deadline arrived the SED published a consultative paper, *The Munn and Dunning Reports: Framework for Decision* (SED, 1982a), which reported on the work of the development programme and set out "implementation proposals" on which comment was invited. This document was important in that it spelt out in detail how the new system would operate and laid down a timetable for its implementation up to 1989 – ten years after the publication of the feasibility study. Finally, in April 1983 Circular 1093 (SED, 1983c) announced that the "new system", as outlined in *Framework for Decision*, would be implemented "as soon as possible".

The aim of the reformers was to create a common curriculum framework for the 14-16 stage, but one which would still allow pupils to develop their "interests and aptitudes", and a common scheme of assessment which would recognise the wide range of achievement among 16 year olds. Thus the core curriculum advocated by Munn could be followed at a variety of levels, as could the optional courses which gave pupils additional scope for choice (some choice being offered to all within the core); and the Foundation, General and Credit courses would each be accorded public recognition on the certificate, after a common process of assessment. But many problems remained: for example, would it really be possible to develop courses at each "level" with such a degree of overlap that pupils could readily transfer from one level to another in either direction? Would a common scheme of assessment prove feasible and acceptable? And – most crucially – would the new Foundation courses, which at last were to provide public recognition and support for the type of work which had always been the Cinderella of school curriculum planning, be seen as worthwhile by their clients and by the public at large?

The significance of the reforms for the curriculum of the third and fourth years, and the working out of the scheme from the 1977 reports to the 1983 proposals, will be discussed in chapter 3.

Sixteen to eighteen

The debate about post-compulsory schooling has been conducted within two alternative frames of reference. The first of these, which dominated the debate at least until the late 1970s, has attempted to resolve the internal structural dilemmas of a traditional academic conception of schooling. In this conception the modal student stayed on after 16, completed a five-subject course at 17, and then progressed to higher education, possibly after spending an extra year in school for a less pressured and more mature form of study. Such issues as the vocational relevance of post-compulsory schooling, or its relation to alternative institutional sources of post-16 provision, have not arisen within this frame of reference. In recent years its main concerns have been the type of pedagogy, the number of examinations and the pacing of courses. The examination system has been at the centre of the debate.

The enduring feature of Scottish post-compulsory education is the Higher examination. This is the main qualification for entrance to higher education in Scotland. It is normally taken in fifth year, at age 17, although nearly half of fifth-year pupils stay on for a sixth year, and most of these either attempt new Highers or re-sit old ones. Highers have been in their present form since 1962; pupils previously took a combination of Highers and Lowers, typically five subjects altogether, in their fifth year. In 1959 a Working Party recommended that Lowers should be replaced by a new O-grade exam, to be taken in fourth year (at 16); the "normal" fifth year was therefore to be filled by Highers only, with five subjects continuing as the norm (SED, 1959). These recommendations were implemented in 1962.

With the introduction of the O-grade, the numbers staying on to 16 rose rapidly. The numbers staying on to 17 also rose, and by the early 1970s about 30 per cent of each year group attempted Highers. An Advisory Council Report in 1960 argued that one or two Highers passes should be a legitimate objective of a large number of fifth-year pupils; this was one of the reasons for maintaining an examination at 17 years (SED, 1960). Proposals for an "Advanced grade" at 18 years were rejected due to widespread opposition, especially from teachers. However in 1968 a new Certificate of Sixth Year Studies (CSYS) was introduced, for pupils who had passed Highers in the relevant subjects. The CSYS was designed to foster independent study, something for which the examination-dominated structure of fourth and fifth years allowed little opportunity. However, the pressure of competition for entrance to higher education has meant that a majority of sixth-year pupils has felt it necessary to re-sit old Highers or attempt new ones; only the most successful pupils have been able to devote the year exclusively to CSYS. This has led to a further diversification of the range of provision in post-fourth-year schooling.

Competitive pressure and the examination system lie at the root of most current problems concerning SCE courses in post-compulsory schooling. Many commentators diagnose "over-examination" – with many pupils taking examinations in three consecutive years and with the fifth-year

Highers course effectively reduced to little more than two terms. This in turn reinforces restrictive styles of teaching and learning, with the emphasis on dictated and duplicated notes supplied by the teachers, and with little opportunity for private reading or group discussion. The pressure of competition for places in higher education has meant that many pupils have opted to continue in this regime in the sixth year and not take CSYS courses which pupils tend to find intrinsically more satisfying.

It is perhaps symbolic that of all the areas of education covered in this book this alone is not the subject of an explicit policy initiative. For this is the holy ground of Scottish education; those who would enter it must tread carefully, or risk charges of sacrilege or heresy. Early in 1983 the Inspectorate published a report on *Teaching and Learning in the Senior Stages of the Scottish Secondary School* (SED, 1983a), which diagnosed the problems described above. It did not propose any specific solutions but dropped delicate hints that a two-year Highers course might be more appropriate, and cast some doubt over the viability of CSYS. It remains to be seen whether these comments will mature into specific proposals for policy reform; perhaps events will be allowed to run their natural course, and the prolongation of the Highers course and the weak position of CSYS will continue as a consequence of unco-ordinated decisions by schools and students.

In the last few years a second and broader frame of reference has emerged for the continuing debate about post-compulsory schooling. Several factors have contributed to this change. The first is the decline in school rolls. The number of pupils in Scottish education authority secondary schools reached a plateau of about 410,000 in 1978 and 1979. Thereafter it began to decline, towards a projected trough of 290,000 in 1991. The decline will not be evenly spread; some school catchments, especially in the cities, are likely to be affected more than others. The fall in rolls will make it harder for many schools to offer an adequate range of post-compulsory courses, and may necessitate more co-operation among schools and between schools and colleges of further education.

Second, the rise in youth unemployment has also had an effect on post-compulsory schooling. In the late 1970s youth unemployment was already high by post-war standards, but along with adult unemployment it rose sharply again after 1979 (Raffe, 1983a). This in turn provoked an increase in the proportion of 16 year olds staying on into post-compulsory schooling (SED, 1982b). This trend is very recent; the 1980 leavers in this study who left from S5 or S6 were the last to decide to stay on before the trend became pronounced, and the longer-term implications are not yet clear. To some extent the rising staying-on rate may mitigate the effects of falling rolls; but it also creates new problems for schools. Many of the new stayers-on are not the "marginal" academic pupils who might attempt one or two Highers (or the sub-Highers exam mooted by the Inspectorate report: SED, 1983a), but "non-academic" pupils demanding a kind of provision which has traditionally been lacking in the post-compulsory courses of most Scottish schools.

The third factor has been the rising proportion of pupils who are not old enough to leave school at the end of fourth year and are required to stay on for at least a term of a fifth year. Since this group is broadly representative of the whole ability range, it adds to the demand for "non-academic" courses in fifth year.

The fourth factor has been the development of new kinds of provision for 16-18 year olds who are not in school. These measures have aimed either to reduce youth unemployment or to prepare young people for an increasingly difficult entry to working life. The Unified Vocational Preparation (UVP) pilot schemes were launched in 1976 to provide part-time courses of "unified" education and training for young people in jobs which traditionally offered no such provision (JUVPG, 1982). New pre-employment courses were planned, and less frequently provided, in colleges of further education, some of them inspired by the Mansell Report of the Further Education Unit (FEU, 1979). Between 1978 and 1983, by far the largest of these measures was the Youth Opportunities Programme (YOP). This was proposed by the Holland Report (MSC, 1977) as a response to youth unemployment, at a time when the problem affected only a minority of the age group and was still seen as a relatively short-term phenomenon. It provided schemes of work preparation and work experience for the young unemployed, ranging in length from two weeks to a year. At the minimum it gave unemployed young people something to do, and kept them off the streets (and off the register); but it aimed also to develop their awareness, motivation, self-confidence and social skills, in order to make them more attractive to employers and to help them to find and secure employment, or at least to cope more effectively with unemployment. Whether or not these aims were realised is debatable, and the quality of YOP schemes certainly varied widely. However, in aspiration the programme, or parts of it, clearly identified with the emerging philosophy of vocational preparation.

In the event the original aims of the Youth Opportunities Programme were drowned by the rising tide of youth unemployment. Remarkably, this led not to a renewed search for policies to deal with youth unemployment, but to an increased emphasis on education and training (Raffe, 1984). The new philosophy of vocational preparation had two central tenets. The first was that all young people, not only those continuing with formal schooling or entering skilled occupations, should have some sort of vocational preparation at 16-plus. The second was that for many of these young people the preparation should combine many of the features of education and training, should not be specific to a particular occupation, and should impart general skills and knowledge which were relevant not only to a range of occupations but also to all areas of adult life. This philosophy was asserted by the Manpower Services Commission in its New Training Initiative (MSC, 1981a, 1981b) and subsequently incorporated in the Youth Training Scheme (YTS) which replaced YOP from September 1983 (DE, 1981; MSC, 1982a). YTS offers 16 and 17 year olds a year's work experience and preparation, including at least three months' off-the-job education or training. The general nature of the training and range of skills to be developed reflect the philosophy of vocational preparation. Unlike YOP, YTS is designed to cover all 16 year olds entering the labour market, not just the unemployed. It therefore replaces the first year of many apprenticeships and jobs open to 16 year olds.

These developments have had a threefold impact on schools. First, the philosophy of vocational preparation has provided a source of ideas for the kinds of provision which schools might make both for the 14-16 age group and for the less academic youngsters staying on after 16. The Education Resources Unit for YOP, funded by the SED to support YOP schemes, sought also to extend the new ideas into schools. This aim was reflected in its re-birth in 1982 as the Scottish Vocational Preparation Unit. From 1977 to 1983 the Education for the Industrial Society Project explored new ideas about vocational education, although it claimed that this was a broader concept than vocational preparation and required "a broad, general education fully in keeping with the Scottish tradition" (CCC, 1983, p.30). However, schools have been slow to develop new courses for the 16-18 age group, partly because of the rival demands of the Munn/Dunning developments for the 14-16 age group.

Second, the new developments, and YTS in particular, are sometimes viewed as threats, competing with schools for their less academic post-compulsory pupils. YTS certainly has some competitive advantages. It offers a £25 weekly allowance to all its trainees, whereas school bursaries are smaller and much harder to obtain; YTS may also appeal to young people who are bored with education and welcome any introduction, however partial, to the world of work.

Third, the development of new types of courses and new structures for providing them makes more pressing than ever the need for co-ordination across institutional boundaries. There may be a need for co-ordination between the later years of compulsory schooling and the activities that follow it end-on. As relatively few young pupils now make the transition directly from school to employment, so the rationale for some 14-16 courses as terminal courses has to be reassessed. Co-ordination may be equally necessary among the different types of post-16 provision. This would point to a coherent range of opportunities with different institutions co-operating in the planning and provision of courses.

However, for co-ordination to be successful it should cover the more extrinsic aspects of courses as well as their content. These aspects include the system of allowances, which currently vary widely across the range of post-16 opportunities (House of Commons Committee on Scottish Affairs, 1981, para. 55) and the links with the labour market. The routes through different types of vocational provision into different sectors of employment should follow some coherent pattern. There are moreover both national and inter-departmental dimensions to co-ordination. YTS is the product of the Manpower Services Commission, a British agency whose interests are in training rather than education. To co-ordinate it with Scottish educational provision requires that the latent conflicts between Scottish and British levels of policy-making, and between education and training, must be resolved.

These tensions are implicit in the SED's (1983b) Action Plan which proposed that all non-SCE courses for the 16-18 age group should be incorporated within an integrated pattern of modular courses, examined by a single certificate. The Action Plan embraced schools and colleges, including YTS courses, and envisaged greater institutional co-operation. It reasserted both the Scottish and the educational aspects of provision, skilfully identifying the national tradition with educational aspirations in general and with the SED in particular. The questions that remain to be settled are whether the degree of co-ordination proposed by the Action Plan will be realised, and whether it will be sufficient. Will coherence be achieved between pre-16 education and what follows, between academic (SCE) and non-academic courses at 16-plus, among the range of allowances offered to 16-18 year olds, and between educational provision and the increasingly complex tangle of routes into employment?

History and structure

The educational system described in this book has changed rapidly in recent years, and further changes, described above, are in progress. This is at once a challenge and a problem for the researcher. It is a challenge because at times of rapid change it is more than ever important to have a systematic understanding of an educational system, of the ways in which it is changing and of the successes and limitations of different policy initiatives. It is a problem because our understanding is always based on information that is out of date; and the faster the rate of change, the more rapidly does information seemingly lose its currency. This, it must be stressed, is a problem which affects all social knowledge, not only research.

Our understanding of the present (let alone the future) is always based upon projections from information about the past.

In this book we aim not only to describe the recent past of Scottish education, but also to illuminate its present and to suggest the continuities, dilemmas and constraints that will help to shape its future. To the problem of how to study a rapidly changing system we adopt a solution that emphasises history and structure.

The need for an historical perspective may seem evident enough. History may not always proceed in perfectly straight lines, but nor does it often make very sharp turns. In order to know where we are going, it is helpful to know where we have come from. An historical perspective can identify the groups, ideas and forces of circumstance which give events their current momentum; it helps us to guess whether that momentum will be maintained. An historical perspective illuminates the ideas, assumptions and expectations which guide the actions of those who would make changes and of those who seek to resist them.

An historical awareness can also illuminate the second, structural perspective. This perspective resolves the problem of how to study a continually changing system by identifying enduring influences or constraints upon educational change. Many of these influences and constraints arise out of the process of differentiation that occurs among pupils as they progress through schooling, and out of the use of education as an instrument for social (and especially occupational) selection. Most teachers are familiar with the backwash effects of examinations (a major instrument of differentiation) on methods of teaching and learning and on the content of what is being taught. More generally, because selection tends to be based on a single dimension of academic attainment, schools find it difficult to give as much attention as they might wish to other aspects of individual growth and development. Any differentiation of pupils tends to be understood in terms of this "vertical" dimension; the system demands failures. Further dilemmas concern the timing of selection, the level of courses and the motivation of pupils.

Elsewhere we have called this complex of issues the "problems of difficulty, selection and motivation", and we have described at greater length the ways in which the school system has tried to cope with them since 1945 (Gray et al., 1983, chapters 1 and 16). In practice there is no clear distinction between an historical and a structural perspective. Structural constraints can only be fully understood in an historical context; and many of these constraints are created by features which are historically defined. This is true of the ideas, assumptions and expectations both of policy-makers and of key agents such as teachers. For example, those planning and providing particular courses in school tend to do so in terms of preconceived "modal groups" such as future university students, pupils in a certain ability band or "non-academic" pupils. In practice some, perhaps a majority, of the students who actually enter a given course may not belong to the appropriate modal group; there is a problem of misfit between the expectations of those providing education and those of the students who make use of it. This problem is widespread in Scottish secondary education due to the piecemeal nature of its expansion and development: a recurrent theme of this book is the tension between the historically defined expectations of policy-makers and the more heterogeneous reality.

The plan of this book

The chapters of the book follow the progress of the 1980 leavers through and beyond school in broadly chronological sequence. Chapter 2 discusses the third and fourth years of secondary education as a recognisable stage in Scottish schooling. Chapter 3 examines, in the context of the Munn and Dunning proposals, the curriculum of this stage and the way it has been structured by the progressive differentiation of pupils. Chapter 4 describes the reactions of the 1980 leavers to their experiences of this stage.

Compulsory and post-compulsory schooling differ in their nature and in the problems that they face; to reflect this difference we use the term "pupils" to describe those in compulsory schooling and "students" for those in post-compulsory education whether at school or elsewhere. Chapters 5 and 6 deal with the point of transition; chapter 5 analyses the decision to stay on at school in relation to social and educational differences and also in relation to the structure of schooling itself. Chapter 6 looks at the young people's reasons for staying or leaving. Chapter 7 follows the volunteers who stayed on into the fifth year and examines the differentiated pattern of courses that they took. Chapter 8 provides a similar analysis of the sixth year, asking how it adds to the fifth year and looking at differences between the east and west of Scotland.

The last two empirical chapters examine the post-school destinations of the 1980 leavers. Chapter 9 analyses the relation between various dimensions of school attainment and employment among those who entered the labour market. Chapter 10 looks at young people's experiences of, and attitudes to, the Youth Opportunities Programme, in the light of its recent replacement by the Youth Training Scheme. Finally, chapter 11 discusses some of the implications of the book's findings for the future success of current educational policy initiatives.

Each chapter is written by a separate author, who is individually responsible for the judgements and views expressed therein. We have endeavoured to make this book more than just a collection of essays; we have discussed successive drafts of each other's chapters, and the book reflects, perhaps more than we ourselves are aware, shared judgements and understandings. In particular we hope that the book offers a wide and reasonably coherent view of the structure of Scottish education for 14-18s, rather than a series of partial views obtained from successive examinations of its separate parts. The first and last chapters were written by the editor and draw on contributions from, and discussion among, all four authors. In this sense they are offered here as collective productions.

Throughout the book we restrict our attention to young people from education authority schools, since these are most directly the subjects of current policy. We usually use the term "post-compulsory schooling" to refer to courses in the fifth year or beyond attended by pupils who stay on beyond their earliest possible leaving date; those who stay on we describe as "volunteers". We use the shorthand terms S1, S2, and so on up to S6 to describe the years of secondary school from first year (typically entered at age 12) to sixth year (typically entered at age 17). Appendix 2 provides a brief glossary of names and terms which occur frequently in the book.

In writing this book we have sought to apply a particular perspective to the study of educational change – a sociological perspective which identifies structural constraints, in particular those that arise out of the selective function of schooling. In doing so we acknowledge that there are other equally valid perspectives on educational change. Neither ours nor any other perspective can offer a complete and rounded view of education. Nor have we deliberately set out to be contentious or to criticise policy merely for the sake of criticism. Indeed we applaud the current spirit of reform in Scottish education and we share many of its ideals and objectives. Our belief is simply that innovations in education, as in other spheres of life, face constraints that are deeply rooted in the structure of social institutions. In drawing attention in the chapters that follow to such constraints we seek, not to weaken the spirit of reform, but to strengthen it through better understanding.

Chapter 2

Looking at compulsory schooling

Penelope Weston

In this book we are concerned with a particular generation of young people, those who left school in 1979/80. And in this, and the following two chapters, we will be looking at one part of their school experience, the third and fourth years (S3 and S4) of their secondary schooling. Since change in the day-to-day business of school and classroom is usually a gradual affair, and since this sample of leavers was representative of every secondary school in Scotland, their experience could probably be used without further comment to epitomise that stage of schooling in Scotland. But it is more accurate and in practice more interesting to set their experience within the particular historical context of the educational system as they passed through it.

These young people, leaving from the fourth, fifth or sixth year of secondary school, entered the first year between 1974 and 1976; ten years earlier, the Scottish Education Department's Circular 600 (SED, 1965) had given official sanction to the move towards a fully comprehensive secondary-school system. In those intervening years, very great progress had been made in this direction, so that 86 per cent of this group of leavers had entered schools which were already non-selective in their entry and were offering a five-year course to Highers before 1975.The year 1975 was significant in another respect: it was the year in which the Munn and Dunning Committees began the deliberations which were intended to reshape curriculum and assessment for the third and fourth years. But by the time the youngest of our group had left the fourth year in 1980, these effects had scarcely been felt in the schools; trials of new Foundation-level courses in English, maths and science in the 60 "first-line" pilot schools were to start the following term. Not until 1986, more than ten years after the 1980 leavers started secondary school, will third-year pupils in all Scottish secondary schools choose from a range of 26 multi-level Munn/Dunning

14

courses, if current SED plans are fully realised.

As our leavers went through the secondary stage, the schools they attended were at an interesting moment in their development. Most of them had digested the major organisational upheavals consequent on the ending of selection; and while there was no shortage of school-based plans to introduce new courses and new forms of timetabling, nor of evident dissatisfaction over the very problems in the S3/S4 curriculum which were to be discussed in the Munn and Dunning Reports (SED, 1977b, 1977a), most schools were operating a curriculum framework which had become well understood by teachers and pupils. This framework provided, for the first year of the course, a broad range of subjects taught by specialist teachers in 40 to 60-minute lessons, mostly in mixed-ability classes; and resulted, four years later, in a complex, differentiated structure, where groups of pupils pursued varying patterns of examination courses, with varying degrees of success. For the pupils, coming at an impressionable age into an authoritarian system, it is not surprising that this framework and the consequences it might have for their personal future should convey an air of inevitability. The same may be true to some extent for teachers, when they are caught up in the day-to-day management of that system. It is when they have the opportunity to reflect upon it that the network of assumptions underlying the everyday business of teaching comes into focus.

In this chapter we want to review three perceptions about the character of schooling in third and fourth years, and to examine the assumptions which have shaped these perceptions. First, that these are the final years of *compulsory* schooling; second, that they constitute a unit of some kind, a recognisable *stage* of schooling; and third, that in these years *differentiation by ability* becomes explicit as pupils are graded and sorted in terms of national examination-based criteria.

For the pupils themselves perhaps the most obvious common feature of their school experience during the third and fourth years is that their attendance is compulsory. They are supposed to be there at school, during the whole of the school day, for every day of the school term. A simplistic definition of compulsion, in relation to schooling, is that it means full-time attendance by pupils of certain ages at an institution called school. Such a definition has for some time been challenged by schemes such as link courses and work experience which involve pupils in activities outside school while they are still within the compulsory period of schooling. But such arrangements have been up to now peripheral to the mainstream experience of most pupils. Indeed the pattern of full-time attendance at school, established for the period of compulsory schooling, has exerted such an effect on the post-compulsory stage that is has aroused strong comments and criticism in a recent Inspectorate report on the post-S4 stage (SED,

1983a). If it is fairly easy to agree on what compulsory schooling demands, minimally, of the pupil, it is rather more difficult to resolve tidily questions about how long the period of compulsory schooling should be. Strictly speaking, compulsion is related to age, but a three-term year especially combined with a single-entry start for primary school soon creates anomalies for all but the few who become five conveniently near the beginning of the school year. Equally, problems can and do arise when the minimum school-leaving age is reached; this may occur not at the end of the fourth year (the "normal" date) but earlier (Christmas S4) or later (Christmas S5).Compulsion could alternatively be related to the length of the school course, for example, completing a school course of eleven three-term years. For just over half the school population, this three-term school career does coincide with their school starting and leaving dates. But the fact remains that for the rest of a year group the two definitions do not match easily.

Underlying these uneasy compromises about the framework of compulsory schooling is a more fundamental assumption that has grown up in the last two decades, that age and stage are equivalent; that a chronological year group should equal a school year group and that the primary criterion for passing from one school year to the next is increase in age. Compare this with the different set of perspectives that applied in the traditional senior secondary school, in which the main criterion for progress up the school was likely to be academic achievement rather than age. Moreover, in this bipartite school system, the influence of the minimum school-leaving age on course planning differed from one type of school to another, the links being most obvious in the junior secondary school. In the senior secondaries, planning was geared to the norm of a five-year, examination-related course, however much these assumptions might be challenged by the numbers of early leavers whose plight was discussed in the *Report of the Working Party on the Curriculum of the Senior Secondary School* (SED, 1959). By 1972 the growing popularity of O-grade courses (aimed largely at these early leavers) had, in the ten years since their introduction, provided the rationale for a four-year secondary course for almost half the age group. The raising of the school-leaving age (RSLA) to 16, in 1972/73, finally conferred official sanction on the four-year course. Highers now looked more like "doing one more year after O-grade" than "completing a five-year course".

This tidying-up of the framework of compulsory schooling to produce a neatly defined eleven-year course, split into seven years of primary and four years of secondary schooling, has at the same time defined with increasing clarity those groups who do not fit tidily into the pattern. Just because the boundaries are more clearly drawn, the anomalous position of those individuals or groups who fall outside them is the more easily seen. Thus the lack of fit between the chronological definition for compulsory schooling (5-16 years) and the school course definition (11 years of schooling) may be acutely felt by the not inconsiderable minority who are affected by it. How appropriate is it to consider nearly half of the school population as anomalies? It is well worth remembering that a substantial minority of a school year group will actually be undertaking half a year of post-compulsory schooling in order to complete their fourth-year course; although these may not be the terms in which S4 is seen by most pupils, teachers or parents.

In reflecting on the compulsory framework of schooling today, we have already touched on the importance of the idea of "stage" for that framework. Once the school year group had become firmly linked to chronological age, the way was open for a course-planning rationale for the common secondary school, which moved away from the old, goal-related designs underlying the five-year course in the selective system, and took as its baseline the concerns of a whole year group. While it was accepted that the needs and capabilities of the pupils within a single year group might vary widely, it was still felt to be possible (in many subjects) to devise a first- or second-year course which could cater productively for all. As a result, a year group might be defined from two standpoints: "second year" meant, on the one hand, 13-14 year old pupils; it could also mean a curriculum outline which could apply with minor variations to all those pupils. With the school year group established as the building block for curriculum planning within secondary education, it was attractive to complete the pattern by explicitly or implicitly bracketing two or more year groups together into a single stage: for example, the S1/S2 introductory stage characterised by a broad curriculum and many mixed-ability classes. The curriculum papers produced by the Consultative Committee on the Curriculum (CCC) and its working parties in the ten years after its foundation in 1965 illustrate this development. Curriculum Paper 2 (the Ruthven Report: SED, 1967), on courses leading to the Scottish Certificate of Education (SCE), specifically divided secondary schooling into three two-year periods, S1/S2, S3/S4 and S5/S6. While these were recognised as artificial groupings, each was seen to have a degree of coherence. Documents on a number of areas of the curriculum followed, Curriculum Paper 7 on *Science for General Education* (SED, 1969) being one of the earliest and most influential. It introduced the principles and practice of integrated science for S1/S2, an approach which has become widely adopted, at least in outline. By 1976 the course material had been revised in an effort to solve the problems which teachers found in presenting an integrated course to mixed-ability classes. An integrated course for S1/S2 was also recommended for technical education in

Curriculum Paper 10 (SED, 1972). Meanwhile new courses for mixed-ability classes were being developed in social subjects, with geography getting under way early; by the time Curriculum Paper 15 on social subjects (SED, 1976a) discussed the principles of S1/S2 planning, new developments within mixed-ability subject-based courses were already being considered.

In planning for the S3/S4 stage, however, the policy-makers of the CCC came up against the older tradition of basing curriculum planning on the requirements of public examinations. It was primarily for those pupils not covered by the provisions of the Scottish Certificate of Education Examination Board that the CCC's committees were asked to design new third- and fourth-year courses. A number of such courses were produced in the run-up to RSLA (SED, 1968, 1969, 1970) but for a variety of reasons these courses were not well received in the schools. The Inspectors' report on *The Raising of the School Leaving Age in Scotland* (SED, 1976b) explains why:

> Many teachers were actively involved in the curriculum preparation made both nationally and locally, but they were, necessarily, a minority. Of the remainder few made advance preparations for RSLA in any detail. They had a variety of other priorities which they considered more urgent, and they tended to leave the planning of courses for RSLA for their own pupils till a relatively late stage… visits to the schools chosen for inspection showed that very few of them had put into practice the courses which had been prepared. (paras. 5.8, 5.9)

Instead, most headteachers, in spite of some misgivings, argued for expanding O-grade presentation:

> Given the structure of the examination system as it existed at the time, they put forward strong arguments for admitting most pupils to SCE courses. They felt that this policy was a logical consequence of a comprehensive system in which maximum opportunities should be offered to all pupils throughout their secondary education. (para. 5.11)

Statistics for fourth-year O-grade presentation, as discussed in the Dunning Report, provide clear evidence of the strength of this feeling and its effect on pupils. By the time our pupils entered secondary school the last two years of compulsory schooling had become, without doubt, the public-examination stage for a substantial majority of pupils. Once again, the urge to provide a common experience in the common school during the common (because compulsory) period of schooling was having the effect of defining more sharply the boundary between those who at least nominally fitted the common pattern and those who did not, in this case the non-certificate pupils who have shown how keenly they, as well as many of their teachers, recognised this exclusion (Gow and McPherson, 1980).

With the encouragement of the media, powerful images have been developed in the public mind about this stage of schooling. It is a stage ushered in by the offer to pupils of a degree of self-determination through subject choice at 14; punctuated by occasional crises of tests, preliminary examinations and revision; and culminating in the rituals of the examinations themselves and the tense wait for the results envelope. Such a picture – of each generation of 15 and 16 year olds eagerly pressing forward to complete the course in a national contest – is of course grossly over-simplified and therefore inaccurate. In the first place it conveniently ignores not only those who failed to start the race, but also those who fell by the wayside as the contest proceeded. To most teachers, it was always apparent that, in addition to the non-certificate minority, there was a substantial group for whom participation in O-grade courses was likely to lead to frustration and disappointment.

How big is this latter group? The answer to this question depends on how success at O-grade is defined. The Dunning Report referred to the recommendation of the 1959 Working Party on the Curriculum (SED, 1959) that three O-grade passes should be recognised as a criterion for success at O-grade, and points out that 40 per cent of a year group were then (1976) achieving this goal (three A-C awards); by 1981 the proportion had risen to 45 per cent. If this figure is used, as Dunning implies it should be, to indicate the approximate proportion for whom an O-grade course was felt to be a satisfactory experience, then some 35-40 per cent of the age group, in addition to the 15-20 per cent of wholly non-certificate pupils, are pursuing an inappropriate course. As with the question of age and school leaving, the effect of defining a common framework is not only to show up more sharply those who are excluded from it but also to mask from the outside world the extent of variation among those nominally included within the fold.

The popular image sketched above also glosses over an important distinction that divides the runners in the O-grade stakes. Often success at O-level (as it is usually described) has been portrayed as the ticket to a successful start in one's chosen career, almost a guaranteed luncheon voucher. For the 60 per cent of young people who left school by the end of S4 (or as soon as possible thereafter) O-grade is (or was until recently) likely to be seen in these terms. However employers may choose to treat it, for its recipients O-grade is a public validation of their value, and in this sense it is a vocational certificate. For them O-grade is at the same time a terminal assessment, marking the transition from school to the labour market. For others – about a quarter of the age group in all – O-grade is only a first-round event, a qualifying round which some would prefer to omit in order to concentrate on the crucial fifth-year contest. Even before the summer term of S4 has ended they have embarked on the run-up to their first significant vocational goal: obtaining the Highers which will serve as a passport to higher education and/or a satisfying white-collar job. To view O-grade as "terminal assessment" for these pupils is to twist the meaning of words. For most of them, the third and fourth years constitute an intermediate stage of schooling, and the end of compulsion brings increased pressure and few signs of liberation. Even among those who can hope for some success at O-grade, expectations for the post-S4 period may vary widely; we shall have to see how this affects their perceptions of the last two years of compulsory schooling.

The S3/S4 stage of schooling has become recognised, then, as the O-grade stage, whatever anomalies this creates for some pupils. Against this single common yardstick all are measured, in one way or another. Perhaps it would be more accurate to say that the measuring instrument is used to grade them, like eggs, size 1 to 5 (or unfit for sale). Given public recognition of the importance of this grading process at the end of S4, the demand for differentiation in the years from 14 to 16 – the attempt to identify likely runners and predict outcomes – is inexorable. How is the process managed in school?

There is no problem for teachers in recognising and publicly acknowledging that pupils vary markedly from each other. Since only one variable – age – is held more or less constant within a given stage of schooling, it can be expected that in every other respect there will be a wide range of variation among pupils, for example, physically, emotionally and attitudinally. All such variations will no doubt be taken into account, where relevant, by any experienced teacher. Indeed, most statements of school aims stress the importance of helping pupils to recognise and develop their individual pattern of talents and skills. Formal recognition of several dimensions of development which may contribute to academic achievement, and on which pupils will vary, has been made in many schools' internal assessment schemes which award grades on reports for "effort" and "classroom attitude" as well as "attainment". In practice, however, it is this third dimension of "attainment", and its powerful *alter ego* "ability", that has come to dominate decisions about what pupils should do in school during the final years of compulsory schooling.

The importance of the concept of ability in shaping teachers' judgements about pupils cannot be confined to one stage of schooling, nor indeed to Scottish schools. Ryrie *et al.* (1979) have argued that such judgements, made during the first and second years of secondary school, are more influential than any other single factor in shaping pupil outcomes at the end of S4; and Weston (1977) in a study of English secondary schools illustrated the importance of decisions at this early stage in constraining subject choices at 14 plus. What is meant here by ability, and how is it used as a criterion for organising pupil experience?

By ability we are referring to a judgement about a pupil's capacity to succeed in some field of endeavour. The judgement is formed on the basis of past success (or failure) but it principally refers to the future. In the selective system of earlier years such classifications would be made at various stages of schooling largely on the basis of externally produced and officially recognised tests of general ability. Now the O-grade results themselves, the first public verdict on a pupil's academic attainment, provide a formal criterion for selection to Highers courses:

> Conditions for admission to Higher grade courses in S5 vary somewhat from school to school, but normally pupils are admitted to them if they hold SCE in the Ordinary grade at band C or above in three or more subjects. (SED, 1983a, para. 2.5)

Within the framework of the compulsory period of education in the comprehensive school, however, most of the burden of judgement lies on the teachers themselves. In the secondary school, because teaching is organised by subject areas the judgement is initially related to a specific subject (ability in maths or history), but several pressures encourage the tendency to generalise across subject-related judgements in order to distill some more global judgement of "general ability". While the judgement may initially be criterion-referenced, in that it is based on the pupil's ability to achieve some defined level of performance, the customary habit of informally rank-ordering any class group of pupils tends to push the judgement towards a norm-referenced standard, with pupils being described as "in the top (or bottom) ten per cent", "just above average", and so on. Pupils, of course, also make their own judgements of their ability, but these are likely to be strongly influenced by the messages, formal and informal, which they receive from their teachers. In practice, problems may arise in some cases where the average level of "ability" in the class or year group is below the national average, so that teachers have to explain to pupils and parents that an A or B in S2 does not necessarily mean that the pupil is going to succeed on an O-grade course; in other words, as teachers have to shift from a school- or class-based norm to the national norms that underlie the O-grade system.

The rationale for this approach to the differentiation of pupils is to be found in the long-established psychometric tradition of a continuum of ability, a single measurable latent dimension on which each pupil can be placed relative to all other pupils in an age group. This tradition has placed "ability" in an unassailable position qualitatively different from any specific ability to perform a given task (McIntyre, 1978). Over the last 50 years it has found expression in every "reform" of the structure of schooling for the years before 16, whether of the national system of schooling (bi- or tripartite allocation of pupils to schools), of the organisation of pupils within the school (streaming or banding) or within the class (ability grouping). Quite often empirical or theoretical support has been found for dividing the continuum into three categories: more able, average, less able. Even administrative structures devised within the school to counteract this tendency can gradually be reshaped to represent it (Weston, 1979).

Differentiation by ability provides a way of grading *pupils;* it is they who are to be categorised in terms of their predicted attainment or ability. But in practice ability has to be translated into ability in maths or woodwork or biology and so on. One pupil may not be equally "able" in all subjects; and however strongly teachers may defend their own subject, they have to recognise that subjects are also graded in terms of their "difficulty", a form of categorisation that has found empirical suppport in studies of O-grade outcomes (Kelly, 1976). Differentiation has therefore been extended from pupils to *subjects,* with the result that the two interact, as Ryrie *et al.* (1979) among others have shown, with more able pupils taking (on the whole) more difficult subjects. The place of any one subject within this hierarchy may of course change over time; perhaps computer studies, for example, will move upwards over time, receiving O-grade recognition as it rises. Indeed, considerable energy is expended by subject lobbies to maintain or enhance the standing of their subject. Such shifts, however, leave the conceptual framework untouched, with the result that the fully differentiated pupils who emerge from S4 can be distinguished by the level of course they have followed, the grades (if any) they have obtained and the difficulty of the subjects they have studied.

A compulsory stage of examination-related schooling, common to all schools, during which pupils are progressively differentiated and publicly graded in line with their "ability": these, we would argue, are some of the important assumptions which have shaped the system experienced by our 1980 leavers, and which we shall try to take account of in the following two chapters. And yet there is a contrasting tradition about the purpose and practice of secondary schooling which found powerful expression in the 1947 report on *Secondary Education* (SED, 1947), which "advocated a form of pedagogy that owed much to an essentially learner-centred philosophy of liberal education" (Gray *et al.*, 1983, p.33).The report called for a national system of assessment at 16, but this was to be a system developed and directed by the teachers, since "the teaching professon had 'come of age' and could be trusted to develop a general education for the new era" (*ibid.*, p.34). In reviewing the final stage of compulsory schooling, as it stands at present, and considering the changes which are proposed for the curriculum, it will be useful to bear in mind the challenge of this alternative view of the purposes of secondary education.

In the next two chapters we want, first, to assess the significance of the assumptions we have discussed here for the young people whose experiences we shall be describing. Chapter 3 will examine the issues of differentiation in the third and fourth years, as it operates at present, while chapter 4 will take up leavers' own evaluations of their experience, particularly of fourth year, and of the day-to-day process of learning as they recalled it. The mismatch between age and stage will be reviewed in more detail in chapter 5, but the views of early leavers, those who did not complete S4, will be noted in chapter 4. Second, we wish to review the proposed changes in the curriculum and examination structure of this stage of schooling and relate them to current practice. How far do these reforms challenge the assumptions we have outlined? And if the assumptions are challenged, what provision is there in the proposals to ensure that administrative changes are accompanied by measures to bring out the necessary changes in attitude and practice? In order to tackle these questions we shall go beyond a review of the proposals themselves and try to anticipate some possible effects of their implementation by building a model of the new system; by treating the present (or recently past) pupil experiences as if they were constrained by the demands of the new structure.

Much has been written in recent years about the third- and fourth-year stage of secondary schooling, and as plans to restructure the learning experience of that stage are put into effect, the attention of commentators has already moved to the post-compulsory stage, where the issues and institutional realities are even more complex and the current circumstances of young people infinitely more problematic. In this situation, therefore, a review of what happened in the third and fourth years of Scottish secondary schools between 1977 and 1980 might seem doubly redundant. We think this is not the case, first, because the Scottish School Leavers Survey uniquely provides information on how individual pupils experienced this two-year period, what they studied and how, the outcome in examination results and their evalution of that experience. This alone makes it possible to monitor and explore the effects of current policies on the participants themselves. The RSLA report of 1976 (SED, 1976b) provides eloquent testimony to the importance of anticipating intelligently how proposed innovations will fit with the realities of teacher and pupil expectations, by discovering in advance as much as possible about those realities. It therefore seems highly relevant to explore the implications of current structures and assumptions as preparations are made to launch a national programme of curriculum reorganisation. Second, while no one can seriously anticipate the accounts which will be given by future leavers about their schooling, we can employ the definitions already being made about how a reformed structure will operate in order to model some possible effects of changes in the system. This system after all will operate for the most part in the same schools and with much the same teaching force as our 1979/80 leavers knew when they were at school, and we should be able to learn important and practical lessons from what these young people have told us about their experience of compulsory schooling.

Chapter 3

Learning their place: differentiation and the S3/S4 curriculum in practice and prospect

Penelope Weston

In this chapter we want to look at what pupils study during the final stage of compulsory schooling, and how their curriculum has been, and may continue to be, shaped by the process of differentiation. The investigation is based primarily on the experience of young people in Scotland who have fairly recently worked their way through this stage of schooling.

The nature of our data on the third- and fourth-year (S3 and S4) curriculum from the 1981 School Leavers Survey will of course colour the kind of description that we can give. First, and most importantly, the curriculum will be described almost entirely in terms of one type of unit or building block: the *subject*. The majority of these units are nationally recognised O-grade subjects, where the name of the subject carries with it a total package of externally defined syllabus, a set of procedures and more or less agreed standards of achievement. Given that we were asking young people to recall their school experience over a period of at least two years, it was important to use a currency they would recognise and which would aid recall. Respondents were presented with a list of 21 subjects, including the most popular O-grade subjects (and some non-examined subjects), and were asked to record, subject by subject, what they had attempted at each of four stages: studying a subject in third and/or fourth year, and sitting the preliminary examination and/or the O-grade examination itself. In addition, they were invited to enter the O-grade award (if any) obtained in the subject in S4. Subjects not listed could be written in and recorded in a similar way. Because this subject record, which covers several time points, is held for each pupil it is possible to describe in some detail the current

system as it is experienced by pupils; for example, to explore subject
combinations and to review curricular differences between sub-groups
defined by individual, regional or school-type criteria. We could test, on a
national scale, the conclusions of more focused investigations such as
Ryrie's (1981) study of the progress of third- and fourth-year pupils in eight
comprehensive schools (see Weston, 1982a), or Spencer's (1983) enquiry
into writing across the curriculum. Second, it should be remembered that
the leavers in our sample came from three year groups and would have been
in S4 in 1977/78, 1978/79 or 1979/80. As they describe their experience of
S3 and S4 they therefore represent a composite year group. This approach
has advantages and disadvantages. On the one hand, small year-to-year
fluctuations are averaged out, giving more stable results; on the other hand,
if important changes took place in schools during those three years, they too
will be averaged out and their impact lost.

We have chosen to use the data on the S3/S4 curriculum in order to
investigate the process of differentiation by ability, as it operates now and
as it might operate in the future, making a link between the current
curriculum framework in schools and the new structure which will soon
replace it. We shall look at two aspects of the Munn and Dunning proposals:
the general shape of the curriculum, as recommended by the Munn
Committee, and the differentiation of that curriculum (and therefore of the
pupils in relation to it) into three course levels as put forward by the
Dunning Committee. By examining the development of the proposals on
these two themes, from the publication of the Dunning and Munn reports
(SED, 1977a, 1977b) to the appearance of Circular 1093 (SED, 1983c), we
can define a model of how the new system might look if superimposed on
the present experience of pupils. We can describe what happened to the
school leavers of 1980 "as if" they had had to operate within a Munn/
Dunning framework. A more descriptive account of the process of learning
within the current framework, as pupils experienced it, will be given in
chapter 4.

National policy and the structure of the curriculum

While the subject has retained its supremacy almost unchallenged as the
organisational unit for learning within the secondary school, numerous
attempts have been made (of which the Munn Report is simply one of the
more recent and, in Scotland, the best known) to prescribe or at least to
recommend in broader or more analytically satisfying terms than mere lists
of subjects, what content and competencies should be studied in this stage
of schooling, and in what proportions. But though the Munn Report spelt
out in some detail the kind of learning experiences which it was thought that
all pupils should be offered, in practice the committee decided that many

of these experiences and modes of learning were realisable, after all, through and within established subjects. The Munn Committee arrived at the broader perspective which their deliberations had envisaged by grouping subjects into eight areas consonant with their eight "modes of activity", and they recommended that all pupils should have substantial experience in each of these areas (by studying one or more of the subjects which represented them) during the third and fourth years. Later discussion documents, and in particular *Framework for Decision* (SED, 1982a), preserved this schema, which has more recently been endorsed in Circular 1093 (SED, 1983c) announcing the implementation of the government's proposals.

In reviewing the curriculum of the 1980 leavers we wanted to make use of this schema, partly in order to test further the claim made by many schools after 1977 that they were "doing Munn already". In practice there are some interesting variations between the two relevant sections of the Munn Report and *Framework for Decision* in the content and presentation of the "modes" of study and in suggestions of how these should be realised. Figure 3.1 shows the titles given to (1) the eight modes of the Munn Report, chapter 4, (2) the seven "areas of activity" in Munn, chapter 5, and (3) the seven modes put forward by the Central Committee on the Curriculum (CCC) as reported in *Framework for Decision*. The differences in order between lists (1) and (2) arise from the fact that the authors decided to list first those areas which were most likely to be represented by a single subject (core subject), followed by the three areas where choice was offered among several subjects thought to represent the area (core fields: Hurman, 1978). This order of the study areas is maintained, with two minor changes, in the third list from *Framework for Decision*, but the title of the first area has once more become the broader "linguistic and literary studies" rather than English. That these changes are not wholly trivial is suggested by Figure 3.2. which shows how the authors of the two documents consider that the modes or areas should be translated into subjects. This specification of subjects reveals some of the thinking behind the classification, and also highlights a number of problems. The most obvious of these, in relation to the diet of subjects currently studied, is the position of modern languages and technical subjects, both of which are jettisoned to the elective part of the Munn curriculum and therefore do not appear in the seven areas which represent the core curriculum. In the *Framework for Decision* schema, which has a more comprehensive list of subjects, modern languages are reinstated in the linguistic and literary studies area, but the position of technical subjects is still a little unclear. Under the new course titles a number appear in the scientific studies area (for example, craft and design, home economics, and social and vocational skills). Business studies is listed

FIGURE 3.1
Modes and areas of study, from the Munn Report to Framework for Decision

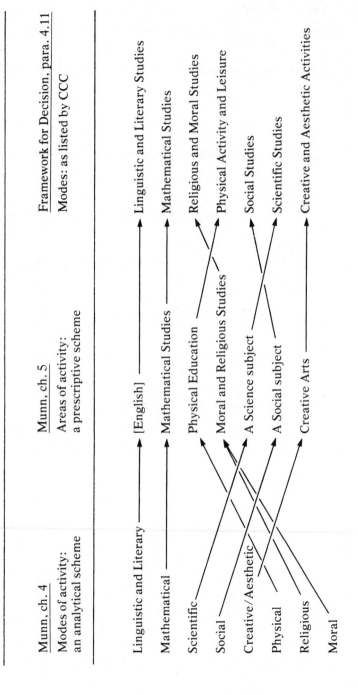

Munn, ch. 4
Modes of activity:
an analytical scheme

Munn, ch. 5
Areas of activity:
a prescriptive scheme

Framework for Decision, para. 4.11
Modes: as listed by CCC

Linguistic and Literary — [English] — Linguistic and Literary Studies

Mathematical — Mathematical Studies — Mathematical Studies

Scientific — Physical Education — Religious and Moral Studies

Social — Moral and Religious Studies — Physical Activity and Leisure

Creative/Aesthetic — A Science subject — Social Studies

Physical — A Social subject — Scientific Studies

Religious — Creative Arts — Creative and Aesthetic Activities

Moral

FIGURE 3.2

Subjects (or courses) representing areas or modes of activity from Figure 3.1

	Munn, ch.5	Framework for Decision Annex B	Neo-Munn schema	
LINGUISTIC AND LITERARY	English	English Gaelic Latin French German	English Gaelic Latin French German	Spanish Russian Italian Greek any other language
MATHEMATICAL	Mathematics	Mathematics *Computing	Maths Arithmetic Computer Studies	Statistics
SCIENTIFIC	Physics Biology Chemistry General Science Anatomy and Physiology Engineering Science Food Science	Science Biology Chemistry Physics *Craft and Design *Home Economics *Social and Vocational Skills *Health Studies	**Science 'A' (Science Studies)** Science/General Science Biology Anatomy, Physiology and Health Chemistry Engineering Science Physics Horticulture Agricultural Science Environmental Studies Geology **Science 'B' (Applied Studies)** Home Economics (F&F, F&N) Building Drawing Secretarial Studies Typing Engineering Science Metalwork Navigation Integrated Craft Woodwork	
SOCIAL	Geography History Modern Studies Economics (core study course)	Geography History Modern Studies Economics *Business Studies Contemporary Social Studies	Economics Economic History Social Studies European Studies Budgetting Careers Education Geography Business Studies History Modern Studies	
CREATIVE/ AESTHETIC	Art Music Drama Dance Creative Craft	Art and Design Music	Art and Design Music Drama	
PHYSICAL	Physical Education	Physical Education	Physical Education Outdoor Education Gymnastics	
RELIGIOUS/ MORAL	Study of moral and religious issues	Religious Studies	Religious Education Guidance Social Education Health Education	

* "Pupils would not be allowed to represent the area by these subjects only."

under social studies, and woodwork, metalwork, and technical drawing are not included.

In investigating current practice in schools we want to discover how far pupils really are "doing Munn already", or at least operating within the defined framework of the government's proposals. Our own attempt to group subjects in Munn-type modes was constrained first by the list of existing subjects that we were classifying and second by the kind of unresolved problems referred to above. The solution we adopted which we will call the "neo-Munn schema" was to follow the *Framework for Decision* schema as far as possible, but to split scientific studies into two areas. The first (science 'A' (science studies)) consists of (mainly traditional) non-applied sciences; the second (science 'B' (applied studies)) includes all technical/practical subjects not allotted elsewhere. The placing of the social and vocational skills course in scientific studies in the government-approved schema was used as a criterion for decisions about practical subjects when we divided this study area.

National policy and the structure of differentiation

Just as the Munn Report in its earlier, theoretical chapters voiced a plea for a balanced general education for all up to 16, so the Dunning Report introduced a radical view of assessment which focused on measuring what has been learned rather than on the rank-ordering of the learners. The significance of diagnostic assessment as a pedagogic tool for teachers was emphasised and the need to develop a range of assessment procedures for all pupils was discussed. But while such ideas have gained some currency among teachers, these aspects of the report made less immediate public impact than the recommendations for the development and assessment of a three-level course structure in S3 and S4.

The design of the scheme focused on the differentiation of courses and syllabuses, not of pupils, but inevitably the different course *levels* were defined to suit pupils of various *levels* of ability. Both reports accepted without reservation the idea of a continuum of ability (SED, 1977a, para.4.17; SED, 1977b, para.6.10). For some reason (unexplained) the Munn Committee was clear that in order to provide for the whole age group three levels would be needed (*ibid.*, para.6.9).

How then were course levels to be defined and what were the implications for pupil differentiation in the new system? Government-initiated discussion documents, from the Dunning Report (1977a) onwards have considered the question of differentiation, underlined the importance of overlap between course levels, and stressed the need for flexibility in deciding what proportion of pupils should be considered eligible for a given course level. But the Dunning Report did not shrink from putting forward target percentages for its three course levels:

Some 25 to 30 per cent of the cohort will be assessed at the
Foundation level...
Some 50 to 65 per cent of the cohort will be assessed at the
General level...
Some 15 to 25 per cent of the cohort will be assessed at
Credit level. (SED, 1977a, p.76, Notes on Figure 8.1)

The report had, however, also offered a Scottish Certificate of Education
(SCE)-related criterion for success at Credit level: a satisfactory
performance could be expected from "pupils likely to gain at least a band
C at H grade in S5" (para. 8.19).

The *Feasibility Study* of 1979 (SED, 1979a) did not attempt any detailed
definitions, commenting that "target populations will have to be defined".
But it went further in relating proposed "Dunning" awards to current O-
grade bands, recommending that "the standard of a Credit award could be
defined as that obtainable by those who at present gain A and about half
of those who gain B at O-grade in each subject" (para. 2.45). General-level
awards would be appropriate for the balance of pupils pursuing an O-grade
course in S4 whether or not they were presented. By definition, Foundation-
level courses should be for those currently on non-O-grade courses, or who
drop out of those courses during S3. The various groups of consultants
whose deliberations are reported in the 1982 document, *Framework for
Decision*, also found great difficulty in making "definite statements about
target populations for the different levels" (SED, 1982a, para.3.4)), and it
was decided instead to define the achievements related to each level, in
order to find out in practice what proportions of pupils could tackle each
level successfully. These post-Dunning discussions hesitated between all-
embracing definitions of course levels or awards ("if grade 2 is a credit in
the Dunning sense, *ie* signifying a candidate who is going to take Higher in
one year" (*ibid.*, para.3.14)) and subject-related statements which indicated
the very different type of target populations which might be expected in
subjects such as English and physics, once O-grade-related criteria had been
translated into Dunning course levels.

   In order to model the possible effects of a three-level course structure on
current practice, we wanted to devise a scheme which was, as far as possible,
in keeping with post-Dunning recommendations but which took account of
the "continuum of ability" concept embedded in those proposals. Other
analyses of pupil progress and differentiation have, understandably,
categorised pupils on some realisation of this continuum, since this is how
differentiation operates within the school. Ryrie *et al.* (1979), for example,
used teachers' grades given to pupils in S2 to distinguish their ability groups,
and many studies have drawn on pupils' VRQ (verbal reasoning quotient)

scores already held by schools, or have administered similar tests themselves. Had such data been available for our respondents, it would have been tempting to follow a similar course, recreating perhaps the familiar three-category format: high, middle and low ability. Such a categorisation is in fact statistically inappropriate for a continuous (latent) variable such as "ability" (which runs from low to high), as both Munn and Dunning recognised. Furthermore it fails to take account of the attempt that was being made in the Munn/Dunning proposals to shift the focus of differentiation from pupils to courses.

How then could we sensibly describe our 1980 leaver cohort in terms of Dunning course levels? We wanted to draw on information about pupils' fourth-year O-grade performance, obtained in the 1981 survey, in order to move towards a Dunning categorisation, and it was important to acknowledge that the essential distinction was not between *pupils* but between *courses taken by pupils*. Thus in theory at least a single individual might be taking three Credit, three General and two Foundation courses in S3 and we wanted to take account of this flexibility in any scheme of categorisation we devised. This precluded any attempt to split the cohort into three discrete groups labelled Credit, General, Foundation, at whatever level the cut-off points were made. In any case, such an approach could rightly be seen as a gross misrepresentation of the planners' intentions, even though it has some support in the Dunning Report itself. But at the same time we wanted to construct a model of how pupil sub-groups at each of the three course levels might fare. We decided that we would get nearest to realising these aims by adopting a system of differential weighting (which would take account of any combination of course levels a pupil was considered to have followed) in order to create hypothetical or "modelled" populations, one for each course level, to which each real pupil in our sample would contribute differentially.

To achieve this we used the information in the post-Dunning documents on O-grade-related criteria for the new course levels in order to reproduce as nearly as possible the intentions of the policy-makers, with one important reservation: no allowance has been made for the relative difficulty of existing subjects, other than that which is already built into the present O-grade assessment system (Kelly, 1976). The same criteria have been used for every examinable subject. The criterion for being on a Credit course has been set as getting an A or a B in O-grade; a General course has been attributed to all those who sat the preliminary examination; and those who studied an examinable subject without sitting prelims have been counted as being on a Foundation course. By calculating the number of Credit (or General or Foundation) courses as a proportion of all the examinable courses started in S3, a weight of between 0 and 1 could be assigned to show the extent to which each pupil was a Credit-level candidate, a General-level candidate and a Foundation-level candidate respectively. Thus the hypothetical individual who had started eight examinable courses in S3, three Credit, three General and two Foundation, would have weights of 0.375 (Credit), 0.375 (General) and 0.25 (Foundation). For each individual the weights would sum to 1.

By applying the weights we were able to create the three hypothetical populations that we sought. Each hypothetical population would represent all the pupils who in varying degrees defined the essence of Credit-ness, General-ness and Foundation-ness. Because this is a weighting mechanism, each individual is potentially a member of each of the defined populations: Credit, General and Foundation. If even one of his (or her) third-year subjects satisfied the criterion for General level (that it had been studied at least up to prelim), then his/her General weighting would be greater than zero. If none of the subjects qualified, and the weighting was therefore zero, then of course in practice that individual would be eliminated from the analyses as soon as the weighting of zero was applied. It is important to stress that most sample members would straddle two or three of these modelled populations. The Foundation population, for example, would be defined in part by those who followed only "Foundation" courses (and therefore on any showing would be defined as Foundation pupils); but it would also be shaped by the characteristics of those who had, on our definition, taken Foundation courses along with General and/or Credit courses. When we speak of the Credit population, therefore, we shall be describing not "real" pupils and their experience, but a composite image to which pupils over a fairly wide range of attainment have contributed. We acknowledge that this is a slippery concept and one which ignores possible differences between subjects in the principles of course allocation; moreover it could be easily misunderstood as precisely that crude categorisation we resolved to avoid. This problem faces all who will be dealing with the new structures. It is difficult to imagine that most teachers have not already created for themselves images of the "typical" Credit, General and Foundation pupil which will influence their judgements. So, to emphasise that the populations which we have created by the differential weighting process are modelled or "ghost" populations, we will refer to them in terms which emphasise their artificiality: they will be known as Modelled POPulations (Credit MPOP, General MPOP and Foundation MPOP). When we want to compare boys with girls we will remind ourselves that these are not real boys and girls by referring to female Credit MPOP, male General MPOP and so on. In this way we can at least lay the groundwork for anticipating changes in the pupils' experience of differentiation. Of course, even if our model approximates at all well to the future allocation of pupils to varying combinations of courses, we can describe the reaction of such pupils only to present (or recently past) experiences. But at this stage of the game that is, for the most part, as much if not more than anyone else can do. With these words of introduction let us now look at the characteristics of the three modelled populations.

Applying the model to the data: characteristics of the three modelled populations

Previous analyses of the Scottish School Leavers Survey data have amply demonstrated the strong association between attainment (as measured, in outcome terms, by SCE qualifications) and family background (Burnhill, 1981; Gray *et al.*, 1983). Because of this relationship it was likely that differences would appear between the MPOPs in analyses related to the respondents' home backgrounds. Table 3.1 presents results for a number of such variables, for each MPOP and for the sample as a whole. These results confirm our expectations. In the Credit MPOP half the weighted membership had fathers whose occupations could be classed as non-manual; for the General MPOP the figure was just over a quarter (28 per cent) and for the Foundation MPOP, half that figure again (13 per cent). The same kind of pattern emerges if we look at the age at which their mothers and fathers had left school, although the contrast between the MPOPs was more marked in relation to fathers than to mothers: in each case, a higher proportion of mothers than fathers have stayed on at school until the age of 16 or older. Even the current employment position of the respondents' fathers revealed a similar pattern, with a 19 per cent gap between the Foundation MPOP and the Credit MPOP in the proportion with fathers currently in a job. In an attempt to facilitate enquiries into the circumstances of single-parent families, respondents were asked a simple question about their residence during fourth year. Only two per cent were unwilling to answer this question, and the results show that the great majority of respondents – over 80 per cent – were living with both parents. But even on this variable, there were differences between the three MPOPs: for example, the proportion living with one parent only was calculated to be 13 per cent in the Foundation MPOP but only seven per cent in the Credit MPOP.

It is not our task here to account for these differences, to attempt to explain how it is that respondents with fathers in non-manual occupations should be so strongly represented within the Credit MPOP. All we can say is that these results provide a kind of reference point for each MPOP; a set of indicators which we can bear in mind as we look at the experience of school through their eyes.

TABLE 3.1

Family background of modelled populations (percentages)

	Modelled population			All
	Credit	General	Foundation	leavers
(a) Father's occupation				
Non-manual	50	28	13	27
Manual	41	59	66	58
Unclassified or not known	9	14	21	16
Total	99	101	100	101
(b) Father's age at leaving school				
15 or under	62	76	80	74
16 or over	28	15	10	16
Not known	19	9	10	10
Total	99	100	100	100
(c) Mother's age at leaving school				
15 or under	60	73	78	72
16 or over	33	20	13	20
Not known	8	8	9	8
Total	101	101	100	100
(d) Father's employment				
In a job	87	80	68	77
Unemployed/unable to work	6	11	22	14
Other	8	9	9	9
Total	101	100	99	100
(e) Family situation in S4: living with …				
… both parents	88	84	79	84
… parent and step-parent	3	3	5	4
… single parent	7	10	13	11
… other or not known	1	2	3	2
Total	99	99	100	101
Unweighted n (of cases with positive MPOP weights)	(2942)	(4223)	(2524)	(5313)

The subject-based curriculum: some initial impressions
   In framing the neo-Munn schema we noted the resilience of the subject
as a conceptual and organisational unit for building the curriculum. As
subjects begin to jockey for position within the new Munn/Dunning
framework the current status of each one will be an important factor: how
many pupils take it, how many sit or pass O-grade and so on. Indeed, that
we can discover so much about each subject and how it fares in the process
of assessment underlines the significance of the subject within the structure
of secondary education. Every year the Scottish Examination Board (SEB)
produces   statistics   showing   the   number   of   fourth-year   O-grade
presentations, by sex, for each subject. These figures can be used to make
comparisons between subjects in any one year, and between years: for
example, trends in modern languages and science presentations over time
can be monitored (Dickson, 1979). Every year, also, the Scottish Education
Department (SED) investigates, at school level, the number of pupils
studying selected subjects at various stages of secondary school. These two
types of data were used to construct for the Dunning Committee an account
of the third- and fourth-year curriculum of a single year group (SED, 1977a,
Table A3). The table in the Dunning Report showed, for 25 subjects, the
number of S3 pupils studying each subject and then, taking that figure as
100 per cent, presented the following statistics:

>   the percentage studying the subject in September of S4
>   the percentage aiming for O-grade in September of S4
>   the percentage presented for O-grade in S4
>   the percentage gaining A-C or D-E awards

The data used were for pupils who were in S4 during the school year 1975/76.
Subjects not available at O-grade, such as physical education and religious
education, were excluded from the table. The 25 subjects which did appear
were grouped in eight subject areas which, interestingly, differed in some
respects from the modes of the Munn Report. Thus the core subjects of
English, arithmetic and maths appeared as one group, and language,
business studies, technical and home economics each appeared as single
subject-group titles.
   We can use these Dunning data on subjects as a point of reference in two
ways: first, they tell us about the curricular *status quo* from which the Munn/
Dunning Committees started out on their deliberations. Second, we can
enquire whether there has been much change in the pattern between 1974/
76 and the end of the decade; were the leavers who took part in the 1981
survey operating within a similar league table of subjects?
   We can begin by looking at the relative position of subjects in S3 in the
Dunning data. This is shown on the left-hand side of Figure 3.3, where each

FIGURE 3.3
Percentage taking certain subjects in S3

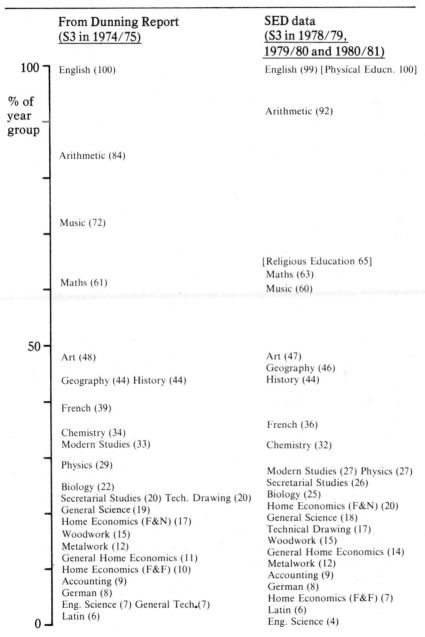

From Dunning Report
(S3 in 1974/75)

SED data
(S3 in 1978/79,
1979/80 and 1980/81)

100 — English (100)   English (99) [Physical Educn. 100]

% of
year   Arithmetic (92)
group

Arithmetic (84)

Music (72)

[Religious Education 65]
Maths (63)
Maths (61)   Music (60)

50 —
Art (48)   Art (47)
                                       Geography (46)
Geography (44) History (44)   History (44)

French (39)
                                       French (36)
Chemistry (34)
Modern Studies (33)   Chemistry (32)

Physics (29)
                                       Modern Studies (27) Physics (27)
Biology (22)   Secretarial Studies (26)
Secretarial Studies (20) Tech. Drawing (20) Biology (25)
General Science (19)   Home Economics (F&N) (20)
Home Economics (F&N) (17)   General Science (18)
Woodwork (15)   Technical Drawing (17)
Metalwork (12)   Woodwork (15)
General Home Economics (11)   General Home Economics (14)
Home Economics (F&F) (10)   Metalwork (12)
Accounting (9)   Accounting (9)
German (8)   German (8)
Eng. Science (7) General Tech.(7)   Home Economics (F&F) (7)
Latin (6)   Latin (6)
0 —   Eng. Science (4)

subject is ranked according to the percentage of the year group who studied it in S3. Only ten of the 25 examinable subjects recorded there were taken by more than 30 per cent of the year group, and this list included only one science subject. French was among the top ten, but the proportion studying any other foreign language was very small: under ten per cent. Both music and art were included; in fact music was taken by almost three quarters of the group (72 per cent), art by almost half (48 per cent). Subjects which we have classified, in the neo-Munn schema, as "applied studies" were mostly studied by between ten and 20 per cent of the age group. In addition to the 22 subjects which could lead to O-grade examinations, there were three "general" headings: general science (19 per cent), general home economics (11 per cent) and general technical subjects (seven per cent); it may be presumed that these were non-examination classes from the beginning of S3.

In order to monitor possible changes in the pattern since the Dunning data were collected, we have drawn on unpublished SED data from the annual School Census. Because detailed information on school subjects at each school stage is confined to a sample of schools, we shall present results averaged over three year groups – a similar approach to the composite year group of the 1981 survey. In this case data are for pupils who were in S3 in 1978/79, 1979/80 and 1980/81. On the right-hand side of Figure 3.3, subjects have been ranked in the same way as for the Dunning data. Two non-O-grade subjects have been included: physical education (assumed to be taken by all the year group) and religious education (65 per cent). These two therefore figure in the list of 11 subjects taken by more than 30 per cent of the year group. Apart from modern studies (27 per cent), the list of examinable subjects in this group is the same as in the Dunning results, and the rank ordering is almost the same, except that music was taken by six out of ten pupils, less than the proportion taking maths. The only science subject in this group (chemistry) was in eleventh place. Some changes had apparently taken place in the percentage of pupils taking some of the applied subjects, but these differences were minor compared with the strong impression of stability conveyed by the two parts of Figure 3.3.

The composite year group we shall be following in most of this chapter using the 1981 survey data represents a slightly earlier date than the composite SED group: the leavers we surveyed were in S3 in 1976/77, 1977/78 or 1978/79. It would be unprofitable to attempt detailed comparisons for all subjects with the Dunning or SED data because of major differences in the way the information was collected for the 1981 survey. However, it is reassuring to note that, following the same approach as in Figure 3.3, the top 11 subjects, that is those studied by over 30 per cent of pupils in S3, were the same as in the SED list. The main difference between the two was that in the 1981 survey results, which were based on leavers' own reports, physical education (87 per cent), music (42 per cent) and art (37 per cent) featured less prominently. In a number of instances, however, the correspondence with the SED list was very close: for example, history, physics, arithmetic and biology, where the differences in percentages was no more than one or two per cent.

In general we can conclude from Figure 3.3 that there has been little change in the relative position of subjects in the S3 curriculum during the period when the 1980 leavers were passing through school. We can also note that the 1981 survey data reflect that picture fairly accurately, particularly for the academic O-grade subjects.

These results open up a very limited perspective on the curriculum; they describe it in terms of separate subjects, and give information on one school year only (S3). To know that modern studies and physics were each studied by 27 per cent of the year group tells us nothing about the ways these subjects were combined with each other or with other subjects, nor about what kind of pupils studied them. To answer questions of this sort we need data which have been recorded by or for each individual, data which are uniquely supplied for Scotland as a whole by the School Leavers Surveys, and which will be used in the rest of the chapter. Before we leave the kind of subject record we have been looking at so far, however, we can learn a little more about what happens to subjects by the end of S4. In particular we can find out how closely a subject was defined by the demands of the O-grade examination by asking whether this was the goal for all or the majority of those who were studying it in S3. Figure 3.4 presents on the left-hand side of the diagram results taken from the Dunning data for five selected subjects. Each subject is drawn from the "top ten" subjects of Figure 3.3 and represents one of the Munn modes or areas of study. The diagram shows the percentage (of the S3 starting group) who were considered to be on an O-grade course at the beginning of S4, and who were presented for the examination at the end of that year. As we might perhaps expect, chemistry was almost exclusively an O-grade subject; nearly 90 per cent of those taking it in S3 were defined as O-grade students in S4, and seven out of ten were presented for the examination. By contrast, only 30 per cent of S3 art pupils were studying for O-grade in S4 with a quarter (24 per cent) proceeding to the exam. Of course these results should be related to the size of the S3 group who started a subject; only 32 per cent of the age group began chemistry compared with almost one in two who were taking art. But it will be seen that the two most "popular" examinable subjects, English and arithmetic, stand out as primarily O-grade subjects, with eight out of ten students on 0-grade courses in S4.

On the right-hand side of Figure 3.4 are presented in comparable fashion some results based on the 1981 survey. Extra caution is needed in this case in making comparisons between the two studies because the time points which define O-grade study are slightly different for the 1981 survey. We asked leavers to tell us if they had "sat" each subject "for prelims", which would imply that they were on an O-grade course at least up to a point which in most schools would fall between November and January of S4 (Dunning has "on O-grade course in September of S4"). "Sat for O-grade" replaces "presented for O-grade" in Dunning. These differences would be likely to result in slightly lower percentages of pupils taking a subject at each point in the 1981 survey results as compared with the Dunning figures. Bearing this in mind, we can see that within-subject developments appear rather similar to those we have already observed for the Dunning data. Chemistry was if anything even more strongly tied to O-grade; so also was art, but in this case the S3 group for the 1981 survey was proportionately smaller (37 per cent) than in the Dunning study and a straight comparison may be misleading. But although we should exercise caution in making comparisons over these two sets of data, the picture that begins to emerge can be outlined with some confidence: subjects differed in the mid 1970s and have continued to differ not only in the proportion of the age group choosing or being directed to study them, but in the extent which they might be defined as wholly "examination" subjects. When a pupil embarked on a subject in S3, would the teacher be expecting him or her to be sitting O-grade with the rest of the group, or would the assumption be that only some pupils (or classes) would be doing so?

If we focus on the 1981 survey results and take the last time point – "sat O-grade" – we can group subjects, in terms of O-grade presentation, as follows: "very high" presentation rate (over 70 per cent of those studying the subject in S3): French, physics, chemistry; "high" presentation rate (60-69 per cent): English, arithmetic, secretarial studies, biology; "medium" presentation rate (50-59 per cent): maths, history, geography, technical drawing; "low" presentation rates (below 50 per cent): modern studies, woodwork, metalwork, music, art. While it would seem plausible to suggest that the "very high" presentation rates reflect a stringent selection process at the beginning of S3, it is interesting to note that the "high" presentation group includes the two core subjects of English and arithmetic, taken by almost all of the S3 populations. The extremely low presentation rates for art and music are of course influenced by the dual role of these subjects for general education and examination purposes. Modern studies had a markedly lower presentation rate than the other two social subjects recorded.

From this evidence we can already anticipate how some areas of our neo-Munn schema will look in general terms; we can expect to find that most pupils were taking "linguistic and literary studies" (ie English) and probably

FIGURE 3.4
Pupils studying certain subjects for O-grade in S4, and taking the O-grade examination, as percentage of pupils starting subject in S3: evidence from the Dunning Report and the 1981 survey

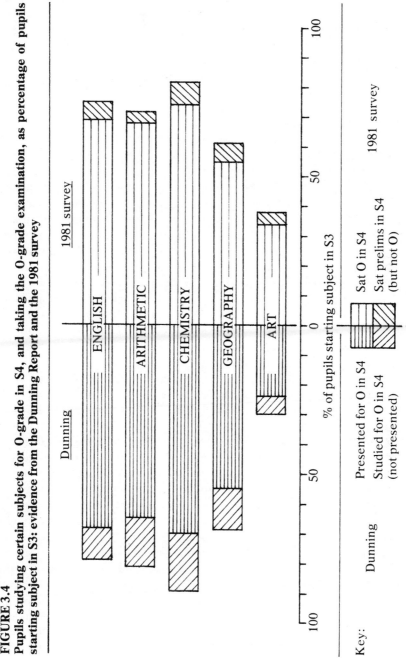

% of pupils starting subject in S3

Key:

Presented for O in S4	Sat O in S4
Studied for O in S4 (not presented)	Sat prelims in S4 (but not O)
Dunning	1981 survey

"mathematical studies" (arithmetic and/or maths), certainly in S3 and probably through to O-grade. We shall probably notice a considerable drop in "aesthetic studies" after S3. But what about the areas of scientific or social studies? How many pupils studied at least one subject in each of these areas? And perhaps more importantly which pupils studied which subjects? It is time to shift the perspective from *subjects* to *pupils* in order to look more closely at how differentiation is realised through the curriculum.

Pupils and their curricula: third year

From this point onwards the discussion will be confined to data from the 1981 survey; and the data will be set within a particular framework. One dimension of that framework defines the content of the curriculum: pupils' curricula will be reviewed in terms of the neo-Munn schema of Figure 3.2. We can look at all or some of the eight areas of that schema, discovering whether pupils studied one or more of the subjects contained in an area, at various moments during the S3/S4 stage of their schooling. The second dimension of the framework concerns the pupils. In addition to looking at the year group as a whole (as we have done so far) we shall want to distinguish representative sub-groups of pupils to see how they fared during this period. We shall do this by employing the modelled populations defined earlier in this chapter. There are two reasons for this approach. First, it places the focus on pupils but enables us to view differentiation at one remove, by seeing what happens to a modelled population which best represents a particular set of criteria or level of ability. Second, the criteria employed to define the population embody definitions made during and since the recommendations of the Munn/Dunning Committees; this means we can relate the experiences of the 1980 leavers to current thinking about differentiation.

Before looking in more detail at the curriculum, we can establish a frame of reference by answering a simpler question: how many subjects, on average, did pupils study altogether? The answer is nine; for the Credit MPOP it was 9.1, slightly higher than for the General MPOP (8.5). One group of respondents, representing approximately 15 per cent of the whole sample, had been given a simpler curriculum record, in which they were asked to tick the subjects they had studied in S4. This form of record was in a short, six-page questionnaire sent to leavers who had not sat O-grade, and probably had not started any O-grade courses. Each of these leavers would therefore have a heavy Foundation weighting and at best only a slight General weighting. The results show that those who completed this questionnaire recorded a higher average number of subjects than the other respondents: 10.7 subjects, compared with 9.4 for the section of the Foundation MPOP who had completed the more detailed curriculum record common to all other respondents. Because of the difference in the form of the curriculum record in the questionnaire and the possibility that this might have resulted in differing patterns of response for this group of leavers, we shall present results for the two sections of the Foundation MPOP separately in a number of tables and figures that follow. Weighted results which are derived from those who completed the full curriculum record will be described under the heading "Foundation MPOP 1"; weighted results based on the simpler record will be ascribed to Foundation MPOP 2.

We can now begin to describe the curriculum followed by the 1980 leavers within the Munn/Dunning model framework we have defined. In Figure 3.5 we show the simplest realisation of this neo-Munn schema for S3. For each of the eight areas, the percentage of pupils studying at least one of the subjects in that area is shown in the diagram. If we look first at results for the whole sample, it can be seen that as might be expected linguistic studies and mathematical studies were already core areas in S3, that is, almost all pupils participated in each of them, and we can safely guess that in practice English and arithmetic (or maths) were the subjects on which these results were primarily based. The other study area – science – which was included in the compulsory core in the government's proposals was in a much weaker position. Less than two thirds of the sample were studying any of the major science subjects, and the science study area was scarcely better supported than the other two lowest ranking areas, religious/moral studies and aesthetic studies. By contrast some kind of social studies, an area not specifically insisted upon as a compulsory component in the government's proposals, was being pursued by 82 per cent of pupils, and three quarters had embarked on at least one subject in the applied studies area.

How general was the experience summarised by these results? By looking at outcomes for the three MPOPs we can get behind the global figures we have used up to now and begin to tackle the underlying issue of this chapter: the character of the curricula experienced by different "types" of pupils during S3/S4.

Two of the eight neo-Munn areas, linguistic studies and mathematical studies, call for little discussion since they were common to the curricula of almost all pupils. Among the Credit MPOP the notable features include the comparatively secure position of science (studied by almost eight out of ten pupils) and the demotion of applied studies (taken by less than half (47 per cent) of this population, the same figure as for aesthetic studies). Indeed, for this group one could define five core areas (linguistic studies, mathematical studies, physical activities, social studies and science studies) and three optional areas (aesthetic studies, applied studies and religious/moral studies). The picture for the general MPOP, not surprisingly, reflects fairly closely the overall results we looked at first and calls for no particular

FIGURE 3.5
Percentage of each modelled population studying at least one subject in each area of the neo-Munn schema in S3

Modelled population

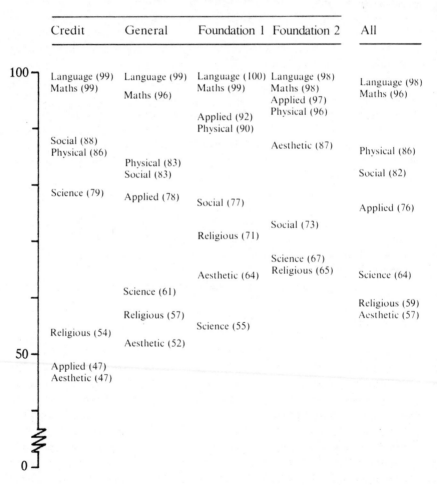

comment. But the pattern for the Foundation MPOP is interesting in several ways. We will distinguish between the Foundation 1 MPOP and the Foundation 2 MPOP, as explained earlier. Foundation 2 results show a high level of participation in each area (65 per cent or more). Within this, applied studies figured prominently (97 per cent studied it) with aesthetic studies also important (87 per cent), while science (taken by two thirds of the group) occupied seventh place. Some part of these results may be attributed to the difference in the form of the curriculum record. But even for the Foundation 1 MPOP (based on the standard curriculum record), applied studies was in third place after linguistic studies and maths. Science this time was in eighth place, studied by just over half the group. In this case, a small core of four areas (linguistic studies, maths, applied studies and physical activities) was coupled with two well supported areas (social and religious studies) and two that were less certain (aesthetic and science studies). These contrasts between the MPOPs in a rather simplified realisation of the S3 curriculum begin to point to well established distinctions between curriculum types and pupil types. But we need to know more about the balance within and between some of these curriculum areas; we also need to consider possible differences between the sexes in the patterns of subjects and studies.

It has already been suggested that doing one or more subjects in "linguistic studies" means in practice almost certainly doing English (and possibly more language subjects). If we are to learn about the study of languages other than English, we need to know just how many subjects were studied within this area. We may also want to know about the proportions taking two or more science subjects, and so on. We decided to stipulate certain combinations of subjects which pupils might take, and to discover how far these patterns were realised. Table 3.2 shows the proportion of each MPOP following each pattern. First we postulated a neo-Munn curriculum in two forms: the first version demanded that pupils should have studied at least one subject in each of the six examinable neo-Munn areas. The second version added the two non-examinable areas of physical activities and religious/moral studies. We can deal quickly with the latter: fewer than one in five pupils were following a full neo-Munn curriculum in S3, except among the Foundation 2 sub-group, where over a third did so. At each course level participation in this full eight-area version was slightly higher among the male MPOP; the lowest participation rate was five per cent in the female Credit MPOP. The examinable neo-Munn curriculum was slightly better supported at each level; interestingly it was the Foundation MPOP who were most likely to qualify on this pattern, with a quarter of the male and slighly less of the female Foundation 1 MPOP following it; results for the Foundation 2 groups show over half of these taking the full range of subjects.

TABLE 3.2

Percentage of each modelled population following selected curriculum patterns in S3, by sex

	Credit		General		Foundation 1		Foundation 2	
	Males	Females	Males	Females	Males	Females	Males	Females
Neo-Munn 1	17	9	22	15	26	21	53	55
Neo-Munn 2	12	5	14	10	18	14	36	36
Science-bias	61	37	28	13	17	8	–	–
Language bias	60	76	26	44	16	29	–	–
Applied-bias	26	19	44	46	70	70	74	89

Key: Neo-Munn 1:   language, maths, social, science, applied, aesthetic (1 or more of each)
Neo-Munn 2:   as above plus religious, physical (1 or more of each)
Science-bias: science (2 or more), language (1 or more), maths (2 or more), social (1 or more)
Language-bias: language (2 or more), maths (2 or more), social (1 or more)
Applied-bias: applied (2 or more), language (1 or more), maths (1 or more)

Three other curriculum patterns were defined and analysed for the MPOPs: a science-biased pattern, a languages-biased pattern and a pattern showing a bias towards applied studies. With the science pattern (which included at least two science subjects) the differences between course levels and between male and female MPOPs are clearly apparent. Among the male Credit MPOP, six out of ten embarked on a science-biased curriculum, but less than four out of ten from the female Credit MPOP did so. Just over a quarter of the male General MPOP started out on this pattern, more than twice as many as in the female General MPOP. For the language-biased pattern, where the main stipulation was that at least two language subjects should be studied (in practice almost certainly English and one other) and no science was required, the pattern was rather similar to the science-biased pattern for each male MPOP: six out of ten for the Credit MPOP, just over a quarter of the General MPOP, and less than 20 per cent of the Foundation 1 MPOP. Among the female MPOPs the pattern was more popular at each level: three quarters of the female Credit MPOP embarked on it and it was a well recognised track for the female General MPOP as well (44 per cent). The third type of curriculum pattern presented here was biased towards applied studies. In this case there was little difference between the sexes. Almost half of the male and of the female General MPOP embarked on a course of this kind which included at least two applied subjects in addition to one language and one mathematical subject. The applied studies curriculum was even more typical for the Foundation MPOP with at least seven out of ten following it. By contrast, only a quarter or less of the Credit MPOP took this combination.

This brief review of third-year curriculum patterns strengthens the impression we have gained from looking at the separate neo-Munn areas, and which has been reported in other studies (Ryrie, 1981): an impression of a curriculum which is differentiated not only by the predominant level of course followed but in the combination of subjects taken by pupils of various "levels" of ability, and in the balance of the curriculum between subject areas. The pattern of differentiation is further complicated by the differences between the sexes in their apparent preferences for and perceptions of some of these subject areas.

Third year to O-grade: the progress of differentiation

So far we have been looking at the S3 curriculum only. What happened to that curriculum in the period up to the end of S4? We can summarise the progress of differentiation for each MPOP, as it currently operates, by looking at the mean number of examinable subjects carried through to the O-grade examination. In the Credit MPOP on average less than one examinable subject was dropped between S3 (7.7) and the examination (6.9), compared with an average decrease, between these time points, of two subjects for the General MPOP (7.0, 5.0). The Foundation 1 MPOP sat an average of 2.5 O-grades, compared with the 7.8 examinable subjects started in S3. For the Credit MPOP "examinable subjects in S3" meant subjects that would almost certainly be sat at O-grade, but for the other two MPOPs there could be no such assurance. Just what had happened over that period we cannot always tell from our data. Those who started non-examined courses may well have completed a two-year course without presenting subjects for examination, and in schools in some areas pupils will have studied for the Certificate of Secondary Education (CSE) rather than O-grade. But the figures serve to remind us that the risk of over-subscription to O-grade courses in S3 has been as persistent a feature of the present system as the over-presentation at O-grade that concerned the Dunning Committee. If, in future, course levels within subjects are defined in S3, it is difficult to see what is to prevent a similar process occurring.

TABLE 3.3

S3 to O-grade: percentage of each modelled population studying at least one subject in eight neo-Munn areas

	Studied in S3	Studied in S4	Sat prelim	Sat O-grade	Obtained A–C award
Credit					
Linguistic	99	99	98	99	88
Mathematical	98	99	98	98	91
Religious/Moral	54	23	–	–	–
Physical	86	41	–	–	–
Social	88	87	87	86	76
Science	79	79	78	77	68
Applied	47	45	43	44	40
Aesthetic	47	26	17	17	15
General					
Linguistic	99	97	94	88	44
Mathematical	96	94	91	84	46
Religious/Moral	57	20	–	–	–
Physical	83	29	–	–	–
Social	83	75	75	65	31
Science	61	58	56	48	21
Applied	78	75	71	65	39
Aesthetic	52	31	23	20	13
Foundation 1					
Linguistic	100	84	61	54	19
Mathematical	99	78	52	47	18
Religious/Moral	71	23	–	–	–
Physical	91	30	–	–	–
Social	77	51	33	29	12
Science	55	37	23	19	8
Applied	92	69	46	41	9
Aesthetic	64	36	16	14	9

We can see how these changes in the scope of the examined curriculum affected its balance by looking at figures for each of the six examinable neo-Munn areas from S3 through to O-grade (Table 3.3) for the Credit and General MPOPs. As we might expect, progress for the Credit MPOP appears smooth, steady and uneventful. By the time the O-grade examination arrived the shape of their curriculum had changed little: of the examinable neo-Munn areas, their four core areas of linguistic, mathematical, social and scientific studies were still almost intact – only two per cent at most of the S3 contingent had dropped out. There was little fall-out either from applied studies; all but three per cent of the S3 students in this area sat O-grade in at least one of its subjects. The two non-examinable areas, religious/moral studies and physical activities, could be monitored as far as study in S4. The results suggest that numbers were halved from S3 to S4; there is no way of checking further on this result from the data and we can only comment that some leavers may have forgotten, or considered it unnecessary to record, studying these subjects in S4. There was also a sharp decrease in aesthetic studies participation at this point, and only 17 per cent of the MPOP proceeded to prelims and O-grade in this area. The same kind of process occurred in aesthetic studies among the General MPOP, with 20 per cent sitting O-grade, compared with the 52 per cent who started in S3. But for the General MPOP this was not the only examinable area where there was a noticeable fall-out between S3 and O-grade. Only linguistic and mathematical studies were carried through by more than seven out of ten pupils, and even in these two areas about one in ten pupils failed to make the O-grade examination. In social studies the figure was almost two in ten. The result was that social and applied studies were attempted at O-grade by just under two thirds of the MPOP, science by less than half. Some pupils, of course, may have been on a non-O-grade course from the outset in some of these subjects, but it is worth noting that in each area except the aesthetic there was a fall-out of between six and 11 per cent after prelims. The Foundation 2 MPOP results have not been included in Table 3.3, since no more than two per cent attempted prelims in any area, and none sat O-grade, but the dropping-out process is well illustrated by the results for the Foundation 1 section. Just over half (54 per cent) sat O-grade in the linguistic studies area (presumably in English); somewhat fewer in mathematical and/or applied studies. For other areas the proportion sitting O-grade was less than three out of ten. Fall-out between prelims and O-grade was no worse, on average, than among the General MPOP, suggesting that pupils had either abandoned an O-grade course at an earlier stage or else never started one. Indeed for this MPOP Table 3.3 shows some substantial drops between S3 and S4; it is impossible to tell for certain whether all these pupils really gave up the subject in that year or failed to record a subject in which they did not attempt O-grade. But the results as a whole for the Foundation MPOP provide a sharp contrast with the steady progress of the Credit MPOP in each of their chosen subject areas towards O-grade – the seal of their two-year course.

These contrasts between the MPOPs of course mask some important variations within each population. Table 3.2 revealed differences between the male and female sections of each MPOP in the pattern of subjects studied in S3, particularly in languages and science. What was the outcome of these choices for each group by the end of S4? The effect within the science and linguistic areas is shown for each sex in the Credit and General MPOPs in Figure 3.6, which traces what happened to the groups for those taking two or more languages, and for two or more sciences, from S3 through to O-grade. In the Credit MPOP, the gap between males and females in the proportion taking two or more languages is clear, but the probability of the pattern being maintained to O-grade is fairly similar for each sex. Among the male General MPOP, less than 30 per cent embarked on two languages; for this minority, drop-out was less severe than among the female General MPOP who were more likely to have followed this course. The results for science reverse these sex differences and show an interesting interaction between sex and level. The proportion starting two or more sciences was almost the same for the female Credit MPOP and the male General MPOP, but drop-out among the latter was more severe. In each of these areas the Foundation 1 MPOP, not included in the diagram, showed a similar pattern to the other two; more of the female Foundation 1 group took two languages than of the male General MPOP; and more of the male Foundation 1 MPOP took two sciences in S3 than the female General MPOP. In each case, however, only a small proportion presented both sciences at O-grade. Choosing subjects in conformity with established sex bias had not worked out particularly well for the General and Foundation MPOP pupils.

Differentiation and the curriculum: profile and prospects
    In this chapter we have tried to investigate the process of differentiation during the final stage of compulsory schooling by setting the record of pupils' experiences against the context of proposed changes in the structure of curriculum and assessment. We briefly reviewed some of the proposals of the Munn and Dunning programme in order to construct a model of the new structures. We were able to do this because the proposals, as currently defined, have been expressed in forms and units which exist in the present system. On the face of it the comparative ease with which we could effect this translation (with some admitted distortions and inaccuracies) is surprising. The impetus for the Munn and Dunning reforms came from a

FIGURE 3.6
Percentage of Credit and General modelled populations following two or more languages, and two or more science subjects, by sex

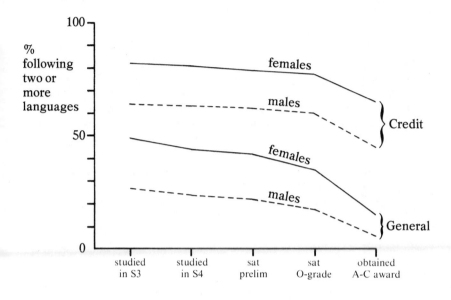

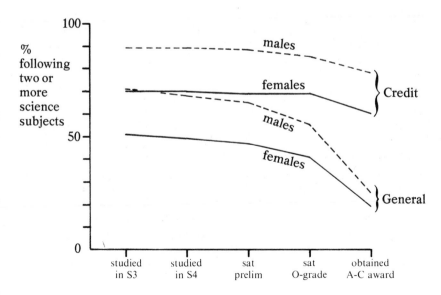

widespread dissatisfaction with the structure of curriculum and examinations that had developed in S3/S4, and one might have expected a correspondingly radical revision of that structure and the terms in which it was defined. How have the committees' proposals, and the later developments of them in the government's programme, met this challenge? And what can we learn from the experience of recent school leavers about the problems and possible consequences of implementing the new structures?

The Munn Committee's concern for a common set of experiences for all pupils and their attempt to spell this out in terms of time allocations for the core curriculum indicated a strong desire to move the S3/S4 curriculum away from the old academic/practical divide and towards a liberal education for all in the final stage of compulsory education. But were administrative specifications sufficient for the purpose? McIntyre (1978) has argued that a crucial weakness of the report was that no attempt was made to formulate detailed pedagogical proposals for implementing the general educational aims outlined in the early chapters. While some interdisciplinary courses were recommended (and are being developed), the bulk of the S3/S4 timetable would continue to be made up of subject units. The responsibility for trying to implement Munn's general aims within and through the subject units would fall on the working parties charged with drawing up national guidelines. Past experience of national curriculum planning for certificate and non-certificate courses would suggest that groups commissioned to plan a course on "science" (General and Foundation) would feel freer to approach their task in the light of the kind of pupil needs referred to in Munn than those formulating proposals for, say, Credit-level French, where the traditional requirements of the subject discipline, especially for those going on to Highers, are already well known. Pressures on and within existing subject disciplines make the task of redirecting the purposes and priorities of the curriculum a difficult one. It seems that in its desire to produce "realistic" proposals which could be implemented as a matter of urgency, the committee passed up the opportunity to challenge the place of the subject in the structure of the curriculum. In doing so they could rightly claim that they were in tune with the views of teachers (Forsyth and Dockrell, 1979). But it could be argued that the only way of realising their general educational aims would have been to find ways of transforming those views before a new administrative structure was formalised.

With the subject firmly established as the building block of the new system, the framework of the Munn modes or areas of study could be adapted to serve as a classification system for all subjects, as we have seen in looking at the detailed list from *Framework for Decision*. No reasons are given in the latter document for the allocation of subjects to areas, the assumption apparently being that the schema is simply a restatement of the Munn Report's proposals. But this is clearly not the case. To start with, the list of subjects is considerably longer. Since the division of the curriculum recommended by Munn into (large) core and (small) elective sections had been virtually abandoned in the government's proposals, the areas or modes now served primarily as an analytical framework for all the subjects in the school's curriculum rather than as a recipe for the obligatory part of each pupil's programme. The effort to fit a collection of school subjects, which have established their identity over the years according to a variety of criteria, into a schema supposedly defined in terms of distinctive modes of experience would challenge the ingenuity of Procrustes, and there is no indication that the task was seriously attempted. As Drever *et al.* (1983) have suggested, "the subjects and modes appear to be little more than labels enabling administratively tidy curriculum plans to be advanced".

The effect of these alterations in the Munn framework is far-reaching. In the Munn proposals all pupils were required to spend about two thirds of their time fairly evenly divided between the seven areas of the core curriculum; the rest could be spent on other subjects in these areas or on subjects not listed there at all. In the government's scheme, on the other hand, the compulsory core is reduced to three subjects (English, maths and science) taking up just over one third of the timetabled week. While "all schools are asked to adopt the curriculum framework provided by the 8 modes of study proposed by the Munn Committee" (SED, 1983c, p.1), some areas or modes are apparently less essential than others, and one of them (language and linguistic studies) has been subdivided into a compulsory element (English) and an optional element (other languages). And while all pupils are expected to work on all seven or eight modes the suggested time allocations mean that the time spent on each could vary widely; Drever *et al.* (1983) have shown how two thirds of pupils' time could be spent on three modes only. In other words, whereas the Munn proposals would have required from all pupils a substantial commitment not only to science but also to aesthetic activities and moral/religious education, the framework of the government's scheme is so loosely defined that schools would have plenty of room to perpetuate whatever sort of differentiated curriculum is currently in operation. Since the recommended compulsory core subjects have now been reduced to three, there seems little incentive for schools to broaden the mainstream (examination) curriculum of most pupils in the way originally envisaged in Munn, especially when other pressures – financial and demographic – are combining to restrict the range of subjects offered in many schools. Even to ensure a minimal compliance with the proposed framework – that all pupils should follow examined courses in English, maths and science, and participate in some way in all the areas of the framework – will require a major effort of planning in the schools where only 64 per cent of the pupils presently participate in a mainstream science subject in S3. And there is nothing in the proposals to ensure that the present heavy commitment to practical subjects among pupils whose courses are likely to be mostly at the General and/or Foundation level would be reduced. Other current problems, such as sex bias in science and languages, are scarcely touched by the proposals.

Concern about the shape of the curriculum after Munn becomes more acute when the experience of our modelled populations is explored. The acceptance by the Dunning Committee of the three-level course structure shaped the character of all that followed. The system of course levels would provide a means for differentiating pupils within each subject or course on a vertical scale (most able --- least able) at some given point in time during S3/S4. The proposal was softened by provision for overlap between levels and by exhortations to course planners to create "as much individual variety as possible" (SED, 1977b, p.45). But other possible strategies for taking account of individual differences in learning – for example, graded courses through which pupils progress at varying rates – were not even suggested. The preferred strategy was rather to define two-year courses of differing levels to which pupils could be directed. From the outset, therefore, the plan for differentiated courses had implications for the differentiation of *pupils*; there were also implications for the differentiation of *subjects*, not all of which would be offered at all three levels. Pupils would be distinguished from each other not only by the level of course they were following but also by the type of subject they were invited to study. That such an approach was in tune with current professional thinking in schools is shown by the fact that 70 per cent of teachers who took part in a survey on this issue endorsed the plan for three course levels (Forsyth and Dockrell, 1979). It is difficult to see what will counteract the long established tradition of over-presentation, which the Dunning Report discussed and deplored and the over-subscription to "higher" level courses in S3. Up to now, when such decisions have had to be made, some teachers have understandably wanted to give borderline pupils the benefit of the doubt, or have been pressed by parents to do so. It will take a firm stand, such as that outlined in the Munn and Dunning Joint Working-Party Report on English (Scottish Examination Board, 1983) in favour of an undifferentiated course structure, to counteract the trend towards more strictly defined course boundaries evident in most of the recommendations, and the consequent need to allocate pupils to a specific course level at some point, even perhaps at the beginning of S3.

It is true that decisions about the system of awards made by the SED and communicated to the SEB in June 1983 are explicitly intended to discourage over-presentation. It is argued that the single seven-point scale of awards will "prevent categorisation of pupils by reference to level of presentation". But it has also been decided that the level of presentation as well as the award band will be shown on the certificate – a decision designed to assist "users of the certificate", including, of course, employers. Indeed, considerable attention is paid to the interests of users who are thought likely to find a single numerical scale "easy to understand" and therefore more acceptable than the alternative stepped scale. For similar reasons a proposal that would have been in keeping with the principles of the Dunning approach to assessment – reversing the direction of the seven-point scale - is rejected. The public are therefore to be offered a more comprehensive and updated version of the familiar scale of cognitive achievement which up to now has been based on O-grade awards (and will remain in part tied to them). It remains to be seen whether "users" are more impressed by the level of award on the scale or the level of presentation; the latter will certainly be of interest when leavers apply for jobs before the results are available. Will the new scheme succeed in insulating decisions about course levels from external pressures? If not, then the reforms will have provided for users not only a more efficient scheme of grading, covering *all* pupils, but also an additional criterion by which aspirants can be differentiated. In a context where pressures for more stringent selection mechanisms have been growing steadily, it seems unlikely that such a tool will not be used.

The third and fourth years have already acquired a well defined public image as the final stage of the compulsory course, a stage when the process of publicly supported learning should be validated by a public and national system of assessment. More recently it has been felt that assessment should be made available for all pupils, as a survey of the profession showed:

> The proposal to have a single national certificate for all pupils completing the fourth year of secondary education was almost universally endorsed, either as a matter of principle (the only acceptable alternative mentioned being to have no national certification at all in S4) or as a matter of practical necessity because employers wanted it, because post-secondary education wanted it, and because parents wanted it. Against these demands the education service was seen as having no sufficient grounds for refusing to measure the quality of its product and gauge the success of its own processes. (Forsyth and Dockrell, 1979, p.7)

Once such an aim – to create a fair system of assessment for all – had been agreed, the task of reformers, though challenging, was well within the capability of Scottish policy makers who had inherited a tradition of national educational assessment which went back at least a hundred years.

But any system of assessment influences and structures the curriculum it is designed to monitor; and alongside the tradition of an examination-steered curriculum there has been another Scottish tradition, of a liberal, general education, which some educationists have considered is the right of all, not just those who succeed in the race. Was it possible to interweave these two strands? Ironically it was the English Certificate of Secondary Education (CSE) which seemed to some Scots to offer the best chance of doing so, since a Mode 3 approach enabled teachers to obtain public assessment for the flexible, broad-based courses which many advocates of general education preferred to traditionally defined examination subjects with their packaged pedagogy. But developments in England have illustrated how an educationally sound innovation in curriculum may become distorted when its assessment scale can be exploited for non-educational purposes. As the pressure of unemployment has grown, the CSE seems to have acquired a bad press as a second-grade qualification which is now hopelessly devalued as job-getting currency in a context where even success at O-level guarantees nothing. Now other attempts are being made to wrench the process of 16-plus assessment away from the one-dimensional scale of cognitive achievement which examinations have come to represent. One of these, the Oxford Certificate of Educational Achievement, which will have sections on graded tests and examples of individual initiative and achievement as well as public examination results, is receiving enthusiastic support from teachers, local policy-makers and researchers in various parts of England (*TES*, 17.6.83). It remains to be seen whether this attempt to record several dimensions of a young person's achievement will be able to withstand the presssures from higher education and from employers for a simple ranking mechanism for selection purposes.

Efforts to include *all* pupils in a single scheme for curriculum and assessment have already brought benefits to the group of pupils who, because their work was not publicly assessed, often received less attention than they should from curriculum planners. The question that remains from our study of the pressures for differentiation wthin the existing system, and our review of the framework that will replace it, is whether the intentions of the policy-makers to create an appropriate, flexible and balanced curriculum for 14-16 year olds will be thwarted by the forces that operate on the school through the choices made by pupils as the period of compulsory schooling comes to an end. All pupils and their teachers rightly want their achievements in learning to be recognised. But how will such achievements be valued and interpreted by others, and consequently by the young people themselves? As one pupil on a Foundation pilot course was heard to remark (*TESS*, 10.6.83), getting a prize which shows you are "good at being stupid" is not really worth working for. If that view were to become widespread it would be a sad epitaph for a decade of reform.

Chapter 4

Reviewing compulsion: pupil perspectives on the fourth-year experience

Penelope Weston

"Better if you could leave school at the age of 14. Because you dont learn nothing after that."

In looking through comments the leavers themselves wrote on their questionnaires it was easy enough to pick out reactions to compulsory schooling which, if less extreme than this one, suggest disenchantment of various kinds with the process of mass education: teachers who were too strict or not strict enough; mixed-ability classes which held back the "bright"; segregation which discriminated against the "thick"; O-grade courses that were too easy (as a preparation for Highers), over-valued by teachers (as a job qualification), monotonous, oppressive, or longed-for (by those not allowed to take them). One girl wrote of her success in beating the system: she managed to obtain permission to leave school, aged 15, at the end of third year (S3) to start a junior secretarial course at college, a step she had not regretted. And yet for the majority the last two years of compulsory schooling seemed to have been accepted readily enough as an apprenticeship for what was to follow, whether in school or outside; an apprenticeship characterised by a willingness to tolerate monotony as long as there were friends to endure it with, and a readiness to recognise and make the most of exceptional characters and events: larger-than-life teachers, subjects which turned out to be "interesting", careers guidance which actually proved useful. Their expectations for this stage of schooling were perhaps more realistic than those of some teachers who managed to convey to their pupils a view of the O-grade examination which endowed that modest educational accreditation (as its creators have perhaps seen it) with all the solemnity of the last judgement:

> Most of the teachers act as if it was an offence to fail an O
> level... they made you think that this was one of the most
> important things that would happen to you in your life,
> which made me all the more nervous when it came to sitting
> the exams.

We have seen in the previous chapter how the demands of the fourth-year examination system have structured the experience of pupils during the last stage of compulsory schooling, confirming for some their experience of success, and demonstrating to others, through a mounting burden of public evidence, their inability to meet its demands. Even if pupils "know the score" fairly well at the beginning of S3, from their interpretation of school grades and the pattern of subjects which they negotiate with their teachers, their position within the year group becomes clarified and all but settled before they sit the O-grade examination. For some, O-grade subjects have been dropped, perhaps as a result of the preliminary examinations. A small minority, already eligible to leave school, will have voted with their feet during the year, thus avoiding the possibility of public certification as "failures". The effects of this process of differentiation are felt and resented not only by those formally excluded from public assessment but also by the self-confessed "average" pupil:

> Everyone says, my parents included, that the school years
> are the best years of a persons life - if that is so, why did
> my parents leave when they were 15! I didn't enjoy my last
> years (4 and 5) in school because the teachers were all
> concerned with helping those they knew would pass all the
> exams. Also the best pupils were given the best teachers,
> thus were more likely to get the *best* results, while the *rest*
> of us were given the worst, therefore we never did very well
> in the exams.... Some teachers made the subjects as
> interesting as possible but they were few and far between.
> I was unlucky enough to get the worst teachers for the most
> important subjects thus as you can see I left school an utter
> failure, thinking what can possibly go wrong now. Anyway,
> I know what I've got to do now, and that is work as hard
> as I can and I've got to get going, I've learned this the hard
> way. Due to the attention paid to the above average,
> myself and many other average pupils have lost out
> somewhere. I'm not ashamed of being average, if only
> other people would consider that we need to feel as though

we're above "average" and we are all individuals, and so
we can go out into the world with a feeling of achievement
instead of failure.

In this chapter we want to investigate the experience of being a fourth-year (S4) pupil through the evaluations of school leavers, as they look back on that stage with the hindsight that almost certainly resulted from their public performance at O-grade. What could they remember of their time in classrooms? What methods of learning had predominated? How would they have liked to learn? What kind of organisation had prevailed in the classroom? What demands had been made on them to work outside lessons, and how far had they complied? And, looking back on that experience, what were their impressions of the final stage of compulsory schooling?

Some of the data to be used come from questions that were asked of all leavers; as far as possible we endeavoured in the 1981 survey to ask common questions about experiences that all had shared. More detailed questions on learning methods and homework were confined to those who had attempted some Scottish Certificate of Education (SCE) examinations at school. The evidence will be reviewed in the light of (actual) S4 O-grade performance, since this is the context in which the evaluation was made. We cannot use these data directly to model the future, but we hope to be able to make some inferences from leavers' evaluations of the experience of differentiated learning as it operates at present. Such inferences could inform policy-making at the school level even when the context for differentiation has changed. Two scales of S4 O-grade performance will be used, depending on the versions of the questionnaire from which the questions came: a six-point scale which distinguishes "early leavers" from other non-qualified pupils, and a broader three-category measure for data which have been less exhaustively analysed.

We shall start by looking behind the curriculum labels of the last chapter, at the kind of learning which was going on in the classroom, and the organisation of the learning process in and out of school. We can then move outwards to look at the more general attitudes which were indicated by leavers' responses to structured questions about the last year of compulsory schooling.

The experience of learning

Approaches to learning. All those who had attempted O-grade were asked a set of questions about the opportunities for learning which had been open to them in certain subjects during fourth year. To what extent were they expected to work together as a class? Were opportunities provided for individual initiative? What technical resources were available and how were they used in lessons? And what did the learners make of these experiences? In the two questionnaire versions on which we have focused for this book, questions on methods of learning related to fourth-year lessons in four subjects: geography (or history) and physics (or biology). Respondents who had studied the first of the two subjects listed in the version were asked to relate their answers to that subject; those who were taking the second subject (but not the first) answered for that subject. This approach made it possible to include more subjects in all, but will probably have introduced some (unknown) degree of bias in the sample of those reviewing the second subject of each pair. The ten "learning methods" have been grouped (in Table 4.1) in accordance with the degree of independent initiative accorded to the learner. Thus there is little suggestion of freedom of action in the first group of items: in each case (except possibly listening to a radio or tape recorder) pupils are almost certainly expected to act in concert as a class group. Three learning methods are then grouped together which suggest some degree of independence: learners are expected to organise their own work, under the general guidance of the teacher. Lastly there are three methods which call for the learner to use some piece of equipment (camera, computer, tape recorder) him/herself, rather than to respond, as one of a class audience, to a presentation on equipment operated by others. Respondents were asked whether they had experienced these methods "often", "sometimes" or "never". Results are given for each of the four subjects separately, and for all subjects together. They show the percentage who said they experienced the method "often".

A comparison between the subjects shows some differences: for instance, *watching* (films, slides, TV) was more prevalent in geography and biology than in history, or in physics where only nine per cent said they watched often. Of the pupils who evaluated history methods, one in five often made their own notes, more than for any other subject. But these differences pale into insignificance when set against the sheer weight of uniformity in learning methods *across* subjects: for each subject, between two thirds and three quarters of those who were asked said that they often copied the teacher's notes, and about half often spent time on worksheets or exercises as a class activity. These two types of activities predominated in all four subjects. Methods in the second group were more likely to be experienced "sometimes" than "often" (results not shown) and no more than 23 per cent of pupils had experienced any of them often in any of the four subjects. Methods which called for pupil use of equipment were almost unknown: in each subject no more than three per cent of pupils had *ever* experienced any of these three methods in fourth-year lessons. Such results may not surprise teachers; indeed independent learning methods of this kind may well not

TABLE 4.1

Percentage saying they experienced each learning method "often" in fourth-year lessons in four subjects: leavers who had attempted O-grade and studied the subject

	Geography	Biology	History	Physics	All subjects
Copied down the teacher's notes	73	71	67	72	70
Worked through exercises or worksheets with the rest of the class	50	44	48	55	50
Watched a TV programme, film or slides	27	32	16	9	20
Listened to a tape, record or radio	7	3	1	1	4
Made my own notes	13	16	21	11	14
Used worksheets as a guide for my own work (or in small group work)	21	23	19	23	21
Used books etc from the school library or resource centre for my work	14	18	20	13	16
Used a tape recorder myself	0	0	1	0	0
Used a camera myself	1	0	0	0	0
Used a computer myself	0	1	0	1	1
Unweighted n	(813)	(463)	(714)	(687)	(2677)

be considered appropriate for the task that almost all these pupils faced in fourth year, namely tackling an O-grade examination. In general, the results are also in keeping with the Inspectors' report on *Learning and Teaching in Scottish Secondary Schools* (SED, 1982c) which surveyed practice in schools as this generation of young people was passing through them. It is more difficult to accept that they are in keeping with the aims of the Munn Committee which envisaged that pupils should experience not only a range of subjects but also a range of modes of activity during the final stage of compulsory schooling. Furthermore, while these questions were asked of a restricted sub-set of leavers – those who had attempted O-grade – analyses of the responses within S4 performance categories (not shown here) showed that differences between the groups in the proportions experiencing each method were generally small. In this respect, perhaps, the comprehensive school has brought equality of experience for the great majority of pupils. To what extent is it true that learning methods are governed by the demands of the examination? How far will the new curriculum and examination system envisaged in the government's proposals stimulate or necessitate change in the learning methods which teachers provide? The Inspectors' report suggested that exhortations and examples in curriculum papers had not brought about change, but that there were indications that a new examination syllabus could have a "beneficial effect", perhaps partly by removing the pressures which teachers felt to restrict the methods offered to pupils in order to "cover the syllabus".[1]

We wanted to know how leavers themselves felt about the learning methods they had experienced. They were invited to note those methods they would have liked to have followed *more often*, and those they would have preferred *less often*. The methods excited varying degrees of interest: the percentage commenting on any one range from 29 per cent (using a tape recorder) to 60 per cent (watching) (results not shown). We have summarised these reactions, for all pupils over all four subjects. In Figure 4.1 the items are scaled (vertically) according to frequency of use and the balance of opinion has been summarised by presenting the difference between those who wanted the method more and less often. Only one method comes out a clear loser: pupils did not, on balance, appreciate the emphasis on directly provided notes, although they may have tolerated this approach as an inevitable concomitant of O-grade courses. But not all methods which were widely used were rejected in this way. On the contrary "watching", on average the third most frequently used approach, was the one which evoked the highest degree of support. Cynics may attribute this result to the idleness of a "television generation"; more charitably this result may point to an understandable desire for more visual stimulus in a context where the balance was weighted heavily in favour of listening and talking.

FIGURE 4.1
Attitudes to methods of study in fourth year: all leavers who attempted
O-grade and studied selected subjects

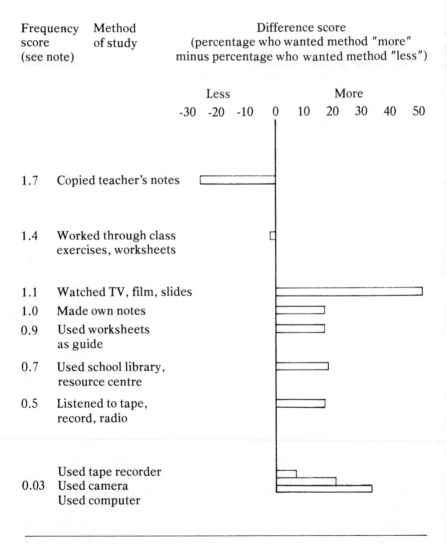

Note: The score for the vertical scale is a mean score for the frequency
with which each method was used, where often = 2, sometimes =
1 , never = 0.

Pupil opinion favoured (to a much more modest extent) the methods which called for more individual initiative in learning; and while some support might have been expected for the novel methods which few had experienced it will be noticed that discrimination was shown, with much more enthusiasm for computers than for cameras or tape recorders.

Classroom organisation. For the majority of secondary pupils and teachers the classroom is the main theatre of action; this is where that particular kind of social world, so forcibly pictured by Waller (1965), and re-created in a new generation of ethnomethodological studies of classroom life (*eg* Stubbs and Delamont, 1976), is continually reconstructed. It has been argued by Rutter and his colleagues (1979) that effectiveness in schooling is associated with a number of aspects of classroom life including the punctuality of the teacher, the efficient use of classroom time and the setting of homework. To investigate some of these aspects of classroom life we presented leavers with a set of items on the organisation of the classroom in fourth year. In order to help respondents to answer as specifically as possible we asked them to talk about lessons in one subject, choosing a subject which virtually all pupils would have studied in fourth year: English. The eight questions which were asked about English are listed in Table 4.2. They have been grouped there into four pairs: two questions on how well leavers thought their teacher knew the class; two about control of the class and its work; two items designed to act as indicators of good planning on the part of the teacher and/or the school: these concern the punctuality of lessons and adequate provision of resources; and two about homework (which we discuss later). On the second pair of items, a higher proportion of girls than boys considered that the teacher could keep order and mark work regularly, but on most of the other items the difference between the sexes was small, and therefore in Table 4.2 results have been presented for boys and girls together. The proportion saying each statement was (on balance) "true" is shown for three sub-groups categorised by fourth-year O-grade attainment, and then for all pupils.

Looking first at results for the whole group, it seems that for all but a small minority of pupils, the English classroom in fourth year was a stable social world: they had their "own" teacher who knew them by name. There was less certainty about the teacher's grip on the class, as indicated by the next two items in the table. In each case less than two thirds of the sample thought the statement was true. Nor was there general agreement about the two "planning" items; in each case between a half and two thirds agreed with the statements. On average, then, we can form the picture of the English room as a predictable context but one that could in some instances be better ordered. There were differences between the attainment sub-groups in the confidence they showed about their English lessons. On every item there

TABLE 4.2

Classroom organisation in fourth-year English lessons; percentage saying each statement was "true", by fourth-year SCE attainment: all school leavers

	5+ O-grades (A – C)	1-4 O-grades (A – C)	No O-grades at A – C	All
The teacher knew our names	95	94	86	91
We nearly always had the proper teacher	95	89	78	86
The teacher could keep order in class	81	67	56	62
The teacher marked our work regularly	81	69	53	63
The teacher started the lessons on time	68	53	55	57
There were enough books or materials to go round	72	59	57	64
We were regularly given homework	74	63	31	53
The teacher made sure we did any homework that was set (percentage of those given homework)	55	67	51	60
Unweighted n	(1573)	(1831)	(1842)	(5246)

was a stronger positive response from the higher-attaining sub-groups. For those who obtained five or more A-C awards, the English classroom had been not only familiar but orderly. By contrast, only half of those who failed to obtain any A-C awards thought the English teacher could keep order or mark their work regularly, although more than eight out of ten in this sub-group agreed that the teacher knew their names. Only among the highest attainment group did more than two thirds consider that their English lessons generally started on time with adequate resources for the class. We cannot draw any conclusions from these results about the reasons for the relative dissatisfaction of low-attaining pupils, even less suggest cause and effect. But that evident dissatisfaction calls for further investigation and provides a baseline for monitoring the effect of classroom organisation once new (and more appropriate) courses have been introduced for pupils for whom present O-grade courses are considered unsuitable.

Learning beyond the classroom. For most third- and fourth-year pupils, schools provided few opportunities for learning in other kinds of context than the classroom. Only 14 per cent had had work experience while they were at school (not necessarily in the fourth year); ten per cent had been on a link course. For most pupils, school work outside the classroom meant work at home, usually on tasks that had been defined and prescribed by teachers.

Homework has been one of the most productive and least discussed growth industries of the comprehensive school. Equalising opportunities in the comprehensive school, including the opportunity to be presented for examination, has generally included equalising the opportunity or requirement for study at home. What was the extent of this obligation among fourth-year pupils? How much time did they spend on homework and was this in keeping with what their teachers expected? In the results we present here we do not expect total accuracy in the recall of what "generally" happened in fourth year, but there is no reason to doubt the relative figures for the different sub-groups of pupils. These questions were asked only of leavers who had attempted O-grade, and the results are shown for boys and girls at three levels of fourth-year SCE attainment (Table 4.3). Two patterns emerge: girls claimed to be more industrious than boys, with almost half (47 per cent) saying that they did one hour or more of homework on weekdays, compared with only just over a quarter (27 per cent) of boys. Secondly, there was an association between attainment and the average amount of homework done. This was true for both sexes. This pattern is in keeping with other surveys of homework (*eg* Keeves, 1972). Even among leavers who sat O-grade but failed to obtain any A-C awards, over a quarter of the girls claimed to have spent an hour or more on homework on a weekday – a not inconsiderable investment of effort. And in each attainment group (taking boys and girls together) just under half of the pupils felt that their teacher had expected them to do even more than they did. Comments on English homework (see Table 4.2) suggest that homework was not always closely monitored; even among high-attaining pupils, who were the most likely to be given homework regularly, one third recalled that their teacher had not always ensured that it was done.

How much attention has been paid to the purposes which homework is intended to serve? How often does it mimic the classroom pattern with pupils being required to carry out routine class exercises? Or is it used to even out the unequal performance in mixed-ability classes, so that slower pupils have to "make up" at home what their quicker peers have already finished in the lesson? Homework, it seems, has become an important aspect of life for most third- and fourth-year pupils, and it is an area where the demands of compulsory schooling spill over into home life.

One way of trying to find out more about how homework fits into the pupils' pattern of learning is to look at the sort of extra help and support that is provided by the family and others, in and out of school. A few simple questions were included in the survey in order to obtain some indications about these kinds of help or tuition. The percentages of leavers who recalled having "extra teaching" in fourth year are shown (for boys and girls separately) in Table 4.3c. While the proportions specifying various kinds of assistance were small, in all 14 per cent of the girls who had attempted O-grades, and ten per cent of the boys, said they had received some kind of extra teaching in fourth year. Among the high attainers (five or more A-C awards) the proportions were even higher: 20 and 17 per cent respectively. The help had most commonly come either from a teacher at school, outside ordinary lessons, or from one of the family, but six per cent of high-attaining girls mentioned a paid tutor. As efforts are made to assess the effectiveness of schools in helping pupils to reach their examination goals, perhaps more attention should be paid to the not inconsiderable ancillary support that may be provided by the family and the professionals. If "home work" in the broadest sense is to be recognised as an integral part of the curriculum for most pupils, ways need to be found of evaluating how it functions and of mobilising the considerable degree of support that families seem prepared to give, if encouraged and supported by (hard-pressed) teachers.

Attitudes to fourth year

From the evidence on learning we can form an impression of fourth-year classroom life for the majority as a period of highly regulated experience, defined by the teacher's requirements, which were themselves constrained by the demands of the O-grade examination. The more successful pupils could expect greater pressure and consistency in the demands made upon

TABLE 4.3

Homework and extra tuition in fourth year, by fourth-year SCE attainment: leavers who had attempted O-grade (percentages)

	5+ O-grades (A – C)		1–4 O-grades (A – C)		No O-grades at A – C		All	
	Males	Females	Males	Females	Males	Females	Males	Females
a) "How much time did you usually spend doing homework on weekdays?"								
None	9	2	25	10	44	28	24	11
Less than an hour	50	35	33	45	41	45	49	42
One hour or more	41	63	23	45	16	27	27	47
Total	100	100	101	100	101	100	100	100
Unweighted n	(746)	(817)	(819)	(926)	(407)	(497)	(1972)	(2276)
b) "And how much homework did your teachers expect you to do?"								
About what I did	49	62	43	56	53	54	47	58
More than I did	51	38	57	44	47	46	53	42
Total (pupils doing homework)	100	100	100	100	100	100	100	100
c) "Did you have any extra teaching, out-with school hours, from …" (Percentage "yes")								
…any of your teachers?	7	8	5	10	2	3	5	7
…any of your family?	5	7	5	8	5	9	5	8
…a paid teacher?	3	2	1	2	6	2	1	3
…someone else?	1	2	2	3	1	2	1	2
Any extra tuition	17	20	11	19	4	6	10	4

them. How did young people interpret and evaluate what had happened, in and out of the classroom? How did they see the fourth-year experience, as they looked back on it?

TABLE 4.4

"Here are some things people have said about their fourth year at school. We want to know want you think about your fourth year. Tick the 'true' or 'untrue' box for each one." Percentage endorsing each statement: all school leavers

	Males	Females	All
(1) I had plenty of friends to be with at school	93	93	93
(2) School work was worth doing	75	83	79
(3) My teachers helped me to do my best	67	74	71
(4) My friends took school seriously	38	50	44
(5) There were too many trouble-makers in my class	35	30	33
(6) School was a waste of time for me	22	16	19
(7) My teachers didn't care about me	18	12	16
(8) Teachers were always picking on me	10	5	8
Unweighted n	(2539)	(2774)	(5313)

Notes: In the questionnaire the statements were presented in the order: 2, 8, 5, 3, 1, 7, 4, 6.

Leavers at all levels of attainment were presented with a set of statements about what it had felt like to be in fourth year. They were asked to say whether each of these statements was (on balance) "true" or "not true" for them. Responses on each of these eight statements are given for all pupils, and for boys and girls separately in Table 4.4. The picture of fourth year that emerges is on the whole a positive one, particularly from the girls, with about three quarters of them seeing their work as worthwhile, and their teachers as supportive. Moreover, negative evaluations of teachers (the last two items in the table) were rejected by all but a small minority. The importance of friendship in everyday school life is underlined by the almost universal endorsement of the item on friends. Less than half the leavers, however, thought their friends took school seriously; further investigation may cast more light on what was implied by responses to this item.

There were other questions asked of all leavers which may provide a perspective on the fourth-year experience. In particular, two thirds (66 per cent) of all those who were asked felt that their fourth year had been "worthwhile", with more girls giving a positive evaluation than boys (70 per cent, 63 per cent). Leavers were also asked to comment on their approach, as they recalled it, to the decision about whether to stay on at school after fourth year. This issue will be looked at in detail in chapter 6, but at this stage it is worth noting that 56 per cent considered that they had been actively looking for a job during fourth year, and 44 per cent thought that their friends had intended to stay on to fifth year.

We can expect that the leavers' experience as well as their evaluation of it will have been influenced by their performance up to and at the end of fourth year. Results on the eight attitudinal items have been computed for five fourth-year O-grade achievement bands, for all those who completed fourth year: five or more, three or four, one or two A-C awards; no A-C awards but at least two subjects sat for prelims and/or O-grade; and a non-SCE group who had at most taken one O-grade subject as far as prelims. A sixth category includes all those who did not complete fourth year, since their experience was inevitably rather different from the rest of the year group. Figure 4.2 presents results for boys and girls within each of these categories. Two points can be made initially about these results. First, six of the eight items show a marked association between approval of school and attainment; and second, the tendency of girls to view their experience more positively than boys holds good on almost every item. The two instances where there was not much difference between the attainment groups were on item 1, where there was little scope for variation since only seven per cent overall did not claim to have had plenty of friends, and on leavers' evaluations of the help received from teachers: between 70 and 80 per cent of girls thought teachers had helped them to do their best (60 to 70 per cent of boys). Otherwise, for all who completed S4 (we will look at the attitudes of early leavers shortly) there was a positive association between attainment and favourable attitudes (items 2, 3 and 4) and a negative association with unfavourable attitudes (items 6, 7 and 8). Higher-attaining pupils were more likely to think that their work had been worth doing, and to agree that their friends took school seriously; lower-attaining pupils were more likely to complain about trouble-makers, to consider that school had been a waste of time, that teachers didn't care about them and

FIGURE 4.2
Attitudes to fourth year: percentage endorsing each statement as "true", by fourth-year SCE attainment and sex

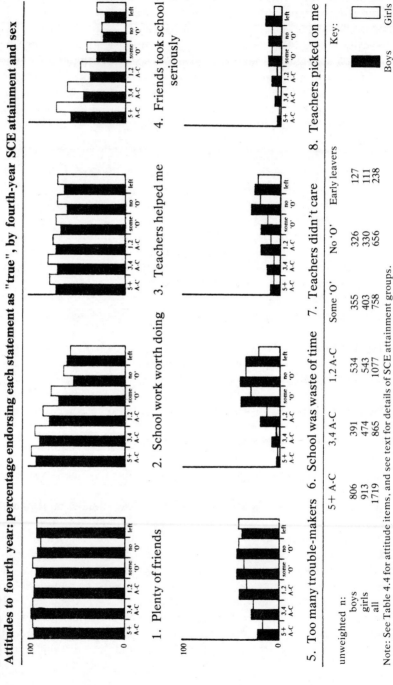

	5+ A-C	3,4 A-C	1,2 A-C	Some 'O'	No 'O'	Early leavers
unweighted n:						
boys	806	391	534	355	326	127
girls	913	474	543	403	330	111
all	1719	865	1077	758	656	238

Note: See Table 4.4 for attitude items, and see text for details of SCE attainment groups.

that they had been "picked on" by teachers. It should be noted, however, that the proportions holding these hostile views were small, even among lowest-attaining boys who were the most critical of school. The rejection by this group of the last year of compulsory schooling is indicated forcefully by one statistic: almost four out of ten (39 per cent) of those who obtained no A-C awards (groups four and five in Figure 4.2) thought that school had been a waste of time for them. Were they the "trouble-makers" who disturbed some of the low attainers? Or was their disaffection fomented by frustration with pointless work in classes where there was little incentive for anyone to learn? "Making trouble", at first something to complain about in others, could become a kind of release for all:

> I was always in thick class and I wish I was never. What I think about the courses I did in my last year (S4) rubbish teachers didn't give a damn what happened to you... all the remedial classes were too slow dull and boring. Then I said to myself well if they arn't going to help me then I wont help them by doing any work. You see I loved English but they put me off by doing things so slow I hated that I wanted to do things the same as my (w)hole year – oh no we did things 1st years.

To investigate the inter-relationship of attitudes further, the association between each pair of items was computed, using the statistic gamma which measures the degree and direction of association for categorical variables from -1.00 to +1.00. Negative associations as well as positive associations are shown in the matrix in Table 4.5, which includes, in addition to the eight items we have been looking at, two other items about fourth year which were referred to earlier: "In the fourth year were most of your friends intending to stay on?" and "In the fourth year were you seriously looking for a job?" The polarisation between hostile and favourable attitudes to school can readily be seen from these results. The inter-correlations between items 6, 7 and 8 are all over 0.70, while the pattern of gammas for the three positive items (2, 3 and 4), though not so strong statistically, is still convincing. The strongest negative association was between item 2 (school work was worth doing) and item 6 (school was a waste of time for me), with a gamma value of –0.83, but the matrix shows a cluster of other negative values of –0.50 or stronger. The minority who agreed with "anti-school" statements were to be found, as Figure 4.2 showed, mainly among those who experienced little success at O-grade, especially boys. The pattern of association with the item on job-hunting suggests that rejection of school was linked with the search for a place in the world outside, although other less alienated leavers might be looking for that as well. By contrast, a definite commitment to school and its demands is marked by the strong positive association between statements 2, 4 and the other additional item about staying on to fifth year: that is, between having friends who took school seriously, and were intending to stay to fifth year, and considering school work worth doing.

Figure 4.2 showed that pupils at all levels of attainment saw school as a

---

TABLE 4.5

Attitudes to fourth year: associations between items measured by gamma

	(7)	(6)	(5)	(1)	(3)	(4)	(2)	(S5F)	(JOB)
(8) Picked on	.78	.73	.41	.09	−.63	−.53	−.63	−.48	.43
(7) Teachers didn't care		.70	.30	−.11	−.76	−.40	−.64	−.33	.27
(6) School waste of time			.30	−.24	−.52	−.59	−.83	−.63	.55
(5) Too many trouble-makers				−.28	−.16	−.27	−.18	−.28	.27
(1) Plenty of friends					.49	.50	.49	.25	.06
(3) Teachers helped						.44	.56	.17	.00
(4) Friends took school seriously							.57	.65	−.37
(2) School work worth doing								.57	−.41
(S5F) Friends intended to stay on									−.68
(JOB) Seriously looking for job									

Notes: Items are numbered as in Table 4.4. The matrix contains values for gamma which measures the strength of association between variables. Values lie between −1.0 and +1.0.

All variables were coded dichotomously before the gamma values were computed: 1 = true, 2 = untrue, no response.

---

place to be with friends, and that the majority accepted the good intentions of teachers. The matrix indicates that associations between these views and the two additional items about post-S4 intentions were positive but low: in other words, that such views cut across the divide between those still committed to school and those already turning to the search for jobs. The other variable that does not fit very neatly into the hostile/favourable pattern is item 5 on "trouble-makers"; the gamma values suggest there was a link between this and other school-rejecting attitudes, but values are all under 0.50. Just what constituted "trouble" and how much it was resented may have varied considerably from one pupil to another.

Before leaving the question of attitudes to fourth year, we will look at the views of two minority groups: first, the "early leavers", the minority of older pupils who took the opportunity that was open to them to leave school without finishing fourth year – usually at Christmas time. The second minority group are rather different: they are a sub-set of the majority who completed fourth year, but their experience differed from the usual pattern in one respect – they had studied for CSE, the (English) Certificate of Secondary Education.

Results for the early leavers have already been presented in Figure 4.2 and can be summarised fairly simply: early leavers (who were of course "unqualified") had views similar to other leavers who had failed to obtain O-grade awards, but in some respects they were slightly more favourably disposed towards their limited fourth-year experience than the lowest attainment group who had completed the year. For instance only 22 per cent of early-leaving girls thought school was a waste of time, compared with 35 per cent of the lowest SCE group. Their reasons for leaving school will be investigated in chapters 5 and 6, but these results do not suggest that they had rejected school more decisively than low attainers who had stayed on. But this assumes that early leavers were drawn from the non-certificate group. In fact, we do not know very much about early leavers: in principle they could have included able pupils who simply chose to exercise their right to leave school, even though they were forfeiting the opportunity to sit O-grade with the majority for whom the end of the course coincided with their reaching school-leaving age. That such a course of action should not necessarily be seen as "dropping out" of education is indicated by the story of the S3 leaver that we referred to at the beginning of this chapter. As an example of individual perseverance and initiative it is worth quoting:

> I never completed my school education – I left at the end of my third year. I thought that I was wasting time doing subjects I didn't enjoy and decided to get an exceptional entry for [] college of FE. I was successful and left school at the age of 15 to join a junior secretarial course.
>
> At my old school I was given the chance to select my subjects at the end of my second year. The choice was bad and I ended up opting for subjects that I didn't really like rather than take others I believed to be a complete waste of time or subjects that I hated. By the end of my third year I became totaly disillusioned. Any hope of becoming a photographer had gone and I decided I'd be better off leaving school and doing something which would help me get a job. As [] High did not have a business studies

department to enable me to take a secretarial course, I finally decided to do everything I could to leave school. I tried to find out through my guidance teacher if I could leave school at the end of third year and go to collge. The guidance teacher told me it was not possible. Luckily I did not pay attention to her and got proper advice and information from [] college Lecturers who came to [] High from [] college to give a talk about further education. There were many pupils from the third year who wanted to go to the meeting but the Depute Rector told us it was for fourth year only. Once again I had to go behind the teachers back and along with some other third year pupils, we went to hear the talk by the lecturer. We found it very interesting and useful. The Depute Rector caught us coming out of the hall we were given a telling off. When we told the Depute there was a chance we could leave school, he said it was absolutely impossible. But this proved to be wrong. Amongst all the others I know who left school early – at the end of third year – none of them regret going to college.

By 1980 42 schools in Scotland were presenting pupils for CSE, and many more were preparing to do so (over 100 by 1982). Overall, 39 per cent of the leavers from the 42 CSE schools who were in the 1981 sample used for this study had experienced CSE courses; 14 per cent had studied for CSE and not for O-grade (that is, they had not taken any O-grade preliminary examinations); the rest had combined CSE with O-grade courses. Since an important educational aim of the local authorities and schools who had introduced CSE was to provide meaningful courses for pupils for whom O-grade courses were inappropriate, it would be interesting to know whether the innovation had had any discernible effect in improving such pupils' attitudes to school. In practice such a comparison is almost impossible to make from survey data, because of the difficulty of defining "similar" groups to compare, and of making inferences from any differences between the results obtained for such groups. We have looked at the results on the eight attitude items of Table 4.4 for a small sub-group of CSE pupils from the 42 CSE schools who had not taken O-grade courses (table not shown here). These results do not give any ground for undue optimism about the possible "effects" of CSE for such pupils. On most of the items their attitudes to school were similar to those of the lowest SCE group, but a higher proportion thought that school had been a waste of time in fourth year, and about half had been bothered by trouble-makers in class. While it would be wrong to attribute these results to the experience of CSE, we can only conclude that there was little evidence of markedly more favourable attitudes from this group. On this slender evidence, the case for CSE as a means of improving attitudes to school for "less able" pupils is not proven.

The fourth-year experience: summary

In exploring some aspects of third- and fourth-year life at school we have come to focus more closely on the process of learning, in and out of the classroom. Our results point to a considerable degree of tolerance, among pupils, for a learning regime which appears at times monotonous and for some burdensome. The prospect of a light at the end of the tunnel was enough to cheer some on their way:

> I liked 4th year better (than) 1, 2 3 it was my leaving year
> and subjects started to go very quickly... the teachers were
> very patient with us and stood for a lot.

For others, two years to O-grade meant marking time: "O grades were too easy when compared with Highers. In fact O grades are too easy on the whole for two years work." Similarly another Highers-qualified leaver felt that O-grade courses were "not very useful for myself" except as "a basis on which to study for Highers".

The realities of fourth-year learning suggest a surprising uniformity of approach for most pupils in a number of subjects. But there can be sharp contrasts in how these realities are experienced, for those who are successfully pursuing what is recognised as a prestigious curriculum, and those who are struggling to achieve a modest success, or who are aware from the very courses and labels they are given that they have already failed.

> After secondary ONE they past the class in two for maths
> & French. The clever & stupid. I was A stupid. After that
> you Dident care what happened you Started to carry on
> making fools of ourselves. They as much as laughed when
> I said I wated to take food & nutrition O level which makes
> one more confidant to show them up, when I left school I
> went furthure education & that showed them when I
> passed that with flying colours that I was not so stupid as
> they thought.

The attitudes of leavers towards fourth year show discrimination and realism. Among the great majority there was a readiness to recognise the effort and commitment of teachers who helped pupils to "do their best", and an acknowledgement of the importance of school as a social context, a place where friends were readily available. But in reflecting on the "value" of fourth year, attitudes were consistently shaped by the experience of differentiation: the more successful the leavers had been, the more likely they were to see school work as worth doing, the less likely to write off school as a waste of time. Will the "prizes" offered in the Munn and Dunning proposals be sufficiently alluring to convince *all* the pupils that their work is worthwhile?

Chapter 5

The ragged edge of compulsory schooling

Peter Burnhill

Introduction

In the remaining chapters of the book we look beyond compulsory education at the post-fourth-year alternatives and the decisions young people make; at the fifth and sixth years (S5 and S6) of secondary schooling; and at young people's transition into the labour market. In chapters 2, 3 and 4 the third and fourth years of secondary school were regarded as a recognisable stage of schooling, the final element in eleven years of compulsory attendance at school. A recurring theme was that throughout that stage a selection process graded and sifted young people, particularly with respect to their potential for progress towards the completion of five (or more) years of secondary schooling and thence on to higher education. That process, set against the background of the idealised five-year academic course which had been followed in the senior secondary schools, and which culminated in the award of the Scottish Certificate of Education (SCE) Higher, provides a context of social and educational selection for post-compulsory schooling.

The current debate about the provision of post-compulsory education was triggered by the rise in youth unemployment, but the debate has rekindled a questioning of the adequacy of initial vocational preparation within school, and also, therefore, a questioning of the purposes that can be served by post-compulsory schooling. Also thrown into relief is the comparative failure of employers and the education service to provide training in occupational skills. In part because of this the transition between school and work has been chosen by a government agency outwith the education service, the Manpower Services Commission (MSC), as a suitable base from which to influence the initial years of work and (directly or indirectly) the latter years of compulsory schooling also. This intervention bears on the debate about the 16-18 age group. The education service in Scotland has responded through the document *16-18s in Scotland: An Action Plan* (SED, 1983b), but an earlier Scottish Education Department document, *From School to Further Education* (SED, 1963), also reported on provision to aid the transition from school to work. The (Brunton) Working Party responsible for that document was charged in 1961 with "improving the arrangements for co-ordinating the later stages of secondary courses and the earlier stages of vocational further education", the latter being taken by members of the Working Party to require recommendations for the pre-employment courses provided by colleges of further education and to permit comment on the (still unfulfilled) intention that employers should be required to allow day-release for all their young employees. In "the 18 years since it was published, some limited progress has been made in attacking the problems which it indicated" (SED and SEB, 1982). Twenty years after the publication of the Brunton Report (and in England and Wales that of the Henniker-Heaton Report) the young people who do not stay on beyond the minimum school-leaving age have become part of a major policy concern. The Action Plan states that "the Government attach great importance to the development of education and training for the 16-18 age group" (SED, 1983b). Elsewhere we read that provision for the (16-19) age group should be "unified, universal, comprehensive and continuing" (Labour Party, 1982); and a discussion paper entitled *A Strategy for Post-Compulsory Education and Training* reports that "(a) major area of immediate concern... (is)... the (set of) opportunities available to the 16-18 age group" (Strathclyde Regional Council, 1981, p.6).

In the debate about provision for the 16-18 year olds it is important to be aware of the extent of current uptake of education and training provision. This may be portrayed in several different ways. One may examine the activities of 16-18 year olds or of 16 year olds, or one may examine instead the pattern of post-fourth-year destinations or of post-school destinations. Different pictures result. The distribution of the 16-18 age group who were in school or further education (full-time and part-time) in autumn 1980 is shown in Figure 5.1a. One third of the target age group was in full-time education and, with part-time courses added, the proportion becomes one half. However, this particular snapshot includes people from three age groups, some of whom had been out of school for two or more years. If the focus is restricted to the activities of 16 year olds, that is, to the activities immediately beyond compulsory schooling, about half were in full-time education and, with part-time courses included, this proportion rises to two thirds (Figure 5.1b). The target age group might also be regarded from a slightly different standpoint. Although the current debate is defined in terms of the minimum school-leaving age of 16, the provision and uptake of education and training is organised into blocks which do not neatly

FIGURE 5.1
Activities of young people in September/October 1980

(a) 16-18 year olds   (b) 16 year olds

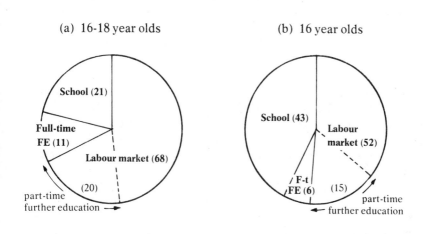

(c) Post fourth year   (d) School leavers

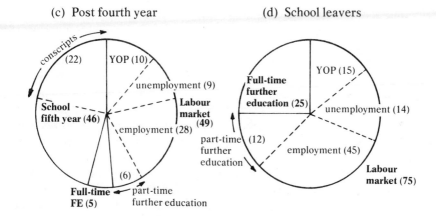

Sources:	(a) and (b) SED School Census and Further Education Student Record (September 1980)
	(c) SED School Census (September 1980) and Scottish School Leavers Survey (October 1980)
	(d) Scottish School Leavers Survey (October 1980)
Notes:	Percentaged distributions are shown in brackets. The term "further education" (FE) is taken to include courses of further and higher education. The term "conscripts" denotes young people who were too young to leave after fourth year and had to stay on into fifth year.

coincide with chronological age. A similar but not precisely equivalent picture to that obtaining in Figure 5.1b is given in Figure 5.1c. Here the focus is on post-fourth-year activity. Over half of this particular year group went on to full-time courses of education, about two thirds if part-time courses are counted. A fourth perspective is provided by looking at the destinations of school leavers, shown in Figure 5.1d. In this picture about one quarter of young people continued with full-time education; the proportion on recognised courses of education and training was about one third with part-time attendance included. These are four quite legitimate ways of looking at the target population in the 16-18s debate; but the pictures vary, with the estimates of the proportion in full-time education ranging from one quarter to one half and those of the proportion in full- or part-time education ranging from about one third to two thirds.

These four snapshots also highlight two important issues which are taken up in the remaining chapters of this book. Firstly, there is the analytical distinction between voluntary schooling (that is, attendance at school beyond the age of 16) and school attendance beyond fourth year.[1] In particular, Figure 5.1c has revealed the sizeable proportion of young people who entered fifth year involuntarily. This is an important category of young persons, whom we shall refer to as "S5 conscripts". Their anomalous position is investigated in this chapter and in chapter 6.

The second issue relates to the element of training and education that is present in the day-to-day work of the young employed and in the special courses provided for the young unemployed. The advent of mass youth unemployment and of the government's special schemes has made the categories of post-compulsory provision more numerous and much less distinct. The trichotomy of post-compulsory academic schooling (at school), full-time vocational education (at a college of further education) and entry to the labour market now seems analytically less appropriate than before. The category of further education always fell uneasily between school and work, principally because "further education" was not an homogeneous category of activities, and because much post-school education and training was done part-time. It was also a minority post-fourth-year option. In 1980 only some five per cent of 16 year olds were to be found in full-time further education, although a further 15 per cent were to be found on part-time courses.[2] Some courses of further education extended the general components of schooling beyond the school gates whilst other courses were vocational to the point of being designed with specific occupations, sometimes specific firms, in mind. The practices which particular industries required in the pre-occupational training of their entrants varied. For example, most young people who wished to be hairdressers or secretaries attended college full-time at their own initiative and as students not as employees; whereas others, those wishing to be waiters or kitchen staff in the hotel and catering industry, for example, attended colleges of further education part-time as employees. Armed-service recruits, nursing staff and some apprentices underwent their off-the-job training as employees within the confines of the industry itself, although sometimes in special and identifiable training centres.

Youth unemployment has brought about changes that might make the institutional walls separating the three categories yet more permeable. For the 1980 school leaver, entry to the labour market was no longer synonymous with starting a job. Participation on one of the MSC's special schemes (the Youth Opportunities Programme) is shown in Figures 5.1c and 5.1d. The Youth Opportunities Programme (YOP), conceived as a temporary remedy for a temporary affliction, was not regarded by its providers or its participants as a serious contender in the post-fourth-year choice. Moreover, the quality of education and training on YOP was contested. The position may change with the introduction of the Youth Training Scheme (YTS), which was conceived with an eye to permanence and as a major post-fourth-year option through which school leavers would enter the labour market. In formal terms, the education and training content of YTS will require a provision for at least twice as many 16 year olds as were provided for through existing part-time further education in 1980. An alternative schema to that suggested by the institutional categories of school, college and work may therefore be required. For the 1980 leaver, however, the post-fourth-year choice was predominantly between continuation of school and direct entry to the labour market.

In the rest of this chapter, the twin perspectives of Figures 5.1b and of 5.1c are shown not to be identical, and it is argued that the lack of fit between the statutory (minimum) school-leaving age and the organisation of schooling by years or stages has important implications for post-fourth-year policy. A persistent feature in the analysis is the greater propensity for girls to stay on at school but this is commented upon only in passing. The propensity to stay on into fifth year is also shown to vary according to factors deriving from the contexts of home and school, and it is suggested that the social differential in staying-on rates will undermine the provision of six-year all-through comprehensive schools over the next decade as school rolls fall.

An anatomy of staying-on rates

Data. In common with other chapters in this book use is made of the sample data from the Scottish School Leavers Survey which was conducted in spring 1981. The target population for that survey was the young people in Scotland who left school during the school session 1979/80. These data are not entirely appropriate for the task of estimating the proportions staying on into post-compulsory school because school leavers include young people who left school after four, five or six years of secondary school and who therefore made their decisions about their post-fourth-year destinations during three separate years. For this reason, in the part of the chapter which is concerned with the demographic characteristics of the S4/ S5 transition and with their change over time, an analysis of the School Census returns is given, aggregated across each of the schools maintained by the Scottish education authorities. Use of this data source has permitted a focus on a particular entry cohort, and an analysis of the age composition and the staying-on behaviour of the young people in that cohort. In the latter part of the chapter the purpose is to show the processes which influence staying-on rates and which are relevant in projecting future rates of participation, for which the data from the Scottish School Leavers Survey are well suited.

Historical background. The decision about whether to stay at school beyond the minimum school-leaving age and the decision about what to do after fourth year represent two conceptually distinct decisions about staying on. Before 1962 there was only one staying-on decision; whether or not to attend school voluntarily. After the age of 15 young people could leave school or stay. The context for the decision was provided by a selective system of secondary schooling. Those in junior secondary schools generally left at age 15.[3] Their decision had been pre-empted, having been made earlier at the point of transfer from primary school; and that tended not to have been an occasion for decision, by parent or offspring, but an occasion for selective allocation. However, among the 30 to 40 per cent or so who had entered senior secondary schools at 12 years old, decisions about voluntary (post-15) schooling had not been wholly determined at the point of transfer.

Voluntary schooling was required to complete the five-year academic course and not all of those in senior secondary schools progressed to complete the five-year course.[4] About two thirds of those who started the five-year course did not stay on for the two post-compulsory years needed to complete it. The educational community regarded these latter young people as having left prematurely and they were the subject of concern over "the wastage of ability" (SED, 1954). It was in response to the study of this wastage that the post-fourth-year decision emerged as a "legitimate" decision point for pupils. In Circular 312 (SED, 1955b) it was announced "that the Secretary of State had decided...to enable pupils in the fourth year of an approved course to be presented in as many subjects (at the O-grade) as they were considered...to be fit to attempt...". The Working Party on the Curriculum of the Senior Secondary School was charged with considering "how senior secondary schools should be organised... and (with making) recommendations as to the general conditions which should in consequence govern the award of the Scottish Leaving Certificate on both the new Ordinary grade and the existing Higher grade" (SED, 1959).

The fourth-year O-grade examination was introduced as an incentive to encourage senior-secondary pupils to stay on for at least one extra year. But an ambiguity arose. Was the decision that faced pupils at the end of fourth year one to do with course completion (of the five years for the Highers) or one to do with embarking upon a new course, the previous four years now constituting a course terminated by the O-grade? This ambiguity apart, it should be recalled that the decision about whether to start (or continue into) fifth year was taken by pupils who had already stayed on beyond the minimum school-leaving age of 15, voluntary schooling having been required in order to achieve certification after either four or five years. And the two decisions were there to be taken by only a minority of pupils. For the 65 per cent of young people not on a course leading to the award of the SCE O- or H-grade there were effectively no such decisions to make.

With the raising of the school-leaving age to 16 the two decisions, about voluntary schooling and about a voluntary fifth year, were pushed nearer together in time. The universal and compulsory four-year secondary course coexisted with the five-year academic course, completion of which required voluntary schooling. This has had three important consequences. Commentators have tended to conflate a young person's decision about post-compulsory (*ie* voluntary) schooling with the decision to stay on and do a fifth year course. Second, the raising of the school-leaving age conferred on the O-grade the status of an end-of-compulsory-schooling certificate. Third, a universal and compulsory four-year secondary course coexisted with a five-year academic course, completion of the latter still requiring voluntary schooling. This brought into question the length of the secondary course and hence gave rise to the ambiguity about staying on for a fifth year. Comprehensive reorganisation, with the almost universal provision of six-year, all-through secondary schools, was to give widespread access to the courses that led to four-year (O-grade) certification. Within the reorganised comprehensive schools, continuation of schooling into fifth year became more readily possible, but was it perhaps regarded by pupils as the commencement of a new course and not as course completion?

By the 1970s, then, the completion of compulsory schooling and the end of the O-grade course coincided, not exactly (as shall be discussed below), but sufficiently so for the one to be regarded as shorthand for the other and for the choice at 16 and for the issue of post-fourth-year provision to be common points of debate.

School-Leaving Age groups and voluntary schooling. To what extent can we regard as equivalent, at least for the purpose of public policy and academic argument, young persons' decisions about voluntary schooling and their voluntary participation in a fifth year at secondary school? That is, to what extent can the behaviour of young people be analysed as though all belonged to a modal category for whom the two decisions were one and the same? The use of this approximate equivalence is lent support by the fact that for a majority of pupils in Scotland the first opportunity to leave school occurs at the end of the fourth year. However, this majority is more slender than is generally supposed.

The Education (Scotland) Act of 1980 and its Regulations make provision for two leaving dates during the school session: at Christmas at the end of the first term and in the summer at the end of the third term.[5] This is done in order to allow young people to leave school when they reach, or are in sight of, their sixteenth birthday. By this arrangement there are three school-leaving age groups amongst those entering secondary school: those who reach their sixteenth birthday by the end of the February in fourth year are eligible to leave at Christmas of S4 (or, in some cases, in the summer of S3); those who become 16 before the following October are eligible to leave in the summer of S4; and those whose sixteenth birthday falls in the October of their fifth year, or later, become eligible to leave the following Christmas (or, in some cases, in the summer of S5). If the age span of a school year were exactly 12 months, then, reckoning by the distribution of births across the months of the year, the middle, and in policy terms the modal, category of pupils would comprise about 60 per cent of the year group. However, the exercise of administrative discretion, both at entry to primary school and in the transition from one primary (or secondary) stage to another, and such events as transfers from one authority's school system to another's, give rise to a much greater spread of ages in a given school year group. Using the School Census it has been possible to estimate this age range and the proportion of pupils who are in the three school-leaving age groups. For example, in third year during the 1978/79 school session some pupils were aged 13, some 14 and some 15: and the proportion in the modal category (that category of pupils for whom the summer term of fourth year was the first opportunity to leave) was only about 52 per cent of that school year group, a majority by a small margin indeed. This group is referred to here as School-Leaving Age group II (SLA II); those eligible to leave in the Christmas of fourth year, or earlier, as SLA I, and those not eligible to leave until the Christmas of fifth year, or later, as SLA III. The estimated distribution of pupils in third year in 1978/79 is shown, separately for males and for females, on the left-hand side of Figure 5.2. Although the pupils in SLA I and III were in the minority, both categories were sizeable and important: pupils in the former group (SLA I) needed to "volunteer" in

FIGURE 5.2
Flows through and out of Scottish secondary schools (1976 entrants) by sex and School-Leaving Age group

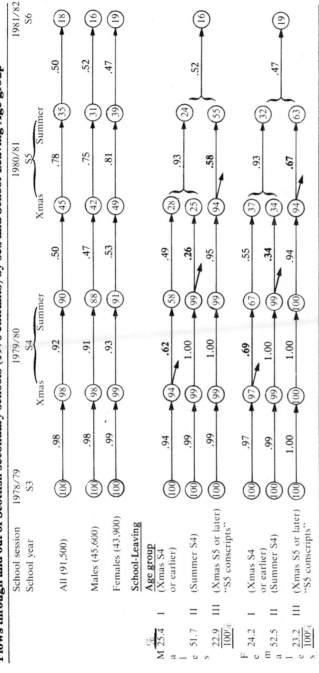

Notes: The principal statistics shown are transition porportions (*eg* .50) and survivor rates (*eg* 45 per cent). The 1976 secondary-school entrants were in S3 during 1978/79 and in S4 during 1979/80. The definition of the School-Leaving Age groups is set out in the text of chapter 5.

Voluntary schooling rates are shown in bold type as transition proportions.

The first opportunity to leave school is indicated by the diagonal arrow.

order to stay on to the end of fourth year (and sit the O-grade), and pupils in the latter group (SLA III) were "conscripted" into fifth year.[6]

Figure 5.2 sets out a series of flow diagrams by which one may observe both the transition proportion from one state to another and the percentage of those who started a third year who "survived" to each particular state. Thus, of the 100 per cent of (the 91,500) pupils who were in S3 in session 1978/79, 90 per cent continued at school until the end of S4, 35 per cent until the end of S5 and 18 per cent until the end of S6. The S4/S5 transition proportion for the cohort was (in 1980) 50 per cent, as was the S5/S6 transition proportion (in 1981). Looking at the flow diagrams separately for males and females, the greater tendency for girls to stay on at school is evident. This is not the occasion to embark on a discussion of gender and its part in educational and occupational careers, but it is worth remarking, as an aside, that a greater percentage of the girls in the third year cohort continued through to each stage. The same is true of all but one of the transition proportions also. Girls are more likely to decide to stay on at every opportunity, save that of the S5/S6 transition.[7]

Set out below these aggregate flow diagrams in Figure 5.2 are the transition proportions and participation rates in each of the three School-Leaving Age groups, shown separately for males and females. A sex difference remains evident, but the differences which are most marked and which are important for the argument presented here are with respect to the three SLA groups. In particular the disaggregation of the S4/S5 transition proportion (which in aggregate was 0.50) will reveal some very different behaviours.

In 1980 47 per cent of boys and 53 per cent of girls who had completed S4 stayed on into fifth year. This crude staying-on rate has had important implications for curricular planning, but it is not an indicator of young people's willingness voluntarily to undertake further schooling. The most obvious reason for this is the "conscription" into fifth year of members of SLA III and the inclusion of these "conscripts" in the numerator. To find a suitable indicator it is necessary to look at the flow diagrams within each SLA group. But first it may be helpful to consider a range of indicators.

One indicator without the defect of wrongly including the "conscription effect" would be that which measured the proportion of young people who stayed on at school beyond the minimum school-leaving age; that is, a weighted average of the proportion in each School-Leaving Age group who stayed on for voluntary schooling. An equally valid alternative would be the proportion starting a fifth year among those for whom this was a voluntary decision; that is, amongst those in SLA I and SLA II. The SED has used various indicators based on age, the current one being the "voluntary" post-16 staying-on rate. This is a combination of the "voluntary schooling" and

"voluntary start to fifth year" indicators. In effect this conflates the
voluntary start to fifth year of those in SLA I and II with the voluntary
completion of fifth year by those in SLA III. The SED's "voluntary" rate
for 1980 was estimated to be 35 per cent for boys and 43 per cent for girls.
If this were used to provide an indicator for the attraction that young people
in Scotland have towards voluntarily embarking on a further stage of
schooling it would result in an over-optimistic view. This is best
demonstrated by first considering only the behaviour (shown in Figure 5.2)
of the young people in the modal category SLA II, for whom the 16-plus
choice coincided with the opportunity to begin a further recognised stage
in the secondary system of schooling. Among the boys only about a quarter
(26 per cent) decided to stay on beyond the age of 16, and among the girls,
among whom the propensity to stay on was consistently greater, the
proportion was still only a third (34 per cent). The reason for the
discrepancy between these figures (26 and 34 per cent) and the set of SED
figures given above (35 and 43 per cent) is to be found in the contrasting
behaviour of those in SLA II and those in the other two groups. Young
people in the SLA II group were less than half as likely to stay on at school
beyond the minimum school-leaving age. Apparently young people not in
the modal group were subject to additional pressures to stay on. For SLA
I (the older pupils in the year group) the rate of voluntary schooling, 62 per
cent among boys and 69 per cent among girls, was not far off the percentage
sitting O-grades. For those on certificate courses there was reason to stay
on voluntarily, but for those who were not there was very little incentive.[8]
The propensity among the SLA III (the "S5 conscripts") to complete the
year voluntarily was also significantly higher, although slightly less so than
among SLA I, perhaps because completion of the fifth year has been
traditionally associated with the more demanding Highers and not with O-
grades.

The willingness of young people voluntarily to begin a new stage of
schooling is much lower than generally thought. For example, in *16-18s in
Scotland: An Action Plan*, a government statement which has commanded
wide support, the continuation of the SCE Higher-grade is recommended
partly on the basis that "(i)t has also become widely accepted that the
availability of a certificate course with a related exit point at the end of the
first post-compulsory year has been a significant inducement to pupils to
return to school, and a major reason why the proportion of such pupils in
Scotland is higher than elsewhere in the United Kingdom" (SED, 1983b,
p.18). The evidence for this is not given directly but by implication some
support is sought from the statement in the subsequent paragraph that "58
per cent of pupils completing S4 in 1981 entered S5". In the Inspectorate
report, *Teaching and Learning in the Senior Stages of the Scottish Secondary*

School, which is given as the source of this statement, the figure is used to "demonstrate that the proportion of S4 pupils staying on in schools remains encouragingly high" (SED, 1983a, p6,15). There are two reasons why this statistic, although not in itself wrong, overstates the relative attractiveness of the fifth year. First, this figure includes those (in SLA III) who were obliged to stay on into fifth year. And second, by including in its base only those who stayed on to complete S4, it excludes consideration of those who had left the previous Christmas and so is based in part on a self-selected group. The statistic which better reflects the extent to which fifth year attracts pupils to return to school is based (paradoxically perhaps) solely on the behaviour of the modal category of leavers (SLA II) for whom the first opportunity to leave school coincided with the opportunity to start a fifth year. This may be demonstrated by example from Figure 5.2. At the beginning of the 1980/81 school session the proportion of pupils who had completed S4 and who then entered S5 was 47 per cent and 53 per cent (boys and girls respectively). But almost half of those who stayed on were conscripts. The proportions of pupils completing S4 and making the transition into fifth year voluntarily, that is excluding the conscripts in SLA III, were 31 per cent and 39 per cent (not shown). These latter proportions are based on the behaviour of SLA I and II, but as can be seen from Figure 5.2 those in SLA I were a self-selected group and the transition proportions for SLA I were high (at 49 and 55 per cent) because of the earlier self-selection at Christmas. It has already been remarked that the corresponding proportions for the modal category (SLA II) were 26 per cent and 34 per cent; coincidentally these were also the percentages of boys and girls from SLA I and II combined who "survived" as far as the start of fifth year. These percentages stand in stark contrast to the figures mentioned above of 47 and 53 per cent. Not only are they very much lower, but in being so they throw into doubt the often repeated view that the "Scottish option to stay on at school for one extra year to attain SCE Highers appears to be more attractive to pupils than the 'A' level alternative requiring two years of study" (Wishart, 1980, p.59; SED and SEB, 1982, p.25; Gray *et al.*, 1983, p.69).

A comparison with south of the border is not completely straightforward but it is worth noting that in 1980 the proportion of boys and girls volunteering to stay on into the sixth form at maintained schools in England and Wales has been estimated at 25 and 29 per cent respectively.[9] The lack of a Christmas leaving date in the south makes this a fair comparison. Moreover, because colleges of further education in England provide full-time courses leading to the award of GCE O- and A-level, the Scottish percentages (of 26 and 34 per cent) might more reasonably be compared with the percentages for England and Wales of 27 and 33 (boys and girls respectively). The result of the comparison should be to overturn the view that it is the Higher, as a qualification obtainable after only one extra year, which leads to a greater level of participation in post-compulsory schooling.

Two additional and related points are worthy of note and have relevance in the 16-18s debate. The first point is that the combination of the raised school-leaving age and the uniform arrangements for entry to primary school have resulted in a situation where about half those entering fifth year in 1980 had been conscripted. In the early 1970s the educational authorities moved to a single entry date for starting primary school. As a consequence there was stricter age-banding on entry and the proportion of pupils in SLA III increased in the early 1980s and the proportion in SLA I decreased. Pupils born in the months of October to December now tend to spend their extra period of compulsory schooling in S5 rather than, say, in repeating part of the first year of primary school. If the law were changed, as was mooted at the start of the decade, so as to abandon the minimum leaving age and require instead young people to undergo four years of secondary schooling, it is most probable that fewer than a third of those conscripts would stay on into fifth year, it being expected that their behaviour would resemble that of their peers in the modal category. Such a change would not only reduce the heterogeneity of the fifth-year intake but it would also, in a period of already falling school rolls, reduce the number of pupils who were at school, both in the first and in the second two terms of fifth year. The proportion of the year group sitting Highers could therefore also be expected to fall. However, in a "coherent provision of education and training for 16-18 year olds" (SED, 1983b, p.26) such a change would remove an important anomaly. For it would also mean that these young people would face the same decision about a fifth year as their peers and, significantly, that they could also enter the labour market and the Youth Training Scheme at the same time of the year.

The second point of note is also to do with compulsion. For in contrast to the low proportion of young people in Scotland who voluntarily started a new, post-compulsory course at school (recall that this was 26 and 34 per cent respectively for males and females) is the much higher proportion (approximately 60 per cent and 68 per cent respectively) who voluntarily completed a course having once started it, the commencement of the course having been compulsory.

Recent trends in voluntary schooling and fifth-year participation

During the period 1978 to 1981 the proportion of young people entering fifth year rose from 44 to 54 per cent among females and from 39 to 47 per cent among males. However, as previously stated, some fifth-year entrants are conscripted; and the proportion of such pupils who were too young to leave at the end of fourth year also rose in the period (1978 to 1981) from 16.7 to 21.3 per cent. These trends are shown at the very top and very bottom of Figure 5.3 and are denoted by AS5(f), AS5(m) and SLA III respectively. Also shown in Figure 5.3 are two other series of staying-on proportions: these correspond to (voluntary) fifth-year participation, denoted VFY(m) and VFY(f), and (approximately) to voluntary (16-plus) schooling, denoted VS16(m) and VS16(f). The latter series shows the proportion of pupils at school who were 16 or more and who had stayed on beyond their first opportunity to leave; the former series is based on the behaviour of young people in the modal School-Leaving Age group (SLA II). From these two series it can be seen that voluntary participation has also been increasing during the period 1978 to 1981 and that this increase has continued into 1982.

The longer VS16 series, shown for the sessions 1973/74 to 1982/83, is the SED's "voluntary" rate.[10] As earlier indicated this conflates the propensity (among young people in SLA I and SLA II) to stay on voluntarily into fifth year with the propensity (among young people in SLA III) to complete the course they are on beyond the age of 16. Nevertheless the general trend in voluntary (16-plus) schooling has been upward since the raising of the school-leaving age took effect. For females this increase has been continuous. For males, there was a slight decrease, in 1977 and in 1978, before the upward trend was renewed. This dip in the series for males coincided with the Education (Scotland) Act of 1976, and the introduction of a uniform definition of school-leaving dates and eligibility (SED, 1976c) but the extent to which there was cause and effect is unclear.[11]

The increase in the SED's "voluntary" rate begs the question whether the increase was because young people have become more likely to stay on to start a fifth year or whether there has been an increase in the propensity to complete a course voluntarily. Looking at the staying-on behaviour of SLA II (for whom the decision to stay on beyond the minimum school-leaving age is the same as the decision to start, or continue into, fifth year) provides an answer. This series, denoted VFY(f) and VFY(m) respectively for females and males, has risen more dramatically over the period than have the other series, and does not show signs of levelling off. Among the young men the increase in the period 1978 to 1981 was from 23.5 to 31.2 per cent and in 1982 it had risen to 35.4 per cent (provisional estimate for 1982). Among young women the increase was from 29.1 to 41.0 per cent (1978-1981) and this had risen further to 44.3 per cent by 1982 (provisional estimate for 1982). Throughout, young women were more likely to stay on than were young men although the two trends have not moved in parallel. Also, 1980 seems to have been something of a watershed year, the big increases occurring at the start of the 1981 and the 1982 sessions.

It is not clear what one should make of the upward trend in each series. What do they indicate for the present and for the future? As was indicated in the previous section, too much can be made of these statistics. In the Inspectorate report on the school system's post-fourth-year provision it is stated that:

> Present staying-on trends are an expression of faith in the schools. Those who return must believe that to do so will serve some purpose, though that may be unclear or only vaguely expressed. (SED, 1983a, para 5.5)

While the decision to stay on may, from the pupils' view (see chapter 6), require an act of faith, it would be wrong to take the trend in (or indeed the level of) staying-on rates as a measure of faith in the school system. To do so, especially on the basis of an upward trend which has derived much (if not all) of its impetus from the awfulness of the youth-labour-market experience, would be illusory. It would also mean that a decrease in the staying-on rate, which may accompany the YTS provision, would then be a measure of failure (or heresy).

Structural influences: educational and social

A young person's decision to leave or to continue with post-compulsory schooling is formed within the two institutions of home and school, albeit that the decision may be taken in the light of employment opportunities. Much of the impetus would seem to come from the organisation and structure of schooling and also to vary markedly with parental characteristics. In this section the strength of these relations are shown, partly as a matter of record, but also in order to highlight how the staying-on rate might be expected to respond both to changes in the structure of schooling and to aggregate changes in parental characteristics. The Munn/Dunning proposals for re-structuring the pattern of differentiation within the compulsory third and fourth years may have major implications for the extent of participation in a voluntary fifth year. In particular, Credit courses re-introduce or formalise the mechanism whereby staying-on behaviour becomes predictable from the allocation of pupils to subject courses at the start of S3. And with the changes in the occupational (class) structure, the class differential in staying-on behaviour also has important policy implications for educational provision in aggregate and for the institutional form that provision takes locally.

Data. For data we have to look beyond the School Census to those generated by the 1981 School Leavers Survey. Using the definition of the three School-Leaving Age groups described earlier, members of SLA III (who are conscripted into fifth year) were excluded from the analyses; and by focusing, in large part, on members of SLA II, the confounding due to the earlier opportunity to leave school at Christmas S4 (by members of SLA I) is avoided.

Schooling and attainment. One popular model of the schooling process is that of a hurdle race in which progress within school is achieved by successively passing examinations or some other form of educational tests, including those implied by teacher assessment. If fourth year were to be characterised as the end of a stage in schooling, and fifth year were to be

---

TABLE 5.1

Percentage volunteering to stay into fifth year, by fourth-year O-grade success, and by (a) School-Leaving Age group and (b) Munn/Dunning level

		Number of O-grades at A–C									
		0	1	2	3	4	5	6	7	8+	All
(a) SLA group											
I	Males	6	9	23	27	48	63	74	83	97	28
	Females	3	19	25	47	59	53	72	91	94	37
II	Males	2	8	18	38	44	55	70	88	95	26
	Females	4	18	23	39	58	67	83	96	99	34
(b) Munn/Dunning level (SLA II only)											
"Credit"	Males	–	–	20	30	45	53	74	91	97	73
	Females	–	–	22	41	62	70	86	98	99	82
"General"	Males	5	9	17	33	42	58	65	79	–	25
	Females	8	17	25	35	55	65	84	92	–	34
"Foundation"	Males	1	6	5	28	32	–	–	–	–	6
	Females	3	18	24	32	60	–	–	–	–	10

Notes: See text for definition of School-Leaving Age (SLA) groups and chapter 3 for derivation of Munn/Dunning levels. In order to indicate the distribution of pupils across O-grade success, "box and whisker" plots of the median and the two quartiles have been imposed. The vertical line indicates the O-grade success achieved by at least half the pupils in the sub-group.

characterised as the start of a new stage, then the height of the intervening hurdle could perhaps be measured in O-grades, the end-of-fourth-year qualification. There is no formal requirement to jump the hurdles but, as is noted in chapter 6, everyone knows that they are there.

The percentage (voluntarily) entering fifth year and its variation across fourth-year O-grade success is shown in Table 5.1, separately for the males and females in each of two of the School-Leaving Age groups (I and II) described above. Also shown in Table 5.1 are the median and the two quartiles, to indicate the distribution of sample members in each SLA group across fourth-year O-grade success. For example, three quarters of SLA I and of SLA II obtained five or fewer O-grades in the A-C award bands and at least half the members of SLA II obtained one or no O-grades (A-C award band). The higher staying-on rates were among the quarter who passed five or more O-grades. There was a very strong association between staying on and O-grade success in both SLA groups. However, this does not necessarily indicate causal influence. O-grade success becomes known to pupils after, and not before, the decision to leave school is effectively made (Ryrie, 1981). Moreover, as argued elsewhere (Gray *et al.*, 1983; Ryrie, 1981; Weston, 1982a), O-grade success is partly predicted by an earlier school process: the selection of pupils into subject groups and into certificate and non-certificate classes. It is therefore to be expected that those earlier decisions will also affect staying-on rates.

In *Framework for Decision* (SED, 1982a) the SED proposed changes in the organisation of the curriculum in S3 and S4 and in the form of assessment at the end of the fourth year. Subject courses and examination presentations were proposed to be at three levels: Foundation, General and Credit. The proposed system does not call for the segregation of pupils into separate populations. It is expected that a given pupil will take each of his or her eight or so subjects at one of the three certificate levels. Using the methods described in chapter 3, the Munn/Dunning levels may be represented as three latent or theoretical populations. These were devised, at least in part, with reference to the fourth-year O-grade results: each individual pupil was retrospectively assigned a probability of membership of each Munn/Dunning level on the basis of the awards obtained at O-grade. Because it has been necessary, for the purposes of this analysis, to define the Munn/Dunning latent populations in terms of fourth-year attainment we cannot measure the likely effect of Munn/Dunning on staying-on rates (or on attainment). However, on the assumption that there will be no effect, we can describe in an heuristic manner the concepts of "Foundation", "General" and "Credit" in terms of school attainment and length of schooling.

In the lower portion of Table 5.1 are set out the staying-on rates of the young people in the School-Leaving Age group II, the modal group for whom voluntary schooling starts at the beginning of the fifth year. The propensity to stay on is shown for each of the three Munn/Dunning levels and, within these, by fourth-year O-grade success. The distribution of each Munn/Dunning population is indicated by the median and two quartiles. The "Foundation" population can be fairly directly represented, almost by definition, as those without O-grades, most of whom would be fourth-year minimum-age leavers. The "Credit" population on the other hand, denotes those who pass five or more O-grades (A-C) and who have a high probability of continuing into fifth year, thus reconstituting the five-year academic course. This would be in keeping with the recommendations made in *Assessment for All* (SED, 1977a, paras. 8.19, 8.33) by the review committee chaired by Dunning:

> The Credit award would be intended to challenge those pupils who would aim at the H-grade certificate in S5....
> The pupil who has followed a Credit level syllabus in a subject should in general be better prepared for the progression to H-grade in S5 and CSYS in S6. A Credit award should not be a pre-requisite for presentation in H-grade though we think it likely that pupils who achieve a General level award in S4 would probably require a 2-year course leading to H-grade.

The "General" Munn/Dunning level is a less homogeneous concept, but would seem to embrace the pupils with one, two or three O-grades (A-C). The propensity to stay on into fifth year is low. "General" would therefore seem to translate into the "courses which culminate in the examination on the Ordinary grade". This phrase comes from the 1959 Working Party on the Curriculum of the Senior Secondary School which reported on the introduction of the O-grade (SED, 1959). In a section headed "Pupils Taking Minimal Certificate Courses", the report goes on to state that it "is probable that many pupils will leave school... (at the end of) the fourth year", although some "of the pupils in this category will, however, wish to continue their education at school". While it should of course be remembered that the 1959 Working Party restricted its attention to pupils in senior secondary schools, this comment fairly describes the continuing ambivalent position evident in Table 5.1 of pupils with three or four O-grades with respect to staying-on behaviour.

What then is the likely effect of Munn/Dunning on future staying-on rates? It is probable that pupils who follow "Credit" courses will be following syllabuses in which there is a presumption of a fifth year. In the

Dunning Report it was expected that "some 15-25 per cent of the cohort (would) be assessed at Credit level" (SED, 1977a, p.77). But this was in respect of a single subject. Pupils will study several subjects, not all at the same level. Accordingly the proportion of the age cohort who will follow at least three or four Credit courses may be much more than 25 per cent. Moreover, as argued in chapter 3 there may be expected to be pressure towards over-presentation at the Credit level through the quest for high-status courses. This would increase further the proportion of pupils who would have contact with courses on which the Highers was seen as the end qualification and which would therefore entail some pressure towards

---

TABLE 5.2

Percentage volunteering to stay into fifth year (a) by father's occupational group (Registrar-General's Social Class) and Munn/Dunning level and (b) by parental schooling and Munn/Dunning level

	"Credit"		"General"		"Foundation"		All		Unweighted n
	M	F	M	F	M	F	M	F	
(a) Social Class									
I Professional	98	94	76	71	59	54	88	80	(118)
II Intermediate	83	91	43	58	27	41	57	69	(583)
IIIN Clerical	90	85	40	53	22	37	51	62	(234)
IIIM-V Manual	58	73	19	26	3	9	17	28	(1849)
Other	65	75	18	24	3	4	14	18	(400)
(b) Parental Schooling									
Father "stayed on"	89	93	47	55	24	27	56	63	(525)
Father left at 15	65	75	21	29	4	9	21	29	(2296)
Mother "stayed on"	86	91	39	52	15	27	46	60	(666)
Mother left at 15	65	75	21	29	4	8	21	28	(2240)

Notes: Staying on is expressed as a percentage of the young people in School-Leaving Age group II (see text). The coding of social class follows that set out in OPCS (1980). The "Other" category denotes occupations which were not classifiable under the scheme or were otherwise unknown, and instances where the father was not in employment or was deceased.

staying on into fifth year. While this would point both to the continuation of selective allocation as a force which shapes the decision about whether to stay on, the aggregate staying-on rate depends also on the much larger number of pupils who will not be following one or more Credit courses. For these young people, especially those predominately following General courses, one may speculate that the decision to leave or stay will depend much more on the relative attractiveness of the labour market, YTS and the provision of further education and college. And that is characterised by a high degree of uncertainty.

Social structure. The other extension to the demographic perspective is provided by a brief examination of the extent to which staying on into fifth year is predictable by reference to parental characteristics. Table 5.2 sets out the percentage (among young people in School-Leaving Age group II) volunteering to stay on into fifth year, arranged according to the Registrar-General's Social Class classification (OPCS, 1980) of the reported description of father's occupation. The sons and daughters of men in the professional occupational group, and to a lesser extent of men in other white-collar occupations, were much more likely to stay on than were the sons and daughters of men in manual occupations or of men who were unemployed, disabled or whose occupations were not classifiable. The gradient across these occupational groupings in the uptake of post-fourth-year schooling is very marked.

Parental schooling provides another, not unrelated, indicator of the influence that "home" may be said to have upon "school". This can be seen in the lower half of Table 5.2, which shows the extent to which the decision to stay on for an extra, post-compulsory year mimicked the decision taken by their parents some years earlier. For both sexes, the likelihood of staying on was more than twice as great among the children of past post-compulsory stayers than it was for the children of those who had left as soon as they were allowed.

For about half of the young people in our sample the staying-on behaviour of the father differed from that of the mother (no table shown), thus providing an opportunity to present, as an aside, some evidence for the debate on possible gender considerations in the inter-generational transmission of educational behaviour.This is shown in Table 5.3. With respect to staying on beyond the minimum school-leaving age, sons resembled their fathers more than their mothers. Similarly one might have expected that daughters would have resembled their mothers more than their fathers. Surprisingly, this is not the case. The staying-on behaviour of the fathers appears much more significant. For both sexes, though, if the father had not stayed on beyond 15, the association with the staying-on behaviour of the mother was positive.

TABLE 5.3

Percentage of sons and daughters staying on, by mothers' and fathers' past staying-on behaviour

	Mother "stayed on"	Mother left at 15	All
(a) Sons			
Father "stayed on"	54	57	56
Father left at 15	36	19	21
All	46	21	
(b) Daughters			
Father "stayed on"	64	61	63
Father left at 15	56	25	29
All	60	28	

The relation of staying on with parental characteristics is shown for three reasons. First, as a point of record, it serves as a reminder of the extent to which the benefits of public expenditure on post-compulsory schooling are not evenly shared across the community. Second, it highlights the extent to which educational selection is reproduced inter-generationally.

The third reason for the presentation of staying-on rates within a classification of father's occupation is related to the second. There is much uncertainty about how to organise schooling in the face of falling rolls. This bears on the viability of existing provision within school for 16-18 year olds. Over the period 1980/90 the size of the 16 year age group will fall markedly. In Strathclyde the reduction will be of the order of 30 per cent (Strathclyde Regional Council, 1981). Because staying-on rates differ with respect to social class, the reduction in the variety of provision for subject courses in S5 and S6 will be more critical (Lothian Region Education Department, 1982) and likely to fall below an acceptable minimum in schools which draw mainly on working-class catchment areas. It will be here, in schools which generally have been upgraded from four-year junior secondary schools, that the six-year all-through comprehensive school will be most at risk. However, the number of young people who are expected to stay on in the future is a product of the number in the age group and the staying-on rate, and in Figure 5.3 the trend was shown to be upward. Because aggregate "staying-on rates may be influenced by changes in the social class composition of the population" (DES, 1983, p.5), there is reason to believe that this upward trend will continue. In Scotland, as in England and Wales, the number of births fell for most of the 1960s and 1970s. At the same time there was a shift in employment towards white-collar occupations. Occupations classed as Social Class I and II grew as a proportion of the population. As a result births in Scotland occurring to fathers in Social Classes I and II rose as a proportion of all births from 15 per cent in 1964 to 18 per cent in 1970 and to 24 per cent in 1977. Children born in 1964 became 16, and therefore old enough to leave school or stay on voluntarily in 1980. Since that date the staying-on rate in Scotland has increased markedly.

While the major part of that increase is due to changes in occupational opportunities for young people it may be necessary, in order to predict future staying-on rates and understand past behaviour, to pay more attention to the impact that social structure has on educational behaviour through parental occupation and attitude. Shifts towards white-collar employment, where educational certification might be more widely regarded as worthwhile, would be expected to increase the staying-on rate.

Summary and conclusion

The pupil's post-fourth-year choice is influenced by two sets of considerations. The first set has come from within the educational system and results from the cumulative effect of such changes as the introduction of the O-grade, the raising of the minimum school-leaving age, the "comprehensive" reform in school organisation and, more recently, with the fall in the size of secondary school rolls. The other set originates from outwith the school system and has been a mix of effects emanating from the social and economic structure of the country, including those of youth unemployment and concern about the level and quality of education and training provided for the 16-18 age group.

The provision of special schemes for the young unemployed meant that the range of post-fourth-year options was more complex than hitherto. Nevertheless, in 1980 the major choice was still between staying on at school and entering the labour market. Whether this will remain so after the introduction of the Youth Training Scheme and the various elements in the Action Plan is problematic, despite the fact that the staying-on rates have increased sharply of late. In 1980 estimates of the extent of participation in full- or part-time education and training depended very much on which part of the 16-18 group one focused on, and one may speculate that future

FIGURE 5.3
Percentage staying on at school in Scotland, 1970-1982, in education-authority schools

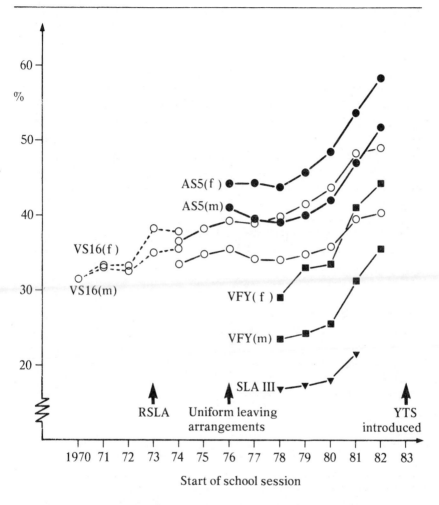

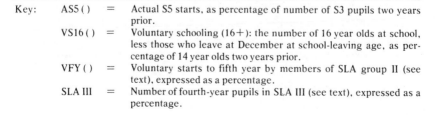

Key: AS5 ( )   =   Actual S5 starts, as percentage of number of S3 pupils two years prior.
        VS16 ( )   =   Voluntary schooling (16+): the number of 16 year olds at school, less those who leave at December at school-leaving age, as percentage of 14 year olds two years prior.
        VFY ( )   =   Voluntary starts to fifth year by members of SLA group II (see text), expressed as a percentage.
        SLA III   =   Number of fourth-year pupils in SLA III (see text), expressed as a percentage.

estimates will depend more on how the classification is made. Even so, and notwithstanding a thoroughgoing "comprehensive" reorganisation of the institutional provision of education and training for the age group, attendance at school would seem likely to remain the major method of participation in post-compulsory education.

Any study of staying-on rates necessarily involves an appreciation of the two issues of course provision and certification. Introduced as a response to official worries over early leaving from the five-year academic course, the O-grade had, by 1980, come to be regarded as an end-of-compulsory-schooling certificate. And with the raising of the school-leaving age the two decisions, whether to stay on at school voluntarily beyond the minimum school-leaving age and whether to start an extra (fifth) year of schooling, although conceptually distinct, had become conflated in public debate. From a policy point of view it is important that considerations of these two decisions are not conflated. For only a slender majority of young people do the two coincide, and when their behaviour is studied, the willingness of young people voluntarily to begin an extra stage of schooling is seen to have been much lower than generally thought. This brings into question the value, in terms of an inducement to young people to stay on at school, of the SCE H-grade, a qualification obtainable after only one extra and voluntary year. The distinction between voluntary schooling and the voluntary start to fifth year has also helped underline the anomalous position of the S5 conscripts. With the adoption of a single date for recruitment to primary school and an apparent desire on the part of the government and the educational authorities to make more coherent the post-fourth-year provision, it would seem rational to amend the law, in order to require eleven years of schooling (or some such) rather than require attendance until the age of 16.

The continuation of the misfit between chronological age and course provision also seems less sensible with the introduction, through Munn/Dunning, of a universal system of fourth-year certification. However, for all its rationality, for pupil and educational system, such a move (to end fifth-year conscription) could aggravate the changes that are being forced on the upper secondary school from another quarter. In particular the fall in school-roll size threatens the viability of some six-year all-through comprehensives. The effect of this fall in cohort size may be partly offset by the increased voluntary participation in fifth year, but, *ceteris paribus*, the removal of the obligation on some young people to stay for a fifth year at school, for reasons of age alone, would cut by about 20-25 per cent the number of young people starting a fifth year. The effect would also be felt beyond the Christmas term of S5 since the S5 conscripts were seen to have a high probability of staying on voluntarily in order to complete the year.

The number and proportion of the age group sitting the Higher would in consequence also be expected to fall. Perhaps the Scottish school system depends unduly on the continuation of the anomaly.

The very strong association between father's occupation and young people's staying-on behaviour means that changes in staying-on rates and in roll sizes will affect each school differently. In schools which have catchment areas with a predominance of young people with fathers who were in manual occupations or who were unemployed, as few as one in five pupils stayed on voluntarily into the fifth year. In the predominantly professional middle-class catchment areas three in five, or perhaps as many as four in five, did so. Maintaining a viable fifth year, in terms of an economic teacher-pupil ratio and an educationally acceptable range of subjects, would seem more difficult in working-class schools.

However, while the fall in roll due to the smaller cohort size threatens the viability of the six-year school in working-class areas, one may speculate that it is in those areas that there has been most increase in the staying-on rate. Certainly there was more scope there for improvement in the take-up of post-fourth-year school provision.

The Action Plan opens up a multiplicity of post-fourth-year alternatives but because of the variety of institutional settings envisaged it is not clear how the staying-on rate will change, or indeed be defined. Nevertheless, while the staying-on rate may depend upon the attractiveness of provision within the new fifth year relative to entering the labour market, also important is the structure of courses in third and fourth year, the selection that takes place there and the connection between that selection and the courses offered in fifth year. The projection of the proposed Munn/Dunning system of curriculum and assessment on the experiences of the 1981 leavers sample (in Table 5.1) highlighted the potential connection between the allocation to Credit courses and the probability of staying on into fifth year. It may be that through attendance on Credit courses young people will come to share the presumption of their continuation into fifth year. However, even with the pressure for over-presentation (at Credit level), the majority of courses taken will be at General level. And it is an open question what these courses should be preparatory for, and how far pupils will have in mind staying on for a two-year Higher, or for whatever courses are provided within the orbit of the Action Plan.

Chapter 6

Young people's reflections on staying or leaving

Peter Burnhill

Introduction

In the previous chapter the decision to stay on at school or leave was investigated from the vantage point of the educational system. Census returns were analysed to show the misfit between chronological age and the provision of a four-year course of secondary schooling, and to demonstrate that the proportion of young people who voluntarily started a fifth year was much lower than had been generally thought. Data from the 1981 Scottish School Leavers Survey were used to show how social selection, and the educational selection within secondary schooling, served to structure staying-on behaviour. Staying-on rates were predictable by such factors as age, sex, family characteristics and, importantly, by the selection mechanism of the schooling process itself. We may regard this strong correlational association as evidence to be used in support of arguments of "how the system works", but we require further evidence to shed light on arguments about why young people stay on or leave. In this chapter we re-investigate the issue of staying on through the reasons the young people themselves gave for leaving or staying. It will be evident that their reasons were indeed framed in the context of educational and social selection. The sense of relief amongst those who left at the earliest opportunity comes across very strongly. But their leaving was often just a formal acknowledgement of an earlier exclusion from the "moral community of school" (Gray et al., 1983, p.170; Gow and McPherson, 1980). Also called into question will be the obligation that our children should stay at school until the age of 16. At present the law gives some young people an opportunity to leave before the end of fourth year. For others the obligation to stay on extends into fifth year.

Data

The investigation in this chapter will be pursued through the analysis of responses to such direct questions as "Why did you start a fifth year?" and (if a fifth year was not started) "Why did you leave when you did?". Also regarded as data will be the difference between fourth-year leavers and fifth-year volunteers in their response to other behavioural and attitudinal questions. Extensive reference will also be made to the open-ended statements that the young people in our sample made on the back pages of their questionnaires.[1]

The data presented come from the 1981 Scottish School Leavers Survey, a sample survey administered to young people some ten months after they had left school. The responses therefore admit a strong element of retrospection. This implies both errors of recall and varying degrees of rationalisation which may have their locus in the post-school destination of the young person. The fact that those who stayed on into fifth year eventually left school from fifth or sixth year also means that their reasons for staying on at school required a considerable recall on the part of the respondents and related to decisions taken either in 1979 or 1978. The reasons given for leaving from fourth year on the other hand refer to decisions taken in 1980 and admit less retrospection.

Context: family, school and friends

When reviewing the motives the young people in 1980 might have had for staying on at school, or for leaving school, it is important to understand that in addition to the context of schooling, motives were formed and decisions made in other, social and economic, contexts. Principal among these were those of family and friends. Leaving school is not entirely an educational matter. The family is a medium for the transmission of values. And values bear on how a young person associates intrinsic and extrinsic rewards with continued schooling. But a young person of 16 is growing up and, if not yet a grown-up, is near to a point of departure from the family and may well want to establish an independence. Contemporaneous with socialisation by the family is the socialisation that takes place outwith the family, particularly through the culture of the peer group. The adolescent peer group may be a particularly potent influence as the dependence on parents is challenged and as an adult identity is sought. However, in many cases the impact of family or of friends on an adolescent's decision are not easy to discern, primarily because a given young person has characteristics which are similar both to family and to members of the peer group. Influence may be unspoken. Only when there is conflict between family, school and friends in the demands on a young person are the respective degrees of influence made explicit. This does of course pose problems for interpretation and for the imputation of motive, and explains, perhaps requires, certain contradictions between correlational evidence and evidence of a less quantitative kind.

There is a further context in which the decision to stay on or leave school could have been placed. Staying on at school means postponing entry to the labour market. To an extent the decision to leave school after fourth year can be seen as vocational in character. Moreover, when the alternative to staying on was paid employment, the (opportunity) cost of staying on at school which was borne by the individual (or the family) could be measured in terms of the wages foregone. And the benefits of further schooling which accrued to the individual could be measured in terms of the better wages that might result from the extra qualifications had by staying on at school. The perceived net value of the extra year at school depended critically upon the period of time over which the benefits were counted and the rate at which the benefits were discounted, that is, the rate at which the present was preferred to the future. The longer the time horizon an individual had, the greater was the tendency to stay on. Similarly, the propensity to stay on at school would be higher among those who were prepared to "defer gratification", and among those who saw intrinsic value in the extra year of schooling and who could therefore count this as an immediate benefit. While this approach to the analysis of staying-on behaviour might have suggested a mechanism whereby staying-on behaviour had been transmitted intergenerationally, the rise in youth unemployment had by 1980 increased the uncertainty surrounding both the perceived costs and the perceived benefits of staying on at school. It is therefore less easy to characterise the decision about whether to stay on at school as an investment decision, or at least one for which there were stable and rational behaviours to be observed. More concretely, there is some evidence that the "vocational impulse" led some 1980 school leavers to leave in order to secure a job "while I had the chance", and led others to stay on in order to avoid unemployment and in the hope of improving job prospects. Uncertainty shortens time horizons and the rate at which future benefits are discounted; getting a job (perhaps any job) became relatively more important as an objective than having a good career, at least for those who, at about the age of 16, felt that they had occupational decisions to make. The relation between staying on and the avoidance of unemployment is investigated in chapter 9 through the statistical technique of multiple regression. In this chapter it is the vocational motive rather than the vocational value of staying on or leaving which is referred to.

Family. At 16 there are changes in the formal and informal rights and obligations of parents, education authorities and young people. Until a young person becomes 16 the parents have been legally obliged to see that the child is given schooling. Being 16 confers on the young person the opportunity to leave school; one of the rights that symbolises transition into adulthood. And leaving school for some young people in 1980 coincided with entry into the labour market, with earning a living, with leaving home, with getting married and with starting a family. However, parental authority and responsibility did not fully end until the age of 18. We may consider that the young person remained part of the family and that the various members of the family were affected by the decisions taken by their 16 year old. (And we conjecture that this occasion may be a particularly stressful time for families.) In turn, members of the family could be expected to have affected these decisions and we should expect to find evidence of this.

The correlational evidence of parental influence was presented in chapter 5. Staying-on behaviour was very strongly related to parental characteristics. For example, the likelihood of staying on was at least twice as great where either the mother, or the father, had stayed on at school beyond the age of 15. The differential was even greater with respect to the father's occupation. The likelihood of staying on was between two and three times as great where the father was in a white-collar job (see Table 5.2). The data were drawn from a survey of young people and there was no questioning of the parents. This must limit what can validly be inferred about parental intention. Nevertheless, when asked what their parents wanted them to do, stay on into fifth year or leave, the extent of agreement between action and (albeit retrospective) perceptions of parental wishes was remarkably high, particularly among those who stayed on; nearly all these volunteers (92 per cent of boys, 94 per cent of girls) indicated that staying into fifth year was what their parents had wanted. (See Table 6.1 for these and other items referred to in this section on context.) Very few (seven per cent, and five per cent) indicated the contrary. In contrast, among those who left as soon as allowed, over half (56, 53) thought that their parents had wanted them to leave, about a third (32, 34) indicated that their parents had wanted them to stay on, with the remainder (12, 13) implicitly recording no parental view. Rather than overt parental pressure, this may have reflected "an acquiescence on the part of the parent with an action initiated by the young person" (report of comments made by the 1954 survey of headteachers with respect to early leaving (SED, 1954)). This in itself would not rule out a longer-term and more all-pervasive influence of parents, but it does underline the point that it is the young person who had the decision to take. Although there is little doubt that various members of a young person's family may help in the formation of an attitude toward post-compulsory schooling (Thomas and Wetherall, 1974; Weir and Nolan, 1977; Ryrie, 1981), there was no written evidence of young people having

TABLE 6.1

Potential influences on the decision to stay on into fifth year, shown separately for fourth-year leavers and fifth-year volunteers, and by sex

	Fourth-year leavers		Fifth-year volunteers	
	Males	Females	Males	Females
(a) Pressures to stay "In fourth year ..."				
... did your parents want you to stay on for another year? (% yes)	32	34	92	94
... did any of your teachers want you to stay on? (% yes)	27	37	83	90
... did most of your friends decide to stay on for a fifth year at school? (% yes)	20	31	77	81
School work was worth doing (% true)	71	79	91	96
Did you take O-grade exams at school? (% yes)	40	69	98	99
On the whole, do you feel your (fourth year) at school was worthwhile? (% yes)	50	55	92	96
(b) Pressures to leave "In fourth year ..."				
... did your parents want you to leave? (% yes)	56	53	7	5
... did any of your teachers advise you to leave? (% yes)	16	10	4	2
my teachers didn't care about me (% true)	22	15	13	7
school was a waste of time for me (% true)	32	23	5	3
were you seriously looking for a job? (% yes)	85	78	17	12
Unweighted n	(1367)	(1331)	(955)	(1231)

stayed or left just to satisfy their parents. As one fourth-year O-grade (male) leaver wrote:

> I left school at 16 years of age, strictly by my own choice. Leaving school was in my opinion the right decision to make. With the results I got there was NO way that it would have been worth my while staying on for another year, a waste of a year I would say. My parents were in favour of me leaving when they learned of how poorly I had done in the O-grade.

School. The school also figures in the decision-making as the agent of the education authority which must ensure that the obligation to provide education for young people aged five to 16 is carried out. As to the provision of courses for those aged 16 or more, the authority and the school, notably the headteacher, have their own decisions to make about the target group for post-compulsory education, and about the form the provision should take. The members of this target group may be "chosen" directly through scholastic barriers to entry and by limiting course provision, or indirectly through the influence the teachers have on the decisions taken by their pupils. In its turn, the school, as a community, is affected by the decisions taken by the 16 year olds. Nearly all (83 per cent, 90 per cent) of those who volunteered to stay on reported that their teachers had wanted them to do so. And a sizeable minority (27, 37) of those who had left as soon as possible also reported that their teachers had wanted them to stay. Clearly the differences are as expected. Very infrequently were teachers reported as having given direct advice to leave. More important perhaps were the indirect signals they gave: of those who left as soon as possible 22 per cent of boys and 15 per cent of girls reported that their "teachers didn't care about me". The young people who volunteered to stay on did not pick up those signals to the same extent. Sizeable proportions (32, 23) of fourth-year leavers thought that school "was a waste of time"; not so the volunteers. The explanation, or at least explanation by identification, is to be found yet again in certification. Among the minimum-age leavers, those who had sat the Scottish Certificate of Education (SCE) O-grade were much more likely than non-certificate leavers to have thought that the fourth year was worthwhile, that school work was worth doing and that fourth year was enjoyable (no table shown). Examinations were what fourth year was all about for pupils, and according to the pupils, for teachers as well. (A more extensive investigation of the pupil's view of fourth year is presented in chapter 4.)

Friends. Lastly, the young people were influenced by their peers, and by shared perceptions of the alternatives and of what was expected of them.

Reports of what friends do are not, however, of themselves indicative of strong influence: paradoxically this is because friends are so much "people like me". Common staying-on behaviour among friends is indicative of common influences as well as of mutual peer influence. However, for young people especially, friends do matter. In chapter 4 reference was made to the importance of friends at school and in Table 6.1 we find that school leaving rarely separated friends. Very large numbers took the same decisions as their friends. The importance of the peer group is also evident from the extensive reference made to friends in the comments written on the back pages of the survey questionnaires. One, who stayed on into fifth year, began her written comment, "Firstly, school was a social meeting place". Another, who left with O-grades, ended her remarks, "P.S. The thing I miss about school is my friends". The strength of individual motivation that lay behind the high level of agreement between friends (shown in Table 6.1) is illustrated by comments from two other fourth-year leavers:

> I didn't really want to leave school but all my friends had left and believe it or not that really made a difference. Before I left school I started to come up with very good results in small tests and my teacher .... encouraged me to stay on but as I said my friend(s) left so I had to leave because I didn't like being lonely. (Female, receptionist with one O-grade)
> I miss my friends who are still at school but they are leaving now which means that I can feel in the same boat. (Male, clerical assistant with O-grades)

The decision to stay

So why do young people stay on into fifth year? As we have noted (in chapter 5) about four out of every ten who stayed on in 1980 did so because they had to; being formally too young to leave they were conscripted into fifth year. Of the young people who were given the choice only a minority (26 per cent of boys and 34 per cent of girls) decided to stay on into fifth year voluntarily. (See chapter 5 for full details of staying-on behaviour in 1980.) The reasons stated by those who volunteered to stay on are set out in Table 6.2. (Strictly speaking these data do not encompass all volunteers. Excluded are those who stayed on into fifth year voluntarily, but who had not obtained at least one O-grade in the A-C award band.) Respondents were asked "Why (did you) start a fifth year?" and invited to tick any of the eight reasons listed, seven of which are shown in Table 6.2: they were also asked to nominate the most important reason. Other research, based on data generated through longitudinal study of a sample of young people

TABLE 6.2

"Why (did you) start a fifth year?" Fifth-year volunteers who had obtained one or more O-grades at A–C while in S4

	Percentage who ticked item as a "reason"		Percentage who underlined item as "most important"	
	Males	**Females**	**Males**	**Females**
I planned to do subjects for Highers	91	93	62	67
I had always assumed I would start a fifth year	57	62	5	4
I enjoyed school life	35	47	2	2
I hadn't decided on my future education or career	54	49	14	12
I was too young to enter the job or course I'd chosen	8	17	2	3
There were no jobs available that I wanted	15	12	5	2
I wanted to get more or better O-grades	38	42	<u>10</u>	<u>10</u>
			100	100
Unweighted n			(958)	(1259)

Notes: The items are not listed here in the order that they appeared in the survey questionnaire. That order is indicated by the sequence 1, 8, 5, 7, 6, 4, 2. Thus the item "I enjoyed school life" was listed fifth. The item which was listed third in the questionnaire, but which is not listed here, read "I was too young to leave at the end of fourth year".

in north Lanarkshire and the Borders, has suggested that pupils' decisions were not rationally thought out (Ryrie, 1981, pp.51-56). The *post hoc* reasoning obtained here by retrospective questioning is likely to be the product of more mature reflection but we cannot pretend that the reasons indicated were necessarily the reasons that led to the action of staying on. The answers given must contain unknown, and potentially large, elements of rationalisation. Nevertheless, it is interesting that although different routes were followed to generate the data, the results presented here are remarkably similar to those of Ryrie. The results from our research are given in Table 6.2 in the form of percentages. Clearly the most important reason given was the intention to sit for Highers. Nine out of ten gave this as a reason for having stayed on and over six out of every ten rated this as the most important reason. The pattern of response given by boys was similar but not identical to that given by girls. For example, the majority of boys (57 per cent) and of girls (62 per cent) reported that they had always assumed that they would stay on. And about half (54 per cent of boys and 49 per cent of girls) said that they had stayed on because they were undecided about their future career. Indeed these young people had not been obliged to decide on their future career and for them the S4/S5 transition point seems not to have been an occasion for decision; they were following the five- (or six-) year academic course. There were very few back-page comments specifically on reasons for staying on into fifth year. Perhaps this was because for these young people staying on was unremarkable, or perhaps it was because the S4/S5 transition was history to the fifth- and sixth-year leavers. One young woman put it this way:

> Most people are encouraged to stay on at school at the end of fourth year... indeed so much emphasis was placed in my school on those studying for Highers and preparing for Further Education, that the others were pushed aside. (Female, studying at university)

The force of the schooling process on the decision to continue into fifth year may be judged by the effort that one young man needed when attempting to swim against the tide:

> After doing my O grade exams, I decided to leave. My teachers were all shocked because they had assumed that I would stay on and sit the highers and then go on to university... we talked in his office for about 2-3 hours... but I did not change my mind ..... The principal guidance teacher telephoned my mother and asked her to bring me to the school to talk it over. I gained 7 O grade passes all at A bands but almost every job I applied for I was told I was overqualified ..... I thought it over, and decided to go back to school to sit higher. (Male, now apprentice quantity surveyor)

The decision to stay on had, to some large extent, been made earlier, at the start of S3 when pupils were allocated to certificate and non-certificate classes. By and large, those who stayed on did so in order to complete their five-year academic course. Only a small minority indicated that other reasons were more important. The principal group amongst this minority said that they had stayed on because there were no suitable jobs available and that they had wanted to stay and improve their O-grades:

> I repeated fourth year because I failed 3 of my O grades. For me, personally, repeating fourth year was very worthwhile. (Female clerical assistant with O-grades)

Very few, less than one in twenty, did so principally because of the lack of suitable jobs, although this did weigh in the balance (having been stated as a reason by about one in seven). These motives were not shared by those who had always presumed a fifth year and who had always intended sitting Highers, even though a third of those who stayed did so in order both to improve O-grade and sit for the Higher (no table shown). Importantly, this was not always a successful strategy:

> I stayed on so I could sit my Highers with a chance that I could get the job I wanted when I left at the end of fifth year. But so far I have not been able to find work. (Male with one Higher, unemployed)

The decision to leave

What of those who left school at the end of fourth year? How marginal were their decisions to stay or leave? It would follow from the arguments advanced elsewhere (Ryrie, 1981, chapter 5) that for most the decision to leave had indeed been made earlier and was there just for the taking:

> I enjoyed school very much but not being clever I did not attain any certificates. I would have stayed on at school but I didn't think it would benefit me. I feel children in lower classes like myself don't get the same attention as in the better classes. (Female on secretarial course at college)

Young people understand well that what takes place at school constitutes social and educational selection:

> I found that school was good for people with exam potential but was a waste of time for others. (Female with O-grades currently on YOP)

It starts early when kids not up to academic standard... are placed in what is commonly known as the *Daft* group where they learn Humileation.... I watched the kids around me clam up and.... (allow) themselves to become inferior. (Male, non-certificate, unemployed)

I would have liked teachers at school to put... more time to help pupils like myself who weren't clever to do better. The teachers were more interested in the clever ones and the not so clever were forgotten about. (Male, non-certificate, currently a medical clerk)

A sense of exclusion and a lack of identification with the aims of the school would mean that the distinction made in chapter 5 between voluntary schooling (schooling beyond the minimum school-leaving age of 16) and the voluntary start to fifth year would be much more salient, especially for those not in the "better classes". As one Highers leaver observed, "too many people see school as a 'waste of time' and merely mark time until they are 16" (female, Highers, studying law at university). Up until the age of 16 schooling was compulsory, but some pupils had effectively left before then; "(I) never went very mutch" wrote one non-certificate male, currently unemployed. Some others complied, but only under compulsion: "if it wasn't for the law I wouldn't have been at school" wrote another young man, this time one with O-grades and employed. Although not universally the case, the sense of relief felt by the lifting of compulsion was evident in much of the written comment by fourth-year leavers:

Since leaving school...

...life has never been better. (Female, O-grade, hairdresser at college)

...I have never looked back. (Male, O-grades, apprentice)

...my life has been better. (Male, non-certificate, YOP)

...I've felt more grown up and I'm treated like an adult. (Female, O-grade, works in bank)

...I have enjoyed life. (Male, non-certificate, window cleaner)

However, for some young people unemployment marred that sense of relief:

Since leaving school...

...my life has been dull and boring but I would not go back to school. (Female, O-grade, unemployed)

...I have been completely bored and fed up with the whole thing – I used to say to myself, I can't wait to leave, get a job and work for a living, but now all I do is watch T.V. and wait for my brew money to come through.[2] (Female, one O-grade, unemployed)

The harsh climate facing school leavers in 1980 forced many to reflect on their decision to leave school, and one wonders how their experience influenced the decisions of their younger peers who later faced the same decision to stay or leave, and whether there is here some partial explanation of the recent rise in staying-on rates. On occasion, the sense of regret represents a complete *volte-face* from what would appear to be firmly held convictions:

When I left school I was glad to see the back of the place but (I) soon found out I was making a big mistake, I soon signed on the dole. (Male, O-grades, technician)
Since I left school I have felt terrible – no jobs, no money .... I think now that I should have stayed on at school. (Female, O-grades, unemployed)

This sense of regret is qualitatively different from that typified by the following comment, a comment also observed in earlier Scottish School Leavers Surveys:

When I was at school I could not wait to get out and get a job. But now that I have left school I know I should have stuck into the work I did at school and I would like to go back for a second chance. (Male, O-grades, storeman)

The pressure on the excluded non-certificate pupil to leave school as soon as possible may be self-evident but why should those who had been admitted into certification not stay on? For it would be wrong to suppose that school was a hateful place for all:

I enjoyed my four years at secondary school. I am now attending further education and I (am) also enjoying it. (Female, O-grades, secretarial course)
The good thing about (my school) was the way in which the lessons were taught. Most teachers were eager to help you if you were in difficulty.... (Female, O-grades, shop assistant)
The good thing about school was the constant encouragement in your lessons by teachers and pupils. (Male, O-grades, football apprentice)

On the whole I enjoyed school very much. I get on well
with my teachers and my classmates were super. (Female,
O-grades, clerkess)

TABLE 6.3

**"Why (did you) leave school in fourth year?" Fourth-year leavers with one or
more O-grades at A–C**

	Percentage who ticked item as a "reason"		Percentage who underlined item as "most important"	
	Males	Females	Males	Females
I had all the O-grades needed for the job or course I wanted	21	21	5	7
I wanted to start a particular job while I had the chance	51	27	33	17
I did not think I could get any better exam results at school	32	36	9	9
I wanted to get a job and be self-supporting	51	46	21	25
I needed the money from a job	21	17	5	4
I was fed up with school	46	45	13	8
I felt I would prefer life at work or college to life at school	58	70	14	30
My parents advised me to	10	9	*	*
Total			100	100
Unweighted n			(941)	(867)

Notes: The items are not listed here in the order they appeared in the
questionnaire. That order is given by the sequence 3, 5, 1, 8, 2, 4, 7, 6.
* = less than one per cent.

These comments were made by young people who nevertheless left at the
end of fourth year. So what were the various motives for leaving school
allegedly held by the qualified fourth-year O-grade leavers? Fourth-year
leavers with at least one O-grade in the A-C award band were asked to

choose among eight possible reasons for leaving. Their responses are set out in Table 6.3 as percentages. Respondents were asked to indicate which reasons they had had for leaving and then to nominate one as the most important reason. The reason for leaving school most often stated by these young men and women (58 per cent and 70 per cent respectively) was that life at work or college had been thought to be preferable. Among girls this reason was rated as most important by 30 per cent and the desire to "get a job and be self-supporting" was rated most important by 25 per cent. For the boys, leaving "to start a particular job while (they) had the chance" was thought to have been the principal motive of 33 per cent, with the desire to "get a job and be self-supporting" being similarly rated by 21 per cent.

Three out of the four items most often indicated by young men as a reason were a preference for "life at work or college" (58 per cent); leaving "to get a job and be self-supporting" (51 per cent); and being "fed up with school" (46 per cent). This reasoning could be said to be more an expression of adolescence, part of the process of growing up and entering the adult world, rather than being a limited expression of a vocational motive for leaving school. Indeed the three reasons were correlated as items with one another and with the item, "I needed the money from a job" (not shown). Taken as a set of correlated items, such reasons were (collectively) nominated as the most important by the majority (60 per cent), with the quest for a job, thereby being self-supporting, having been nominated as such by about a fifth (21 per cent).

Young people, when thinking about leaving the process of certification, have also to consider what would be lost by delaying entry to the labour market. As stated, the reason for leaving indicated as most important by the largest proportion (33 per cent) of the young men was "the chance to get a particular job".

> I left school because from first year I had set my sights on
> the job I have just now. Fortunately I got the job first time
> and I felt that if I turned it down I (would) never have got
> the opportunity again. (Male, O-grades, craft apprentice)

This was specifically vocational reasoning and was set in relation to a particular job, but it also reflected worry over getting any job.

There are two sides to schooling and selective certification. One has an incremental, or step-like character, whereby about a third of these young people give as their reason for leaving the ladder of certification, "I did not think I could get any better exam results at school". The other side permits the view that one leaves because "I had all the O-grades needed for the job or course I wanted." In an earlier Scottish School Leavers Survey (the 1973 survey of 1971/72 school leavers) 46 per cent of male O-grade leavers said they had left because they were already qualified to do what it was they wanted, and (although the comparison was with a different set of reason items) about a third stated that this was the most influential reason. For the leavers from the 1979/80 session hardly anyone (five per cent) said that this was the most important reason, and relatively few (21 per cent) even indicated that it was influential. Little wonder, for in the intervening period the crisis of youth unemployment could be said to have severely devalued O-grades as a currency. Not that O-grades were unimportant in getting jobs, but the jobs cost more.

Young women would appear to have had a different pattern of reasons for leaving, a sex difference that was not present in the pattern of reasons for staying on. In part the difference between the two patterns may be because a smaller proportion of women than men left at the end of fourth year and those women that left were less well qualified than the young men. Nevertheless the reason thought most important was a preference for life at college or work (30 per cent) and the next largest proportion (25 per cent) rated as most important their desire to get a job and be self-supporting. These two reasons were among the three most often indicated to be influential (70 per cent and 46 per cent, respectively); the other being that "I was fed up with school" (45 per cent).

The expectation that qualifications would not be improved upon by staying at school was slightly greater than among the young men (but in part this was because the better qualified women stayed on in greater proportion than did the men). A similarly low proportion said that they left because they had enough O-grades to suit their purpose (seven per cent rated as most important, 21 per cent as an influence). This too contrasts with the position among the 1971/72 school leavers, when half of the (fourth-year O-grade) young women in the sample indicated that this had been a strong influence on their decision to leave and four in ten had stated this as the most influential reason. Where the young women were noticeably different from the young men in their reasoning, was in the much lower indication (27 per cent as opposed to 51 per cent) that it was the chance to get a particular job that had motivated them, having been about half as likely (17 per cent as opposed to 33 per cent) to have rated this as their main reason for leaving.

The school-leaving age and the end of compulsory schooling

In 1972/73 the minimum school-leaving age was raised from 15 to 16. RSLA had a number of major implications. Firstly, it increased the period of compulsory secondary schooling from an average of three to an average of four years. This increased the level of public spending on education and also extended, and thus increased, the financial (private) cost of school attendance borne by families, a cost against which there was no general compensating bursary (Blaug, 1970). For young people RSLA extended the period of their economic dependence upon their parents and postponed the prospect of entry to the world of work, and seemingly also of adulthood. RSLA also promoted the importance of the O-grade as a fourth-year school-leaving certificate and, together with comprehensive reorganisation, extended the level of its presentation. RSLA also reduced the stock of potential employees in the labour market and, from the young person's viewpoint, shortened the length of their working life by one year. With the present levels of youth unemployment, if RSLA had not been enacted there would surely be mounting pressure for it to be introduced, the opportunity cost for society of such a measure perhaps having never been lower. Leaving aside any consideration of whether the Manpower Services Commission's Youth Training Scheme represents a further raising of the school-leaving age by the back door (in formal terms it surely does not), it is worthwhile reflecting on what young people have to say about the requirement that they should stay at school for so long. No direct questions were asked about this in the survey, but as has already been indicated the element of compulsion was recognised in the written comments to the survey. This should not be surprising since any survey which goes beyond mere observation involves a dialogue with each respondent, even if that dialogue is conducted through the medium of a flow of fixed questions in a self-completion questionnaire. One (perceptive) comment ran:

> On the survey, I feel it asks very appropriate questions. I get the feeling that the questions about S4 were aimed at whether or not the leaving age is too high (or low). If this is the case then may I say that the school leaving age is at present correct for those who are able to achieve O grades. But for those who are really (below) O grade stage – and are perhaps better inclined manually – a practical course in some (other) sort of institution would benefit these people, as I believe some of those people are bored and restless in their last year at school and perhaps this is the cause of any hooliganism in classrooms. (Female, Highers, university)

This was not an isolated comment:

> (The) school leaving age should be reduced because there are some people who just aren't interested in school and are wasting everybody's time including their (own)! (Male, O-grades, student nurse)

> School could be made better by allowing pupils to leave
> when they are about 15 as 3 years at school is enough to
> have a good education. (Male, non-certificate, apprentice
> baker)

A further important implication of RSLA was the continued use of chronological age to determine the length of compulsory schooling. In chapter 5 the size of the modal category of pupils who reached 16 at the end of fourth year was shown to have been barely a majority. The other two major categories of pupils comprised those who were old enough to leave beforehand at Christmas (S4), and those who had to stay on beyond the fourth year but who were then able to leave at Christmas (S5). Those from the first category (referred to in chapter 5 as being in School-Leaving Age (SLA) group I) who chose to leave at the minimum school-leaving age of 16 were generally those in the non-certificate classes. Clearly there was nothing to detain them, and with the prospect of an earlier chance of scarce jobs and their eligibility for Supplementary Benefit there was some reason to leave. Sometimes the balance tipped so heavily as to cause "wastage" from certificate classes:

> In my fourth year I was determined nothing was going to
> stop my leaving in the December lot. You see I was a year
> older than some in my year... I should have sat my 4 O
> grades in the following May. My parents (coaxed) me but
> I was determined I was going to leave. I have never been
> happier since I left. I am unemployed at the moment....
> (Female, non-certificate, unemployed)

Most of the difficulties arose with the growing proportion of those young people who were conscripted into fifth year. Members of this group (referred to as SLA III in chapter 5) knew well the analytic distinction between starting a fifth year and being a volunteer (except perhaps for the minority who regarded themselves as on the five-year academic course which culminated in the Higher). Staying on into fifth year was an anomaly:

> I liked the first 4 years *then I had to stay on for another year*.
> (Male, non-certificate, YOP) (original emphasis)
> I had to stay on until Christmas. In that time I didn't have
> any classes at all. I worked at the zoo on Wednesday, and
> (otherwise) ran messages for all the teachers and the
> secretary. Surely it would have been better if I would have
> been able to leave and look for a job. (Female, O-grades,
> shop assistant)

Summary and conclusions

Decisions about what to do after fourth year appear to have been framed in the context of educational and social selection. They seem to have arisen "fairly directly from the structure and organisation of the schooling process" (Ryrie, 1981, p.64). For those with O-grades staying on was explicable in terms of plans to sit subjects for the Higher, thus completing the five-year academic course. Moreover, among these young people, there was a majority who had felt a presumption of a fifth year. And to repeat a comment quoted earlier, "they had assumed I would stay on and take the highers".

At the other extreme there was another modal group. Here the reasons for leaving school were more forcibly expressed. There were echoes of "glad to be out" (Weir and Nolan, 1977) and "flung aside" (Gow and McPherson, 1981). Even among the fourth-year leavers with O-grades, being fed up with school played a part in the decision making. Much of this would seem to have arisen from a general feeling that young people at school were not treated like young adults.

The written comments of the young people who had to stay on into the fifth year has also lent support to the distinction, made in chapter 5, between voluntary schooling and voluntary participation in fifth year. However, against the pressure of argument that the law should be changed to require four years of secondary schooling, rather than schooling until the age of 16, should be set the observation that those who were obliged to stay on into the fifth year seem to have shown a willingness to complete the course they were embarked upon (see chapter 5).

This and the preceding chapter have focused on the decision to stay on at school for post-compulsory education but it should be noted that schooling does not have to be provided or taken up at school and there has of late been an increase in full-time non-advanced further education. Finally, some young people asked whether school has to be the way it was:

> At College... (they) treat you more like Adults. (Female, O-grades, Secretarial College)
> My old school used to be good because they used to send you out on a training scheme. They could send more people to college. (Male, non-certificate, apprentice plasterer)
> From the start of secondary schooling pupils should pick if they want to go for O levels or a trade (eg electrician). But those opting for a trade must pick at least *3* trades in which to study in secondary school. In the system today too many pupils are rushed into subjects, by teachers and parents, of which they (the pupils) are not interested or know nothing about. (Male, O-grades, electrical fitter)

I found out that school was good for people with exam
potential but a waste of time for others. There should be
more work experience. (Female, O-grades, YOP)

My school education has taught me the basics which I ...
could have learned far quicker if it had not been for all the
pointless exam passing factors which have no use to the
majority of school leavers... except the exams
unfortunately determine (which) particular person (is)
suitable for a job. (Male, O-grades, apprentice)

Chapter 7

Post-compulsory schooling: the fifth year

Andrew McPherson

Introduction

The inter-related problems of difficulty, selection and motivation do not disappear in the post-compulsory stages of schooling but they must be solved in a different context which has itself been changing since the late 1970s. Recapitulating chapter 1 and also Gray *et al.* (1983, chapter 1), we may state these problems as a set of questions: how many pupils should be allowed to take how many courses, at what levels of difficulty, and to prepare in what ways and for how long, for what sorts of examinations and with what prospects of success? If all education were recurrent these dilemmas would not be acute, for people could progress at their own pace and also retrace their steps when a wrong turning had been made. But in "one-off" systems of universal education the solution to any one of these questions limits the options for solving the others; and this interdependence does not disappear with the ending of compulsion at 16 years.

Nevertheless some things do change at this point. Most obviously there is no longer a presumption of universality. Students (as we describe all persons in post-compulsory education, whether or not at school) may now legitimately select themselves into or out of school, and the extent to which they do so influences the school system's room for manoeuvre on the other questions. If, as in the 1950s, few students stay on, there will be less call to differentiate provision, especially if they share goals in common with each other and with the school. If many stay on, the pressures towards differentiation will become greater, especially where students' goals diverge from those held by their fellows and by the school. The emergence of the "new sixth year" in the 1960s and of the "new fifth year" in the 1960s and 1970s are examples. In both cases some schools for a time attempted to protect their more traditional goals by selecting students for the sixth-year and the fifth-year stages on the basis of fifth-year Highers and fourth-year

O-grades respectively; the "new" and less qualified students who stayed on, but who were not selected, were required to repeat the stage of their previous year's work. We can say that such schools responded to new demands by emphasising the selection side of the equation, rather than the provision side on which the difficulty and content of available courses might be adjusted; and we can describe such responses as part of the school system's intended or unintended "management" of the interdependent dilemmas just outlined (Gray *et al.*, 1983, pp.65-69).

A further characteristic of the post-compulsory period is that a new management tool becomes available at 16 years: the student's public examination results. Because they involve publicly administered, standardised procedures, and because they relate to the Highers examinations, examinations at 16 years have higher legitimacy than the internal examinations on which initial selection at 14 years is largely based. Hitherto, few schools have formally used fourth-year results to determine the fifth-year courses of students, although the "guidance" of students' choices in the light of previous examination performance may have effects that approximate formal selection. In some measure, however, schools have tended to err on the side of starting students on post-compulsory courses that may eventually prove to be too difficult for them. Thus, on the "provision" side of the equation, students have been allowed considerable latitude in constructing courses of varying degrees of difficulty using the many permutations of duration (one or two years), level (O, H, CSYS), and numbers of subjects. Options are also increased by choices between easy and difficult subjects (Kelly, 1976); and the contents of courses can also be varied, but mainly so far within the limits of what is largely an "academic" curriculum (Gray *et al.*, 1983, chapters 5 and 6).

This solution, using the provision side of the equation, has proved robust when coping with the problems posed by the "new" fifth and sixth years. Students could use the permutations just described to find their own level, even if that level might be a not-very-advantageous rung on a not-very-appropriate curricular ladder. Of course schools have also guided students' choices in the light of the latters' fourth-year examination performance, but the flexibility of post-fourth-year provision in school has relieved teacher and student alike of some of the onus of irrevocable decisions.

Nevertheless the balance of this equation is now vulnerable to changes in the wider context of post-compulsory schooling. With high youth unemployment a greater range of potential school leavers remains "available" to schools and new needs must be met. At the same time, falling rolls make aspects of this more varied provision uneconomic. Moreover, the very fact that schools' current provision is so varied in terms of load, duration and difficulty exposes them to the argument that other agencies could cater for particular categories of post-compulsory students more efficiently if students were concentrated in more purpose-specific institutions. Such institutions, it is argued, could also offer to their special clientèle an alternative and more appropriate curriculum. If 16 year olds were attracted to such courses in inverse proportion to their chances of success in Highers examinations taken at school, the composition of the population of 16-17 year olds that remained at school might not be very different from that of a school population retained under formal selection procedures. The main difference, of course, is that some element of choice would have been retained.

Thus selection and differentiation are on the agenda for the 16-plus debate. Whilst it is improbable that formal selection analogous to the 12-plus will be introduced at 16 years, it is the case that one option, or one possible eventuality, for post-compulsory schooling is that it concentrate solely on the preparation of students for higher education, with other students catered for elsewhere. If this were the case then the consequences of the self-selection and of the "guided" choices of students with respect to schooling tracks could well approximate a bipartite system: Brunton courses for fifth year, so to speak, rather than for third year (SED, 1963). Alternatively, if post-compulsory schooling were to be recognised as legitimately multi-functional, and were it to serve, as it almost certainly then would, a larger proportion of the age group, a further differentiation of the difficulty of post-compulsory school courses would be required and with it some basis for the selective allocation of students to courses of different levels of difficulty. This would also be the case if there were demands for a standardisation of all post-compulsory provision in the name of some curricular concept such as "a general education" (as has already happened in third and fourth year), or of some political concept such as the "equality of opportunity to acquire academic credentials".

At the time of writing (summer 1983) this last eventuality may seem improbable. For the moment, the wave of egalitarianism released by comprehensive reorganisation has spent itself at the end of fourth year, but not before Munn and Dunning had attempted to carry a form of the common curriculum forward from the first- and second-year stage. Though currently quiescent, egalitarianism may well revive demands for comprehensive post-compulsory provision and, indeed, the Action Plan has already been glossed in these terms.

> The promise in the Action Plan to revise the Highers is more far-reaching than the careful phraseology of the plan might have indicated. In planning for the 16-18s it has in its sights the academically able as well as those who are at

present in further education or who return for a fifth year without an opportunity to tackle Highers.... In the short term the Highers syllabi will be revised to make them fit onto those of the Munn and Dunning courses.... In the long term HM Inspectors have a gleam in their eye. Not usually given to espying the farther shores of radicalism, they see the opportunity of bringing together all post-16 certificates under one roof. In other words, students at further education colleges pursuing modular courses in plumbing would gain a certificate with the same name as academically inclined school pupils deep in Cicero. The comprehensive ideal would move a significant step forwards. (Pickard, 1983)

Strathclyde's blueprint for post-compulsory education and training might be similarly interpreted (Strathclyde Regional Council, 1981).

The two chapters on the fifth and the sixth years of schooling select and describe the data on the sample with the foregoing considerations in mind. A central theme of both chapters concerns the educational anomalies that arise from the school system's present attempt to manage the dilemmas of difficulty, selection and motivation using means fashioned in earlier decades, when post-compulsory schooling was assumed to be predominantly about helping students to qualify for higher education. No one doubts that this is a proper thing for schools to do. Indeed, it might be that, in a context of increasingly varied institutional provision for post-compulsory education, the preparation of students for higher education is the only thing that schools should do. Few, at any rate, would deny that there are tensions between this function of post-compulsory schooling and the functions it must currently fulfil for students who will not, or do not wish to, qualify for higher education. Moreover, other institutions and agencies compete with schools for such students. But how easily can such students be identified and at what stage? What proportion of post-compulsory school students does the "new" fifth year comprise? What do they want, and currently get, from continuing their education at school?

The data can give us perspectives on these questions that can in turn contribute to thinking about the proper place in post-compulsory provision of schooling, and of the present examination system and school curriculum. Among the questions of the moment to which these chapters therefore relate are the following: the place of new certificate examinations in fifth year (whether Credit and General certificates or a quasi-vocational certificate like the Scottish Certificate of Vocational Studies (SCVS)); the goals and viability of the present fifth-year Highers course; whether schools should provide one or two years of post-compulsory schooling (or, indeed, any at all); whether the Certificate of Sixth Year Studies (CSYS) should become a formal qualification for entry to higher education; whether it should be retained in sixth year, and how its principles and practice might be introduced in some form, a year earlier, in fifth year.

In both chapters the discussion of the data is preceded by a brief recent history of policy for the stage in question. But the discussion of the implications of the analysis for policy comes at the end of chapter 8 and in the final chapter.

Policy for fifth year

Earlier chapters have already described some of the developments that have influenced the suitability of current provision for the fifth year. To recapitulate briefly: following the introduction of the O-grade in 1962, more students were encouraged to stay on for a fourth year by the prospect of achieving an examination reward in return for only one year of post-compulsory education. In the ten years that followed, the proportion of students who were persuaded also then to undertake a fifth year roughly doubled to around 30 per cent and almost all of them took at least one course for Highers. The extension of the period of compulsory education to 16 years in 1973 (RSLA) had the effect of making the fifth year into the first year of post-compulsory education. After changes in the entry and leaving regulations in the mid-1970s about a quarter of the age group who were technically too young to leave until Christmas were "conscripted" into the fifth year. But RSLA at first had only a negligible influence on the proportions returning voluntarily. Between 1972 and 1979 the percentages of males in the age group who attempted Highers in the fifth year remained virtually stable whilst the percentages of females rose, but only slightly. Over this period also there was only trivial growth in the proportion of students who completed a fifth year taking only further examinations at the O-grade. It was not until the youth job market collapsed in 1980 that there was an appreciable change in the proportions returning voluntarily for a fifth year, and it was only some time after the advent of the Manpower Services Commission (MSC) in 1974 that education officials began to give serious attention to the structure of fifth-year courses and to their suitability for less able post-compulsory pupils. Indeed, a case can be made for saying that, with the possible exception of the Ruthven Report (SED, 1967), the Inspectorate report *Teaching and Learning in the Senior Stages of the Scottish Secondary School* (SED, 1983a) was the first sustained public review that the fifth year had ever received.

Although this review was the most attractively written educational document to come from St Andrew's House for almost three decades it was, unfortunately, some 20 years overdue. During the 1960s and 1970s provision for the fifth year had been pulled in opposite directions. On the one hand, the rapid expansion of the fifth year in the 1960s had resulted in some differentiation of fifth-year students' backgrounds, interests and abilities. On the other hand, the abolition in 1961 of the Scottish Leaving Certificate, and especially of its fifth-year Lower grade, thereafter meant that the modal course available in fifth year – the Scottish Certificate of Education (SCE) course at the Higher grade – was to be more difficult. It was implicit in the abolition of the Lower that if a pupil were to take a general or broad course of five subjects at a post-compulsory level these were henceforth to be Highers subjects.

Adding to this increase in the difficulty of the modal fifth-year course were the ambitions that the Scottish Education Department (SED) held for the sixth year. In an attempt to clear the sixth year for "advanced" or "post-Higher" work, the SED successfully persuaded schools in the 1960s that first-time presentations for Highers should be made mainly in the fifth year. In the 1950s Highers presentations had more commonly been spread over two years. Thus, at the very time that the fifth year was being opened to a wider range of pupils, there was a sharp increase in the number and level of courses for which most fifth-year pupils were required to prepare. In this sense the fifth year was made more difficult; the school system's expectations of pupils were raised. This move passed largely without contemporary comment and was only publicly acknowledged in a recommendation that some post-O-grade pupils might first present for Highers in sixth year, thereby forming a "slower stream", as it were. At the time an important consideration was the pupil who transferred to a six-year school after sitting O-grades at the type of four-year school that was to be swept away with comprehensive reorganisation. In the event, few Highers pupils have postponed sitting all their Highers until sixth year, though there are hints in the 1983 Inspectorate report that the SED might in the future give more encouragement to the two-year, post-O-grade Highers course (SED, 1983a, paras. 5.18-5.20).

Setting the scene

Figures from the School Census information used for Figure 5.2 indicate that in 1980 45 per cent of the year group returned to school in the August of their fifth year. Eight per cent returned because they were not yet old enough to leave but they thereafter did so at the earliest opportunity. A further 14 per cent eventually stayed on voluntarily although they had initially been required by reason of age to return in August. Adding this group to the 23 per cent who returned voluntarily in August, we can say that 37 per cent of the year group embarked voluntarily on post-compulsory schooling. A separate point is that 62 per cent of those who were "conscripted" into the fifth year by virtue of their being too young to leave in the previous summer, remained voluntarily at school after the first (Christmas) date at which they could leave school.

This chapter is about those students, and only those students, who voluntarily entered post-compulsory schooling in the August of the fifth year, or at some date thereafter. (In schools which attempted to maintain selective entry to the fifth year some students with poor fourth-year O-grade results are asked to "repeat their fourth year". All such are treated here as fifth-year students.) We shall describe this group as "volunteers"; it should be noted that it includes those "conscripts" who were to stay on beyond the Christmas of fifth year and thereby become volunteers. In this chapter, except where the context makes otherwise clear, the percentages mentioned take all volunteers as the 100 per cent base.

This is how one student described her transition to a schooling that, in formal terms, was now voluntary.

> I enjoyed school life until fifth year where I found that there was too much emphasis laid upon passing the exams at the end of the course. I had secured a great deal of enjoyment from my fourth year studies. However, in fifth year I found the pressure of the work immense. I felt that I was merely being programmed to reiterate facts and figures at a later date.

Another said:

> The Higher courses were all rushed far too much. You really only have 6/7 months to do a Higher course with the result that you speed through the course unable to enjoy it because of this, and – what matters much more – unable to properly understand everything.

A third said:

> I found most of the teaching unimaginative, formal and altogether uninspiring. I enjoyed English and History because most of the learning was left to the individual who could develop his own opinions and attitudes to interesting problems.... I feel that throughout my Fourth and Fifth years myself and many others were hindered by teachers who desperately tried to 'cram' the syllabus in as short a

time as possible.

Such comments come as no surprise for the fifth-year Highers course is notorious for the pressures it places upon students. But how widely were these feelings shared? About half the volunteers said that the amount of work required in fifth year "came as a shock"; six out of ten said that their SCE work "dominated their life" and three quarters said that they were unable to "keep up with the work in (their) SCE courses in fifth year" (no table shown). This gives us some measure of the price at which standards in the fifth year are currently bought, a measure which we may juxtapose to the views of the Inspectorate, based upon their observations of some 60 schools between 1979 and 1982.

> The objective of the Higher grade course, given equally high priority by both teachers and pupils, is to achieve the best possible results in the examination. To that end, teachers are not inclined to run risks. They prepare their work thoroughly. They teach hard and directly, to the whole class, at a brisk pace, and in a definite mould.... For their part, the pupils apply themselves conscientiously. They do a great deal of written work, mainly in forms and contexts that are apt to figure in the external examination.... Teachers and pupils are thus conjoined on a common enterprise not lightly regarded by either. The former inform, inculcate, and provide a focus for 'return'. The latter absorb, digest, and meet their deadlines.... Traditional periodic testing and preliminary examinations on the model of the external examination harden the mould.... Almost all of this teaching and learning (perhaps that is the appropriate order) is, after its fashion, efficient.... Significantly, such approaches do not strike all the pupils as dull; most know full well what is at stake, respect their teachers for making great efforts on their behalf, and fret only when the rigour slackens. (SED, 1983a, paras. 3.4-3.6)

One guesses that the rigour did not often slacken, for 83 per cent of students who stayed voluntarily to fifth year afterwards said that it had been worthwhile.

FIGURE 7.1
Differentiation in fourth and fifth year
(a) percentages of volunteers with fourth-year O-grade awards at A-C
(b) percentages of volunteers with Highers passes in fifth year
**(c) associations between proportions of all awards/passes and propor-
tions of volunteers**

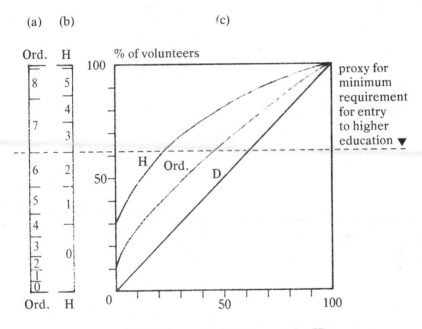

% of SCE awards (Ord.) or passes (H)

Difficulty and differentiation

What SCE qualifications did the volunteers already possess and how
evenly were these qualifications distributed among them? The column
labelled "Ord." on the left of Figure 7.1 shows the percentages of volunteers
who had achieved each number of A-C awards in their fourth-year O-grades
(the percentages may be read off from the adjacent scale labelled "% of

volunteers"). Only a handful had achieved no such awards, but one quarter (25 per cent) had achieved three A-C awards or less. Thirty-eight per cent had got at least seven A-C awards and 53 per cent had got at least six. A year later, however, when the Highers results were known, the picture was to look rather different. The scale labelled "H" shows the percentages of students who achieved Highers passes at the end of the year. Thirty per cent were to pass none and 47 per cent were to pass less than two.

Three Highers passes are commonly taken as a proxy for the threshold entrance qualification for higher education; only 38 per cent of the volunteers were to achieve or surpass this level by the end of fifth year; they lie on or above the horizontal broken line in the figure. This line happens also to demarcate volunteers who had more than six fourth-year O-grade awards at A-C.

In this sense, and under present conditions, a one-year, post-O-grade course that had as its sole purpose the preparation of students for entry to higher education would successfully serve under half of those volunteering for fifth year; and, if a level of difficulty that produced a "failure" rate of about 20 per cent were accepted, then about half the fifth year might be admitted to such a course (*ie* about 40 per cent successful and 10 per cent unsuccessful). Naturally, if one were to extend such a course to two years but leave the threshold qualification unchanged, higher proportions of students might be admitted to it (see the discussion of Figure 8.5 in the next chapter). Thus the consequences of difficulty for the differentiation of students depend partly on the "third d" of duration.

But how far did the fifth year further differentiate students? The main body of Figure 7.1 plots the percentage of volunteers (vertical scale) against the percentage of all awards made (horizontal scale). Fourth-year O-grades and fifth-year H-grades are plotted separately by the two curving lines respectively labelled "Ord." and "H". In either examination, if all students had received the same number of awards the plot would be the diagonal (D), ten per cent of the students receiving ten per cent of the awards, 20 per cent receiving 20 per cent, and so on. The extent to which the curved plots depart from the diagonal is a measure of the tendency for awards to be concentrated among only some students. A tendency in this direction is apparent for fourth-year O-grade awards at A-C; it is even more apparent for fifth-year H-grade awards (by about as much again, the area bounded by H/D being about twice the size of the area bounded by Ord./D). In this sense we can compare the fifth-year Higher with the fourth-year O-grade and say that, among the students who volunteered for post-compulsory schooling, Highers success was unequally distributed to a degree that was roughly double the inequality in the distribution of examination success among the same persons a year earlier. (To be precise, Ord./D is 27 per cent of the area above the diagonal, D, and H/D is 52 per cent.)

This conclusion gives us a measure of the extent to which the difficulty of fifth-year courses was further to differentiate the volunteers, setting them in competition with each other for success. "The school was good", said one student, "because there was a high degree of competition between pupils. Therefore they worked harder; got good results. Teachers encouraged competition." (She also added that her schooling had not helped her afterwards.)

The extent of differentiation before and during fifth year provides a framework or agenda for the presentation of the data. Why did students choose to enter the fifth-year hothouse? How did their examination plans change during the year? How did examination courses constrain the framework for their curriculum? How did fifth year "add" to fourth year in terms of students' further successes and failures? When did the fifth-year leavers decide to leave and what reasons did they give? What had these leavers got out of fifth year and what did they think afterwards of their experience? The remainder of the chapter discusses each of these questions in turn and looks generally at the relationship between students' experiences of fifth year and their performance in public examinations a year earlier.

Why did students volunteer for a fifth year?

This question has already been discussed in chapter 6 (Table 6.2) and the treatment here will be brief. For about six out of ten of the volunteers, Highers was identified as the most important single reason for choosing to stay on; for a further one in ten it was more O-grades; and for a further one in ten it was the fact that they had not decided on their future education or career. Only small percentages indicated that their most important reason concerned their age or the lack of jobs. Six out of ten volunteers had "always assumed" they would start a fifth year (few, however, giving it as the main reason).

However, even if a majority of fifth-year volunteers had entered fifth year primarily to study for Highers and had been planning on this for some time past, there were others for whom Highers had been much less important. By about Christmas of fifth year about one third of the volunteers were studying fewer than three Highers courses and less than a fifth of this group recalled that the acquisition of Highers qualifications had been their main objective in choosing to stay on. Their motives had been various: the acquisition of O-grades was mentioned more often than any other reason, but even this was chosen by fewer than half as their single most important reason (no table shown).

Among students studying three or four Highers, two thirds indicated that Highers had been their main objective in staying on, but four out of ten mentioned that more, or better, O-grades were also a consideration. Only the students starting five or more Highers had seen O-grades as virtually irrelevant but these students only comprised just under a third of the volunteers.

One should not try to be too exact about proportions when discussing these reasons; the data are retrospectively reported and one may summarise them in different ways. Nevertheless it is clear that a large minority of the volunteers did not take courses that could qualify them for entry to higher education in one year; and, to the extent that this minority was concerned with qualifications, the O-grade was more important than the Higher, even though some may have attempted a Higher or two as well.

How did examination plans change?

What light do the data throw on students' progress between August and the summer examinations? How many took the courses they had initially planned? How many took more, and how many less? The discussion in this section focuses on the 92 per cent of volunteers who started at last one course for Highers. In the sections that follow it, however, all volunteers for fifth year again comprise the 100 per cent sample base unless the contrary is explicitly stated.

Eighty per cent said they eventually "studied for the Highers examination" the same number of subjects that, in the August of their fifth year, they had intended to study for Highers; six per cent said they studied more Highers than they had initially intended and 14 per cent said they studied fewer. (Of this last group about half ended up studying only one or two Highers.) There was, therefore, a fairly small net change in numbers of subjects and a net movement towards a lightening of the load. A little under one student in five discontinued the study of at least one subject that they had started to study for Highers, although some, of course, took up other Highers subjects for examination, in fifth or sixth year.

These data were retrospectively reported and this limits the precision with which we can speak. Nevertheless the direction and general magnitude of the net changes, and also their pattern, can be informative as part of the general picture presented in this chapter. Entry to fifth year is now largely open or formally non-selective (though see Ryrie, 1981, p.69). Nevertheless the difficulty of the Highers course means that there is still a job of selection to be done. Most of this occurs at the beginning of the year when teachers and students plan the students' H- and O-grade courses. But a minority of students finds during the course of the year that initial plans have been set too high.

Most school students receive the first formal indication of their progress in fifth year from their performance in the preliminary examinations that individual schools conduct internally, usually just before or just after Christmas. Nine out of ten volunteers said they had taken preliminary examinations. About one third (31 per cent) of all volunteers (*ie* of those who had, and who had not, sat the preliminary examinations) said their plans had been changed by these examinations in some respect: 17 per cent of volunteers said they decided to attempt fewer subjects for Highers in fifth year; ten per cent said their reaction was to "postpone sitting subject(s) at Higher until a sixth year". (Nineteen per cent mentioned one or both of these reactions.) Six per cent decided to attempt more subjects at the O-grade (but most of this six per cent also dropped or postponed Highers). Five per cent dropped one or more O-grade and six per cent said they decided to leave (and most seem to have done so).

What respondents told us about the preliminary examinations therefore accords well with our inferences from the record of their Highers courses. Where students modified their ambitions it was mostly "downwards", in the direction of fewer, or easier, or longer examination courses. Around one fifth cut down their Highers load or reallocated some of it to a possible sixth year. A further few per cent (we cannot be sure how many) may have cut down on their O-grade courses, even though they were not doing Highers. A large part of this lightening of the load seems to have been occasioned by the Christmas preliminary examinations.

How did examination courses constrain the framework for the curriculum?

The level and number of SCE examination courses that students take is a major influence both on the curriculum and, indeed, on their entire experience of schooling. The Inspectorate found in the fifth years of the 60 schools they studied between 1979 and 1982 that:

> (t)he total time pupils spend on subjects for examination
> is rarely less than 75 per cent of the week. Usually it is in
> excess of that.... (SED, 1983a, para.2.18)

This section is concerned only with the SCE courses that were studied in fifth year with a view to presentation at O-grade or H-grade in either fifth or sixth year. (The data do not allow a watertight distinction to be drawn between courses studied before and after Christmas preliminary examinations.) It is not about the content of particular subjects or groups of subjects (for which see SED and SEB, 1982, chapters 4 and 5), nor is it about methods. But it is about the framework for contents and methods that is set by the numbers and levels of examinations that students undertake.

How were fifth-year O-grades combined with H-grade courses? Figure 7.2 answers this question. Each vertical block is drawn proportional to the

FIGURE 7.2
Number of SCE O- and H-grade courses studied throughout fifth year (percentages)

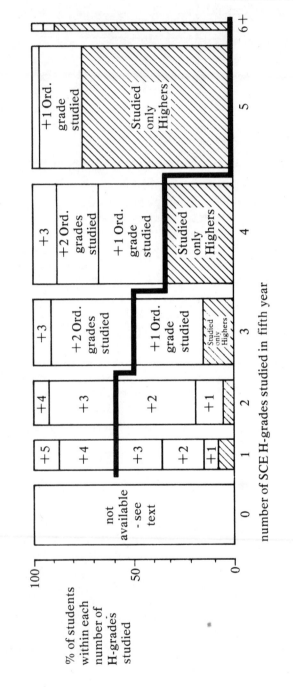

Key: ▬▬▬   'threshold' percentage **below** which fewer than five SCE subjects (at Ord. or H) were studied

        ▨▨▨   studied H-grades but not Ord. grades

percentage of students studying in fifth year the number of Highers courses indicated at its base. Within each block the hatched area shows the percentage taking only H-grade courses, whilst the plain areas above record the percentages taking additional O-grade courses. (The extreme left-hand block indicates the 14 per cent of volunteers who studied no Highers through to examination in fifth year. They include the eight per cent who did not start Highers courses and some of the five per cent who left during the year. The data on the fifth-year O-grade courses of this group as a whole are not yet satisfactory partly because there is some confounding with item non-response. Provisional indications are that most studied fewer than five O-grades, but it is safer to record the information as not available.)

Like Figure 7.1, Figure 7.2 makes it apparent that the fifth-year course was only a course of five or more Highers subjects for a minority of students, some 29 per cent. What it also reveals, however, is the extent to which the fifth-year course comprises less than five SCE subjects, whether at H-grade or O-grade. All the students falling below the heavy black line studied fewer than five SCE subjects. These students total 31 per cent of the volunteers, or 39 per cent of all volunteers for whom a wholly adequate record of fifth-year courses is currently available. Thus the O-grade has a major role in the fifth-year curriculum. Well over half the volunteers studied for the O-grade in fifth year and, statistically, it raised the percentage of students studying five examination courses from the three in ten who did so on the basis of Highers alone, to about six in ten. Without it three fifth-year students in ten could not have attained the potential for breadth that a five-subject course might offer.

Nevertheless, easier than Highers though the O-grade is, it appears from Figure 7.2 that it may not be so easy as to put a five-subject examination course within the reach of all fifth-year pupils. The heavy black line moves stepwise across the levels of Highers and at least a half of those studying three or fewer Highers in fact studied fewer than five examination courses in all. The Inspectorate's study found that fifth-year courses "by and large, consist in the first instance of five subjects for external examination" (SED, 1983a, para.2.15). It seems, however, that "in the second instance" (*ie* after the preliminary examination) the courses of some three or four in ten fifth-year students fall below this standard. One guesses that much of this shortfall results from the difficulty that the less able among the volunteers had in carrying five subjects to SCE presentation level.

FIGURE 7.3
Percentages respectively studying, and passing, three and four H-grade courses in fifth year, by the number of fourth-year O-grade awards at A-C

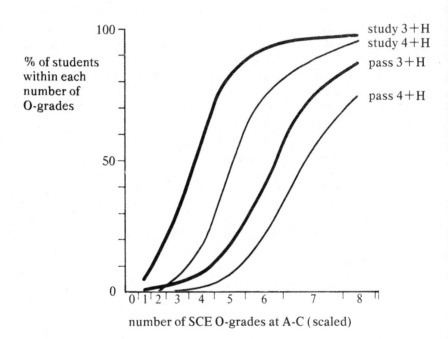

number of SCE O-grades at A-C (scaled)

How did fifth year add to fourth year?

Figure 7.3 offers an overview of events between the summers of fourth and fifth year. The horizontal scale is drawn proportional to the number of fifth-year volunteers who had achieved each number of A-C awards at O-grade in their fourth year. (The five per cent of volunteers recorded as having no such awards are not shown in the diagram although they have been included in the calculations for it.) The vertical scale is the percentage of volunteers at each level of O-grade award. The figure shows: the percentages studying at least three Highers courses (indicated by the top, bold line); the percentages studying at least four Highers (the next line down); the percentages passing at least three Highers (the bold line one up from the bottom); and the percentages passing four Highers (the bottom line).

All the lines move steeply upwards from left to right indicating a strong relationship between fourth-year success and the fifth-year record; and the position of the "thresholds" (indicated by parts of the slopes tending more towards the horizontal) also reflects this relationship. Thus, to take the top line, most volunteers with at least five O-grade awards studied at least three H-grade courses. Between one and five A-C awards the percentage starting three or more Highers courses rises steeply. Taking three H-grade passes as a proxy for the minimum entrance qualification for higher education, we see that schools provided fifth-year courses that could lead to such a qualification by the end of the year for virtually all their volunteer fifth-year who had achieved at least five A-C awards, but for very few of those who had achieved no more than, say, three awards. (Students with four fourth-year awards, among whom roughly half started at least three Highers, clearly posed a problem. They comprised ten per cent of the volunteer fifth year.)

Moving to Highers achievement and the two lower lines, the thresholds for success lie higher up the scale of fourth-year achievement (ie further to the right of the figure). Few volunteers who had less than six A-C O-grade awards achieved three or more Highers passes by the end of fifth year (six per cent). By contrast, two thirds of students with six or more such fourth-year awards did achieve at least three Highers passes a year later (66 per cent). Only just over half the volunteers (54 per cent) had at least six O-grade awards when they started fifth year. If they alone had been admitted to Highers courses and other sorts of courses had been provided for the remainder, three per cent of the volunteers would have been excluded from a course in which they were capable of reaching the threshold achievement for success by the end of fifth year; and 18 per cent would have been admitted to a course which was too difficult for them in only one year. In terms of these criteria and this information, therefore, about one fifth of the volunteers would have been misallocated.

Figure 7.3 also gives us an estimate of the difficulty of the fifth-year Highers examination. The estimate is conservative because it does not use the full range of information on the numbers of attempts and passes. But the vertical distance between the two bold lines (study 3+H; pass 3+H), or between the two other lines, indicates the percentage of volunteers who failed at least one subject. Thus, among volunteers with five A-C awards in their fourth-year O-grades, 82 per cent studied at least three Highers in fifth year but only 16 per cent had passed at least three Highers by the end of the year.

Forty-four per cent of the volunteers achieved A-C awards at O-grade in fifth year, but only 16 per cent gained more than one. Among those who returned to fifth year only with the intention of sitting O-grades, the large majority failed to achieve any A-C awards.

The augmentation of Highers qualifications in sixth year is discussed in the next chapter.

Fifth-year leavers

Only 30 per cent of the sample of volunteers recalled that, at the start of the fifth year, they had intended no more than the one year of post-compulsory schooling; 39 per cent recalled that, at that point, they had firmly intended to do a sixth year also, whilst 31 per cent recalled that they had either been undecided about staying on after the fifth year or had not thought about it (no table shown). (The percentages in this section are based on the 92 per cent of volunteers who started to study at least one Highers course and who therefore received the Highers questionnaire.) In the event 56 per cent left in fifth year, almost all of them in the summer. The net effect of fifth year was therefore to increase the percentage of students who wanted to leave. About half of this effect seems attributable to the Christmas preliminary examinations and much of the rest of it to the fifth-year results themselves. Looking at individuals, 55 per cent actually left or stayed according to their (recalled) plans as they had been before the preliminary examinations; a further five per cent who had initially planned to leave in fact stayed on, as did a further 13 per cent who had initially been undecided or who had not thought about it; a further 18 per cent who had also been undecided in fact left as, finally, did nine per cent who had initially planned to stay on.

Whilst retrospective data such as these probably underestimate the degree of indecision as at the beginning of fifth year, and whilst they probably exaggerate the degree of consistency between initial intentions and eventual behaviour, they are better than mere conjecture. They suggest that the two main effects of the fifth year on educational plans were, first, to confirm them for a slight majority and, second, to encourage otherwise undecided students to think of terminating their post-compulsory schooling after only one year. Two thirds (64 per cent) of the students who were initially undecided in fact left before the sixth year.

The large majority of volunteers (85 per cent) said they had not considered leaving without first taking their SCE examinations, and a further ten per cent said they had considered "early leaving" during the fifth year, but had not done so. Only five per cent of the volunteers left school during the year. A majority of this small group had returned in the previous August with the intention of attempting at least one Higher, but many said that they had been unable to find jobs, were undecided on their future and had planned to take more O-grades meantime. The proportion of volunteers in this position is likely to have risen since the 1981 survey.

Fifty-six per cent of the post-compulsory volunteers did not start a sixth year. What reasons did fifth-year leavers give for leaving school? Thirty per cent indicated that their single most important reason for leaving was that they "had all the Highers or O-grades needed for the job or course (they) wanted"; and a further seven per cent said that their most important reason was that they "did not think (they) would get any better exam results at school". So just over a third gave a main reason that involved qualifications. A further third said they were primarily motivated by job considerations: "I wanted to get a job and be self-supporting" (13 per cent); "I needed the money from a job" (two per cent); or "I wanted to started a particular job while I had the chance" (16 per cent). The remaining third said either that they were "fed up with school" (12 per cent) or that they felt they would "prefer life at work or college to life at school" (19 per cent). Some more information on the factors that weighed with students is given in Table 8.1 in the next chapter.

To what extent had fifth-year leavers among the volunteers improved on their fourth-year qualifications? About 28 per cent of them, or a little under, did not add to their tally of fourth-year passes ("a little under" because five per cent, who had six or more fourth-year O-grade awards at A-C, but who achieved no Highers passes, may have "passed" an extra O-grade or two in fifth year – this detail has not yet become available from the data). A further 15 per cent achieved O-grade awards at A-C in further subjects but passed no Highers. Thus four in ten fifth-year leavers who had chosen to start a fifth-year course did not achieve Highers passes. Three in ten passed one or two Highers and three in ten passed three or more. Less than one third, in other words, had qualifications that met the notional minimum requirement for entry to higher education.

Nevertheless nine months after leaving school, fifth-year leavers looked back on their year in post-compulsory schooling with something akin to cheerful resilience. Three quarters (76 per cent) said their fifth year at school had been "worthwhile". Even among those who had not improved their SCE qualifications over half the leavers (55 per cent) thought their fifth year worthwhile; and so too did 72 per cent of the leavers who had achieved more A-C awards at O-grade, but no H-grades (no table shown). The percentage judging fifth year worthwhile was 79 per cent among fifth-year leavers who achieved one or two Highers passes. But total happiness, it seems, was to pass three or more Highers in fifth year, and then to leave school. Virtually all of this group (97 per cent) said their fifth year had been worthwhile. Of the volunteers who continued to sixth year 90 per cent said this of their fifth year.

Thus, taking all the volunteers, whether or not they stayed for a sixth year, 83 per cent subsequently said that their fifth year had been worthwhile. For all that students found the fifth year pressured and difficult, this endorsement cannot be overlooked by the proponents of change.

Summary and comment

The contents and level of difficulty of fifth-year courses are largely a legacy of post-compulsory schooling's main function of earlier times, the preparation of students for higher education. In the "new" fifth year a course, say, of four or five Highers is too difficult for the majority of students to complete successfully in one year. Courses for the O-grade therefore continued to make a substantial contribution to the curriculum, even of students doing three or four Highers as well. Nevertheless a majority of the students who volunteered for fifth year did not take the five examination courses, whether at O- or H-grade, that would be required to fulfil more traditional prescriptions for a broad or general education.

For the most part students adopted different levels of difficulty for their fifth-year work, choosing a variable number of courses at the two grades of O and H in a way that closely reflected their O-grade achievements in the previous year. But the level of difficulty of their overall course was not fully determined for all students as they started fifth year, for two reasons: first, about a fifth of students dropped at least one Higher during the fifth year, often as a result of their performance in the Christmas preliminary examination; and second, about a third of students starting their fifth year had not at that point decided whether they wanted to do a second year of post-compulsory schooling. Indeed changes of intention during the fifth year meant that barely a half of students ending their fifth year then acted in conformity with their intention of a year earlier.

In other words, whilst fourth-year O-grade performance seemed to determine much of the variation between students in the load of fifth-year courses they assumed, there was also some indeterminacy in the system, especially when viewed in the context of post-compulsory schooling as a whole. The fourth-year O-grade examination was a weighty arbiter of the fifth-year course but schools tended also to encourage students, especially the less able, to keep their aspirations high. A corollary of this, and also of the many graduations of levels of difficulty that can be constructed from the permutations of the O- and H-grade, is that there is no single point at which new-fifth-year students can unarguably be demarcated from old-fifth-year students. If one is looking for such a differentiation it might be found at a point between the third of fifth-year volunteers who did not attempt the three Highers that notionally could constitute a qualification for entry to higher education, and the remainder of students who did. But among the former were some, though not many, who would gain more Highers in sixth year, and among the latter were a considerable number who would fail at least one of their three Highers in fifth year. So the proportions of volunteers who might be designated as the new fifth year ("conscripts" to fifth year who left at Christmas have been excluded from consideration in this chapter) could be somewhat lower than one third, or it could be as high as the 60 per cent who had not achieved three Highers passes by the end of fifth year. Of course, if three Highers passes were taken as too low a proxy for the minimum entrance qualification for higher education, the new fifth year would comprise somewhat more than 60 per cent; and if it were to include all who were not to achieve the five Highers passes of the traditional course then 85 per cent of fifth-year students would be new.

The elasticity of the idea of the new fifth year obviously makes it somewhat unsatisfactory both as a basis for describing the data and also, by extension, as a basis for policy-making. Moreover, what meaning it has it takes, as it were, by default, by being the negative of the old fifth year. This is unsatisfactory for a second reason, because the idea of the old or traditional fifth year is thereby left unexamined. It is assumed to be conceptually unproblematic and descriptively serviceable, and it is not a far cry from this to thinking of the old fifth year as unproblematic and serviceable in an educational sense as well. If anything, indeed, the old fifth year is less a descriptive term than a moral term, an expression of the single and common purpose for post-compulsory schooling that underpinned provision until the early 1960s; a system provided by men of parts for lads o'pairts. Two things may be said here. First, the traditional fifth year of five Highers in fifth year is in fact a tradition of barely two decades standing. Second, studies of school students before this period (*eg* Maxwell, 1969) make it clear that former fifth years also contained a range of ability (though not so wide a range) and, yes, students who wanted university entrance qualifications, but also students who used their achievements in these qualifying examinations to enter the professions, industry and commerce directly from school.

From this perspective, the new fifth year of the 1960s and the 1970s is better understood not as dichotomously distinct from the old, but simply as the old fifth year writ larger.

In 1980, conditions in an already ailing youth labour market worsened rapidly, and we must bear this in mind when considering the wider implications of our findings on the fifth year. But first we must examine the contribution of the sixth year to post-compulsory schooling.

Chapter 8

Post-compulsory schooling: the sixth year

Andrew McPherson

Introduction

Perhaps it is because the sixth year has been asked to serve a variety of purposes that there has been more agreement over what it should not do than over what it should. On the three occasions that the question has been raised in the recent past, the possibility of having a two-year, post-16 course with only one point of exit, at 18 years, has been decisively rejected: in the 1940s, in the late 1950s, and again in the early 1980s. An important consideration here has always been that the system ought to allow students to fulfil the qualifications for entry to higher education at 17 years by the end of their fifth year. (Readers are reminded that the term "student" in this book refers to all persons in education who have passed the minimum age for leaving school.) If school students were required to complete a second post-compulsory year before "qualifying", fewer, it has been thought, would embark on post-compulsory schooling, and access to higher education would suffer.

But agreement that the end of the sixth year should not constitute the only point at which post-compulsory schooling might be concluded clearly leaves much else to be resolved. As mentioned in the previous chapter, official deliberations in the early 1960s sanctioned a "mixed" sixth year serving pupils at several different stages of their education. At one extreme it was to provide the "slower stream" student with the opportunity to complete a two-year, post-O-grade course by presenting for Highers (mostly one or two) for the first time at the end of their sixth year. At the other extreme, it was to provide "genuine" sixth-year students with "genuine" sixth-year courses, platonic ideas to which the Inspectorate still gave currency in 1983 (SED, 1983a, paras. 2.10, 2.11). The assumption here was, and still is, that such students would obtain Highers entry qualifications for higher education by the end of their fifth year. To the universities a "proper" sixth year seemed to offer a sounder preparation for all their prospective students, thereby extending its hitherto more restricted purpose of helping high-fliers to win university bursary awards; and many in the schools did not demur. Others, however, have preferred not to tie the second post-compulsory year to the particulars of the university curriculum, but have wanted it to be a liberalising experience for all sixth-year students, whether or not they were planning to enter higher education.

When it was introduced in 1968 it was this last purpose that the Certificate of Sixth Year Studies (CSYS) was officially meant to fulfil. Whatever its incidental merits as a preparation for higher education, it was initially intended to serve mainly as a liberal conclusion to the period of secondary schooling and as a benign influence on the academic curriculum and didactic methods of both years of post-compulsory schooling. These hopes have been largely disappointed owing to the wishful thinking of the time about the practicalities of qualifying for higher education by means of the fifth-year Highers examination. But the original purpose for the CSYS has been resurrected in the Inspectorate's recent proposals for fifth and sixth years: the CSYS embodied "important educational principles" and it was desirable to "extend their influence into the mainstream of secondary education" (*ibid.*, paras. 3.14, 5.19). The Inspectorate also, however, emphasised the "fairly insecure place occupied by CSYS generally" (about six per cent of the age group took it in 1980) and questioned "the justification for a national apparatus for examinations that can command no more than that order of support". "The final comment on CSYS", it observed, somewhat gloomily, "may have to be that it arrived too late in Scottish secondary education for it to have had a wide effect on teaching and learning generally" (*ibid.*, paras. 2.12, 3.14).

The reasons for this are well enough documented in other studies referred to in this chapter and they require only a brief introduction at this point. As competition for entry to higher education started to intensify in the late 1950s, fewer students who began the sixth year could be sure that their fifth-year Highers awards would secure their admission to higher education and especially to university. More students entered sixth year partly in order to improve on their fifth-year examination qualifications, and more of these did so by presenting again in sixth year for Highers examinations in which they had performed poorly a year earlier. The "slow stream" of students presenting all their Highers for the first time only in sixth year has been negligible (at around one per cent of volunteers in the present survey, although a significant minority of fifth-year Highers presentees deferred the presentation of some subjects to sixth year, as described below). The CSYS had a somewhat ambivalent, if not nugatory, status as a formal qualification for entry to higher education and few sixth-year students, about one in ten, took only CSYS courses. Between these two extremes, of the slow-stream student and the high-flier, one finds the large majority of sixth-year students. For them, and for the sixth year as a whole, therefore, the Higher has remained the dominant element.

This chapter continues the exploration of the themes of difficulty, selection and motivation by examining the ways in which the continuing pursuit of Highers qualifications structured students' experiences of sixth-year courses. In illustrating the influence on schools of selection for higher education, it draws attention to pronounced differences between the west of Scotland and the rest of the country in the functions of sixth year for students who have attained at least three Higher passes by the end of fifth year; and it also shows heuristically an example of the sort of differentiation of students that might be necessary to free post-compulsory schooling from the incubus of excessive external examinations.

Entry to the sixth year

Three quarters of sixth-year entrants recalled having felt at the end of fifth year that they "needed better qualifications for a future job or course". Two thirds said this was a "very important" consideration for them at the end of their fifth year and two thirds said it was a reason for their return to school; 45 per cent said it was the single most important reason for returning, whilst a further 26 per cent said that their most important reason for returning was that they were undecided on their future education or career (no table shown). Answering another question, 29 per cent of entrants to sixth year said that, after they had got their fifth-year results, they were "fairly certain (their) results were good enough" to "qualify (them) for the type of job or course they had in mind"; 26 per cent were "uncertain" and 44 per cent were "certain (their) results were not good enough" (no table shown).

A large majority of students, therefore, started their sixth year in the belief that they had to improve their Highers qualifications and, for at least half, this was the overriding consideration. This and other views of those who stayed to sixth year are shown in Table 8.1, together with the views of fifth-year leavers. A large majority of sixth-year students had clearly thought that improvement was within their capabilities. Only 12 per cent agreed with the statement, "I did not think I would get any better exam results at school", compared with 44 per cent of fifth-year leavers. About one half, or just under, of sixth year students had been undecided on their "future education or career". Interestingly, fifth- and sixth-year leavers did not differ greatly in their perception of the desirability of the jobs they thought available to them at the end of fifth year (one item up from the bottom of the table).

One other comment is prompted by Table 8.1. Six out of ten sixth-year students (57 per cent) said that they had wished "to extend (their) knowledge of subjects (they) had passed at Highers". Of respondents to another questionnaire version, however, somewhat fewer (40 per cent) gave this as a reason (among other reasons) for their return (no table shown);

TABLE 8.1

Selected views at the end of fifth year, by year of leaving (percentages)

	fifth-year leavers				sixth-year leavers			
	disagree	?	agree	total	disagree	?	agree	total
I needed better qualifications for a future job or course	55	11	34	100	21	5	74	100
I did not think I would get any better exam results at school	39	17	44	100	76	12	12	100
I hadn't decided on my future education or career	70	8	22	100	50	6	44	100
I wanted to start a particular job while I had the chance	47	13	40	100	84	12	4	100
I wanted to get a job and be self-supporting	45	12	43	100	80	10	10	100
I needed the money from a job	58	14	28	100	81	12	7	100
There were no jobs available that I wanted	55	20	25	100	43	24	33	100
I wished to extend my knowledge of subjects I had passed at Highers	50	20	30	100	27	16	57	100

Notes: The table collapses the seven-point scale that was used. "?" identifies "can't say or neutral". Not all items are shown, and the order here differs from that on the questionnaire. The definition of the target sample in this table differs slightly from that of the "volunteers" used in chapters 7 and 8.

fewer still (31 per cent) rated this as having been a very important consideration for them at the end of fifth year, and only nine per cent picked this as the single most important reason for starting a sixth year. Also, only ten per cent of the sixth year said that, at the end of the fifth year, the wish to "study new subjects at school" had been "very important" to them.

The most common consideration was therefore the pursuit of further qualifications.

During the past two decades, and probably earlier too, the pattern of entry to the sixth year of schools in west-central Scotland, in the Strathclyde Region, has differed from that elsewhere in the country. A higher proportion of students in Strathclyde with good fifth-year Highers qualifications has left school at the end of fifth year (Gray *et al.*, 1983, Table 5.1). In the early 1960s most entrants to university direct from Scottish schools had completed a sixth year at school but, since then, the two west-central universities of Glasgow and Strathclyde have diverged from the other Scottish universities by selecting almost half of their Scottish entry (coming direct from school) from the fifth year (no table shown).

Altogether 44 per cent of the volunteers returned for a sixth year, 40 per cent in Strathclyde and 48 per cent elsewhere in Scotland. The regional variation is clearly visible in the decisions made by the sample. Figure 8.1 shows the percentages of pupils who returned for a sixth year, disaggregated on the horizontal scale by the number of Highers they had passed in fifth year. (The horizontal axis has been scaled according to the percentage of Scottish volunteers at each level of fifth-year Highers pass.) Across students with fewer than three passes the two halves of Scotland behave almost identically; the percentages returning increase in linear fashion with the number of passes. However, at the threshold of three passes, used in chapters 7 and 8 as a proxy for a national minimum qualification for entry to higher education, the Strathclyde percentage falls and then levels out at 45 per cent, whereas the percentage in the rest of Scotland continues to rise, to 77 per cent.

Among students with three or more fifth-year Highers, there were concomitant regional variations in the advice students said they had received in their fifth year. In Strathclyde, significantly fewer students (in a statistical sense) said that their parents had wanted them to stay on for another year (difference between the percentages for Strathclyde and elsewhere = 16 per cent); or that any of their teachers had wanted them to stay on (difference = 15 per cent); or that their friends had actually stayed on (difference = 17 per cent). More in Strathclyde had been advised to leave by their parents (difference = 16 per cent).

FIGURE 8.1
Percentage returning for a sixth year, by the number of fifth -year Highers passes, and by area of Scotland: all post-compulsory school students

---

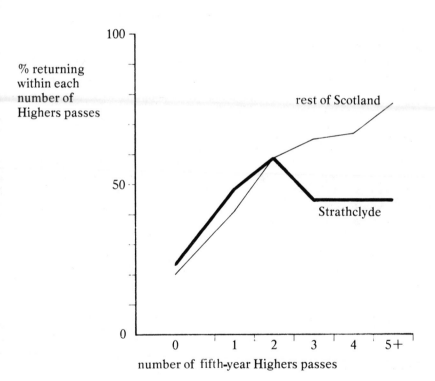

The structure for the sixth-year curriculum

Like its counterpart in chapter 7, this section refers not to curriculum content or methods but to the constraints that the number and level of examination courses place on possibilities for the curriculum. I disregard the GCE A-level throughout this chapter. It was taken by only two per cent of the sixth-year sample.

In the 60 schools which they inspected between 1979 and 1982, the Inspectorate found that the most common sixth-year programme was "some combination of four examination subjects" (SED, 1983a, para.2.10). Our data indicate that this was indeed the case in Scotland as a whole but, even when allowance is made for the possible under-reporting of some courses, they also suggest that the "most common" programme was taken by a minority of sixth-year pupils: only 37 per cent reported that they had studied four subjects for the Scottish Certificate of Education (SCE) O- or H-grade or for the CSYS. Twenty one per cent of sixth-year students reported five or more examinable courses: 27 per cent reported three, and 16 per cent reported fewer than three.

Highers. We have seen that a majority of sixth-year students wished to improve their examination qualifications and it is understandable that they should have done so: only 41 per cent of the Strathclyde sixth-year entry already possessed three or more Highers passes, as did only 55 per cent of sixth-year students elsewhere in Scotland (the lower Strathclyde percentage reflecting the tendency for well qualified students in the west to leave after fifth year).

The 1981 data have not been analysed here to show whether the Highers that students studied in sixth year were second attempts at subjects in which they had failed to gain adequate marks in the fifth-year SCE H-grade examination ("repeats"); or whether they were "new" Highers to be presented for the first time in sixth year, after a one- or two-year course. However, analyses of the sixth year of 1976 (surveyed in 1977) are a fairly certain guide to what the 1981 data would tell us about the sixth year of 1980. They may be summarised as follows: the tendency for sixth-year students to repeat some of their fifth-year Highers presentations has risen since the 1960s (Gray *et al.*, 1983, p.78) and most repeated attempts have led to an improved performance (Blackburn, 1979). Repeats are more common in the "mainstream" subjects (such as English) largely because they are more frequently first taken in fifth year, whereas "minority Highers" are more commonly taken for the first time in sixth year, and taken by sixth-year students whose fourth- and fifth-year performance has tended to be better than that of their sixth-year fellows (*ibid.*; Pascoe, 1979).

Highers and O-grades. The course structure of the sixth year is shown in Figure 8.2 for the two parts of Scotland. More sixth-year students in

FIGURE 8.2
The course structure of the sixth year, by area of Scotland: sixth-year
students (percentages)

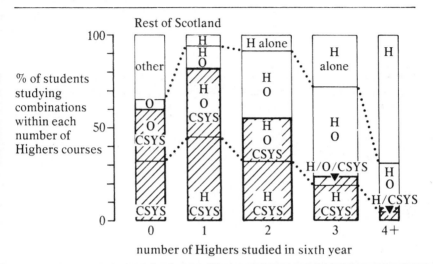

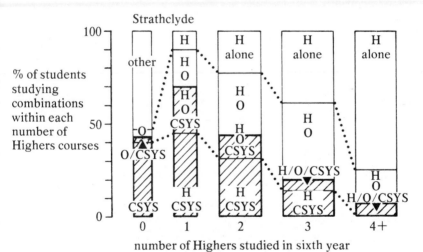

Key: ▨▨▨▨ at least one CSYS course studied

         ⋮⋮⋮⋮   encloses pupils studying SCE O-grades

         H   Highers course in sixth year (1 or more)
         O   O-grade course in sixth year (1 or more)
         CSYS Sixth Year Studies course (1 or more)

Strathclyde studied three or more Highers in sixth year than did so elsewhere (52 per cent and 36 per cent respectively); fewer in Strathclyde studied none or one (24 per cent and 36 per cent respectively). The area within the vertical blocks that is bounded by the dotted line indicates the proportions who studied at least one O-grade course in sixth year. The

---

FIGURE 8.3
Percentage taking at least one CSYS course, by the number of fifth-year Highers passes, and by area of Scotland: all post-compulsory school students

---

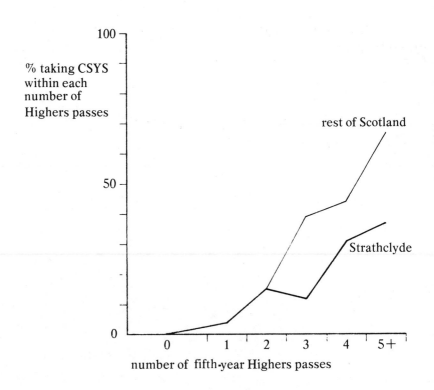

examination in fact served a surprisingly high proportion of the sixth-year sample (43 per cent in all), the proportions being larger for students studying one, two or three Highers, than for those studying either no Highers or more than three. The majority of students studying O-grades in the sixth year, however, studied only one subject at this level (30 per cent of the sixth year). It is probable, therefore, that the O-grade served either to fill up an incomplete timetable, to secure a "useful" pass (say in mathematics or a language), or to offer a relatively easy introduction to a new subject. More students in the rest of Scotland than in Strathclyde took an O-grade course in sixth year (48 per cent and 37 per cent respectively); and more CSYS students in the rest of Scotland combined CSYS with O-grades than did so in Strathclyde, this tendency being the more marked the fewer the sixth-year Highers that were also studied.

Possibly this indicates a greater emphasis outside Strathclyde on the sixth year as a period of diversification, and a greater emphasis within Strathclyde on the acquisition of Highers qualifications alone.

CSYS. A similar comment might also be made about the role of the CSYS courses. They were taken by about a third of sixth-year students in Strathclyde (32 per cent) and by just under half of their counterparts elsewhere in Scotland. Figure 8.2 shows that, whatever the number of Highers courses taken in sixth year, the student in Strathclyde was less likely than his or her counterpart elsewhere in Scotland also to be taking CSYS courses. This tendency, however, is only part of the explanation of the weaker position of the CSYS in the west of Scotland. More important were two other inter-related tendencies: first, the smaller proportion of well qualified pupils who returned in Strathclyde for a sixth year; and second, the smaller proportion of the Strathclyde sixth year that studied two sixth-year Highers or less; for only among such students (students who were not to augment their Highers qualifications to any great extent) did appreciable proportions, of around half or over, embark on work for the CSYS.

Study for the CSYS among all post-compulsory volunteers (fifth- and sixth-year leavers) is shown in Figure 8.3, disaggregated by the number of fifth-year Highers passes (scaled as in Figure 8.1) and by area. Among those with five or more such passes the area difference is marked: 37 per cent of the Strathclyde students took a CSYS course compared with two thirds of students elsewhere in Scotland, most of this difference, however, being contributed by the larger proportion of "early" (fifth-year) leavers in the west. One can readily understand how Strathclyde schools, having fewer well qualified sixth-year students than schools elsewhere, would less often provide CSYS courses for the sixth-year students they did have.

Students are only allowed to study for the CSYS if they have already passed the subject in question at the Higher grade. Hence CSYS students tend to have a better fifth-year academic record. This is part of the explanation of the tendency shown in Figure 8.3 for the proportions studying CSYS to rise with the number of fifth-year Highers passes (the other part being the association between this latter factor and staying to sixth year: see Figure 8.1). Another way of expressing this tendency is to say that among the 59 per cent of sixth-year students who did not take a CSYS course, three quarters (74 per cent) had fewer than three fifth-year Highers passes. Among the 41 per cent who took a CSYS course, 83 per cent had more than three fifth-year Highers passes (no table shown).

We may conjecture that students' beliefs about the qualifying status of CSYS courses also contributed to the tendency for weaker students not to take them. One version of the 1981 survey put this comment and question to students:

> At the end of your fifth year, you were no doubt aware that
> Highers are a generally recognised qualification for entry
> to courses of education, and to a number of jobs. *As it
> seemed to you then*, for how many of these courses and jobs
> was Sixth Year Studies also a recognised qualification for
> entry?

A little more than a quarter of students indicated they were uncertain; just over a further quarter answered "none"; and just over a further quarter indicated "some or few". Only the remaining 15 per cent answered "all" or "most". At the end of their fifth year, therefore, few students regarded the CSYS as a qualification (though in passing it should be noted that the universities do accord some weight to CSYS courses (SUCE, 1981) and that there is evidence that the CSYS can improve a university application's chances of success (McPherson and Neave, 1976, chapter 4)). In the light of these perceptions it is not surprising that many sixth-year students with fewer Highers passes or lower Highers grades than their fellows tended not to take CSYS courses even when the courses were offered and when the students were technically qualified for admission to them. Nor is it surprising that most students who took the CSYS took it in combination with sixth-year Highers courses (Figure 8.2). But the impact of the CSYS on the pedagogy of the sixth year was doubtless blunted in consequence.

The augmentation of Highers qualifications

Analyses of the 1977 survey data have established that the large majority of sixth-year students improved on their fifth-year Highers achievement, a substantial minority adding at least two further Highers passes to their fifth-year tally (Taylor, 1978). Blackburn (1979) has shown that most students who attempted a subject twice for Highers improved on their fifth-year performance, and also that a repeated presentation was generally a better tactic than a first-time presentation that had been deferred to sixth year on the grounds that a student was not "ready" at the end of fifth year.

To what extent did the sixth-year students of 1980 augment their Highers qualifications? Figure 8.4 shows the sixth-year Highers increment according to the number of fifth-year Highers passes already held. Strathclyde is shown separately from the rest of Scotland. The figure describes all post-compulsory volunteers, whether or not they did a sixth year. Fifth-year leavers are shown towards the top of the diagrams (this bit of information is the same as that contained in Figure 8.1). Students adding at least one Highers pass to their fifth-year complement are shown in the hatched areas towards the bottom. The intermediate blank areas indicate sixth-year students who did not gain additional Highers passes (some of whom, of course, studied for the CSYS). From this figure we may judge two things. First, by taking the total area as the 100 per cent base we may judge the contribution of the sixth year to the qualifications achieved by all volunteers for post-compulsory education. Second, by excluding the fifth-year leavers and taking as the 100 per cent base only the volunteers who continued to sixth year we may judge the extent to which the sixth year augmented the qualifications of students who entered it.

To comment, first, on this latter point, it is clear that most sixth-year students gained additional Highers passes. Indeed, in both parts of the country, a majority of sixth-year students with fewer than five fifth-year Highers passes acquired more in their sixth year. This observation is perfectly consistent with the results of analyses of the 1977 survey mentioned earlier in this section. But we should not move too rapidly from the observation that the sixth year helps most students to improve their Highers qualifications to the conclusion that the sixth year must play a part in the system by which students in post-compulsory schooling acquire their leaving qualifications. For what Figure 8.4 also reveals is the lesser extent to which, in the Strathclyde Region, volunteers with more than three fifth-year Highers awards augmented these in sixth year. Of all volunteers gaining four fifth-year passes, for example, 23 per cent in Strathclyde added more passes in sixth year, compared with 45 per cent elsewhere. The figures for students with five fifth-year passes are 26 per cent and 40 per cent respectively. Strathclyde produces as many degree-level students as elsewhere in Scotland (indeed rather more than "expectation" given the less favoured socio-economic circumstances of the Region). A strong implication of Figure 8.4 is therefore that the practice of the universities in the east and the north of selecting the majority of their school entry from the sixth year contributes to an inflation in Highers qualifications (a higher

FIGURE 8.4
Augmentation of fifth-year Highers passes with Highers passed in sixth year, by area of Scotland: all post-compulsory school students (percentages)

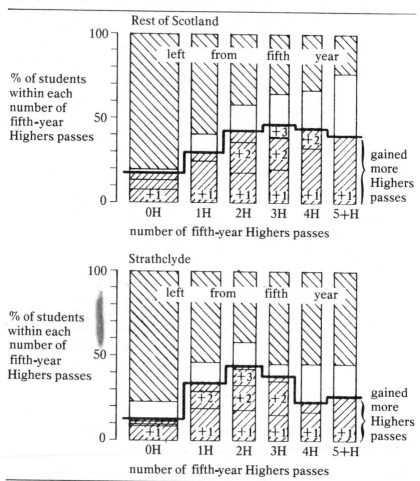

Key: left from fifth year

gained additional Highers passes (i.e. +1, +2, +3)

did sixth year but gained no additional Highers passes

Notes: Sixth-year passes in subjects passed at H-grade in fifth year are not counted. A ceiling of six Highers passes overall was set; thus the percentage of pupils whose Highers are augmented in sixth year may be slightly underestimated among those with 5+ H-grade passes in fifth year.

paper admissions requirement) which, by the standards of the western half of the country, is unnecessary.

One may take this argument further. Entry to higher education is now of course a highly competitive business in which, at the borderline of success with failure, otherwise trivial differences in qualifications may have a lifetime's consequences. From this perspective the augmentation that the sixth year allows is non-trivial, and more especially so in view of the fact that our proxy measure of qualification for higher education, three Highers passes, is often lower than the going rate for particular courses. But it was not always so in Scotland. In 1961 nine out of ten school leavers with at least two Highers and three Lowers entered higher education (Committee on Higher Education, 1963, Appendix 1, p.31). Moreover, in other European countries the attainment of a threshold qualification entitles its holder to university entry. Thus the significance of sixth-year augmentation for many of the individuals who pass further Highers and who are, to repeat, only a minority of post-compulsory students, is itself is a consequence of the variable requirements for entry to higher education.

We may therefore ask the question: if places in higher education were equally available to all students who had surpassed a threshold entry requirement, for how many students in post-compulsory schooling would it be important to have a sixth year that allowed students to augment their fifth-year qualifications? Figure 8.5 offers an answer. It refers to all post-compulsory volunteers and has as its horizontal axis the number of O-grade awards at A-C in fourth year (scaled according to the percentage of volunteers achieving each number of awards). The lower line rising from left to right shows the percentage of volunteers who had passed at least three Highers by the end of fifth year. The upper line shows the percentage who had reached this level by the end of a sixth year (whether or not they did a sixth year). Thus, at each point on the horizontal axis, the vertical distance between the two rising lines shows the contribution made by the additional qualifications (if any) gained in sixth year. For example, at the end of fifth year, 16 per cent of students having five fourth-year O-grades at A-C had passed three or more Highers. Qualifications gained in sixth year raised this to 32 per cent.

The area between the two rising lines (B+C) indicates students who attained or crossed the 3+ Highers threshold as a result of doing a sixth year. It occupies only a small proportion of the total area of the figure. In fact only nine per cent of post-compulsory school students achieved the proxy threshold qualification of three Highers by augmenting their Highers passes in sixth year. Most post-compulsory students had either reached this level in fifth year or left school without reaching it. Also, the sixth year made little impression on the differentiation between post-compulsory students'

FIGURE 8.5
Augmentation of Highers passes, and fourth-year awards — percentages passing at least three Highers after fifth year and after sixth year respectively, by the number of fourth-year O-grade awards at A-C: all post-compulsory school students

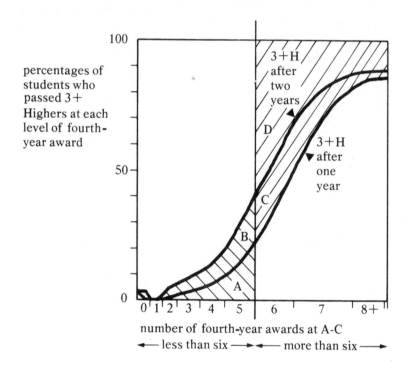

Key:
 "wrongly" excluded from post-
fourth-year course leading to higher education

 "wrongly" included in post-
fourth-year course leading to higher education

qualifications that Figure 7.1 has shown us was produced by fifth-year Highers (no table shown). Yet the augmentation of qualifications was the predominant function of the sixth year for those who entered it and most sixth-year students did indeed improve their Highers qualifications; but not by much, relative to their fellows. (Of course, if we chose a proxy entry requirement other than three Highers, different numbers would result but the overall point would remain unchanged: whatever the threshold requirement, few post-compulsory volunteers achieved it by doing a sixth year. Nor would it be changed by including entry to jobs along with entry to higher education as the reward for achievement, provided, that is, that the assumption of a single threshold requirement is retained.)

Different tracks after fourth year?

The CSYS was intended for students who had achieved all the Highers qualifications they required by the end of fifth year. In practice a majority of sixth-year students either knew that they had not done this, or else were uncertain as to what was required of them, mainly because of the variability of entry qualifications for higher education. If the pursuit of qualifications displaced the goals of the CSYS then *a fortiori* this would apply to attempts to promote an education similar to the CSYS, but in fifth year.

Could such problems in fifth and sixth year be resolved by using fourth-year public examinations to select for courses leading to the probable achievement of higher education entry qualifications after one year, or perhaps after two? What sort of differentiation of courses might be involved in attempting in this way to free fifth and sixth year from the incubus of the qualifications race? In Figure 8.5 the shaded areas to the left of the vertical line and underneath the curved lines show the volunteers who would be "wrongly" excluded if six O-grades at A-C were used as the criterion for selection. They would constitute three per cent by the end of fifth year (area A) and six per cent by the end of sixth year (A+B). (Areas in the figures are approximate. Values quoted in the text have been calculated from the data.) The areas to the right of the vertical line show the percentages who would have been wrongly included in a school course leading to higher education. They constitute 19 per cent after fifth year (C+D) and 12 per cent (D) after sixth year. Thus, by the end of sixth year it would turn out that 18 per cent of volunteers had been misallocated (6+12). Whether these are acceptable levels can only be decided in the light of further considerations. Among these are the subsequent opportunities that are available for transfer between courses, and also the consequences of using the fourth-year examination in this way for course allocation decisions in second and third year, or even earlier. Clearly the use of a selection threshold other than six O-grades at A-C would produce different misallocation percentages, whilst the use of information on grades awarded at O-grade, in addition to information on the number of "passes" would result in fewer misallocations. Finally, the likelihood is that if some such criterion were applied among all 16-17 year olds, and not just among the volunteers, the percentage of misallocations would be considerably lower.

A planned separation of the tracks precisely as modelled in Figure 8.5 is fairly unlikely. Nor would such a separation entirely free fifth and sixth year from the incubus of the qualifications race unless the threshold criterion of three Highers passes were indeed to guarantee admission to most school students' preferred destination after school; and that too is unlikely.

Nevertheless, as will be argued in the section that concludes this chapter, provision decisions must be made concerning how many students are to be allowed to keep open the possibility of acquiring academic qualifications, for how long, and in what sorts of institutions (school or college). Policy may despair of freeing post-compulsory students on the right-hand side of the vertical line in Figure 8.5 from the thrall of the qualifications race, but nevertheless decide that it has an area of discretion among the students lying to the left-hand side of the vertical line, or of a line drawn at some adjacent point. The further to the left this line moves, the larger will be the number of students who take inappropriately "academic" courses; the further to the right it is moved, the larger will be the number of students who will be unable to take courses that might qualify them for entry to higher education, but the larger also will be the number of school students over whom policy made by the public authority in Scotland will have sway.

Perhaps in the end there will be no line, no demarcation, even though the currency of the dichotomous concepts of the "old" and "new" fifth years makes one more probable. But, if there is to be no tracking after fourth year, new courses for the fifth year will have to take their chance in competition with those already established; and that is a formidable context in which to establish a new curricular philosophy (see below).

It is emphasised that the arguments relating to Figure 8.5 are offered heuristically and not as a recommendation for selection by public examination at the end of fourth year. Their purpose is solely to explicate some of the evils between which policy for post-compulsory education must choose, especially in the light of the variable academic qualifications required for entry to favoured positions after school.

The attractions of Sixth Year Studies

Years before CSYS courses were introduced, a substantial minority of well-qualified students in the west left school at the end of fifth year, and they have continued to do so until this day. In Strathclyde in 1980 only 13 per cent of the post-compulsory volunteers eventually studied for the CSYS.

Elsewhere in Scotland, where conditions have been more propitious, 23 per cent did so. But the popularity of CSYS courses with students can no more be inferred simply from the numbers of students who take them than can the popularity of taking Highers in sixth year.

Among the students who took them, CSYS courses emerged from the 1977 survey as highly attractive (Gray and McPherson, 1978); and the 1981 data tell a similar story. In both surveys the large majority of CSYS students (three quarters or more) agreed that their CSYS course(s) had given them "good opportunities to follow up subject interests", "good experience of organising (their) own study", and a "better relationship with (their) subject teacher(s)". In both surveys only a quarter agreed that CSYS courses "proved less worthwhile than taking new Highers or O-grades", and only a tenth agreed that CSYS courses "did not go much further into the subject(s) than the Highers course(s)" (no table shown). It would be difficult for a curriculum to better this record and desirable indeed if the influence of its educational principles were extended "into the mainstream of secondary education" as the Inspectorate recommended (see above).

The 1981 survey also confirmed that Highers students as a whole were largely agreed on the intrinsic attractions of CSYS courses, but were either ambivalent, or unable to agree, about their extrinsic value. They were uncertain or divided over whether CSYS courses were less worthwhile than new SCE courses; on whether CSYS courses had more to offer than other ways of spending the year prior to further education; and on whether it was better to go straight from fifth year into a job or further education (see also *ibid.*).

The present system thereby reduces student demand for an intrinsically attractive CSYS curriculum: fifth-year leaving is too firmly established in the west, and the pursuit of further formal qualifications in sixth year is too common throughout Scotland. Paradoxically, however, if this pursuit were less common, the numbers in sixth year who would be available to take (non-qualifying) CSYS courses would probably be smaller, though much would depend on the policies of those selecting for higher education.

Leavers' evaluations of fifth and sixth year

The impact of the CSYS on teaching and learning, and on morale generally, in the sixth year would have been greater had more than a minority of sixth-year students taken CSYS courses, and had CSYS courses generally comprised more than a minority of the courses of the students who took them. A cause for concern, however, is the fact that sixth-year leavers thought less of their sixth year than they did of their fifth year, and less also than fifth-year leavers thought of their fifth year. Relative to the generally dismissive views of, say, non-certificate leavers on the value of their final year (Gow and McPherson, 1980), the "slump" in sixth year is not large, but it does mean that about one sixth-year student in five thought they had got less out of sixth year than out of fifth year. Answers to other questions about what leavers subsequently wished they had done indicate that 16 per cent of sixth-year leavers wished (when they answered the questionnaire) that they had left after fifth year, whilst 38 per cent felt they had taken a wrong decision about some aspect of their final year's course; the comparable figure for the fifth-year leavers was rather lower, at 16 per cent.

Summary and comment

Much of the present character of the sixth year was determined at the time of the abolition of the Lower in 1962, when the difficulty of the fifth-year course was raised and the Scottish Education Department (SED) and schools pressed most students to fight the battle for qualifications in the confined field of fifth year, rather than spread the campaign in more leisurely fashion over the fifth and sixth years. Behind this move was the wishful expectation that a short sharp engagement in fifth year would prove decisive and that the victors would be home, if not by Christmas, then at least by the following summer, adorned with awards and ready to enjoy a final school year of contemplative study and liberal enrichment in the intellectual territory to which they had won right of entry.

In the event the terrain proved more difficult than plans had first allowed, the army grew larger, and casualties higher, for it transpired that the army was not fighting to gain a fixed objective, but was fighting among itself. The Christmas engagement was, literally, the preliminary; and at the end of the fifth-year campaign, just over half the volunteer force called it a day. Among those who did not re-enlist, a third had fulfilled the rules of the game and were honourably discharged with at least three Highers awards; just under a third got one or two awards; but almost half had no Highers awards at all (though a minority of these did get more O-grade awards). About half of those who did enlist for a further year already had at least three Highers awards but a majority of them were uncertain how they might complete their engagement with honour: three quarters of sixth-year students had felt at the end of fifth year that they needed better awards and most felt that they could achieve some improvement through a further year's endeavour. They were right; a large majority of the sixth year did improve their tally of awards and many raised the grade of particular awards they already held.

Students varied, however, in the burden they carried in sixth year. A little under half attempted three or more Highers but over two thirds attempted at least two. Four out of ten took on the O-grade, but mostly as a skirmish with a single subject; hardly any students studied more than one O-grade.

All this means that only a minority of students spent any time at all in the curriculum fit for heroes: four out of ten sixth-year students (or under two out of ten post-compulsory volunteers) did a course for the CSYS; and students who took the CSYS entirely unencumbered by the pursuit of further Highers qualifications numbered somewhat less than two in ten of all sixth-year students. Most who did the CSYS had already achieved three Highers passes in fifth year; few sixth-year students who did not do the CSYS had three such passes. Opinions of the intrinsic qualities of the CSYS curriculum were high, both among those who experienced it, and among the post-compulsory volunteers as a whole, but the Certificate's uncertain qualifying status reduced its extrinsic attractiveness to students.

In Strathclyde, and also elsewhere in Scotland, students with fewer than three fifth-year Highers awards were equally likely to return for a further year, this propensity rising with the number of awards. However, among those who had achieved a notional minimum qualification for entry into higher education (three or more H-grades), the campaign in the west thereafter differed somewhat from that in the rest of Scotland. In Strathclyde students with three, four and five or more fifth-year Highers passes were no more likely to return for a sixth year than Strathclyde students with one such pass (around 45 per cent). A major factor contributing to the fifth-year leaving of well qualified students in the west was the readiness of higher education selectors in the west of Scotland to accept students directly from fifth year. Elsewhere in Scotland this was uncommon and the proportion returning for a sixth year increased with the number of fifth-year Highers passes, attaining three quarters among those with five passes. The higher proportion of well qualified students returning for a sixth year elsewhere in Scotland provided a more substantial base for CSYS work, but the effects of this propensity on the sixth-year curriculum should not be exaggerated. Most such students also studied for Highers in sixth year and many were only in sixth year and thereby "available" to the CSYS because many selectors would not act on fifth-year qualifications at the end of the student's fifth year. Thus, whilst the sixth year was a period of diversification for more students in the rest of Scotland than it was in Strathclyde, its dominant function in both parts of Scotland was that of the augmentation of Highers qualifications.

The function of augmentation, however, must also be seen in perspective. It flourishes because of the variable entry requirements for courses in higher education and because of the resultant uncertainty or pessimism of students over whether their fifth-year Higher qualifications are adequate to their purpose. If there were a single, threshold requirement for entry to all courses – say three or more Highers passes – the opportunities for augmentation provided by the sixth year would be important only for a small proportion of the post-compulsory volunteers, about one in ten. (Most post compulsory students who were to reach this threshold could be identified by their fourth-year O-grade performance.) This conclusion of course assumes that the adoption of such a threshold would not itself stimulate further students with weaker qualifications at the end of their fifth year to try another year of schooling. Nevertheless it usefully highlights the way in which educational purposes for the final year of post-compulsory schooling are displaced by a contest for qualifications that would be unnecessary if the transition to post-school education were less determined by the requirements of the market in scarce places.

Implications for the fifth and sixth years

Thus consideration of alternatives for the sixth year soon indicates its interdependence not only with the year that follows it, but with the preceding year as well. We may now, therefore, broaden our discussion to consider some of the wider implications of chapters 7 and 8.

Current proposals for the reform of post-compulsory education clearly require a review of the philosophy and structure of fifth-year school courses and especially of Highers courses. These courses have hitherto been explained in terms of what has become a rather vacuous concept of "a general education" (Gray et al., 1983, chapters 5 and 6). Can the idea of general education be filled out, and is it to continue as an ideal? If so, what part is a vocationally oriented education to play in courses that are intended as general and liberalising? Or, alternatively, are common curricular goals to be abandoned in post-compulsory schooling? These are issues that lie outwith the scope of the present discussion, although they clearly underpin both it and the Action Plan. What these two chapters may perhaps contribute is some understanding of the constraints of certification and selection on the possibilities for translating educational aims into curriculum, and also into institutional forms such as schools and colleges.

The failure of CSYS courses to establish themselves more widely has led many to argue that they should become a formal requirement for university entry, and possibly also for entry to other forms of higher education. This would in turn necessitate other changes: either the Certificate would have to be made available also in fifth year, in which case the pre-condition of a Highers pass in the same subject would have to be removed; or the post-fourth-year course would have to be lengthened to two years, with disruptive effects on the pattern of entry to higher education in the west of Scotland, and possibly also on the incidence of entry in Scotland as a whole. What is more, if the CSYS were a universal requirement, selectors would have to discriminate between applicants on the basis of their CSYS grades, and schools in their turn would orient their teaching more towards the achievement of grades, neglecting the other outcomes that the Certificate was intended to promote. Arguably, heavy selection at the end of fourth year might head off such trends, but it would have to err on the side of excluding potential successes rather than of including potential failures if the function of differentiation that post-compulsory schooling currently performs were to be reduced. However, this would go against the grain of present assumptions and practices in the schools by which "weaker" students (roughly in the 15th to 35th percentiles) are encouraged to stay on the academic ladder if they can.

An alternative strategy for creating space in the sixth year for the Certificate would be for higher education selectors to admit solely on the basis of fifth-year Highers achievement but with the condition that a CSYS course be taken. Again this would effectively make two years of post-compulsory schooling mandatory for entrants to higher education, and it would also increase the competitive pressures in fifth year, conceivably producing fifth-year students who, although qualified, had an attitude to study that was less amenable to change in a "proper" sixth year. Of course it would also increase the pressure on schools to make earlier and more differentiated provision for pupils on a Credit track in third and fourth years.

However it were introduced, a post-compulsory course in school that took two years to complete is a more remote prospect now than it was in the expansionist sixties. More than ever, therefore, the fulcrum for post-compulsory reform must be the fifth-year Higher.

At first sight the CSYS and the quasi-vocational courses proposed under the Action Plan seem strange bedfellows. But they share two things in common: both stress to some degree the importance of "internal" or school control of curriculum and assessment; and both have been mooted as a partial answer to the question of what to provide in the first year of post-compulsory schooling. Whatever is to happen to the sixth year, the Inspectorate wishes to preserve and generalise in fifth year much of the principles and practice of the CSYS. An essentially liberalising experience designed for an elite of 17-18 year olds in school should, they imply, be made more widely available to school students a year younger. More immediately, it seems that courses for the Scottish Certificate of Vocational Studies (SCVS), a quasi-vocational qualification, are to be conjoined with existing fifth-year courses through the proposed modularisation of all post-compulsory provision in a sort of *marriage à la module*. The part to be played by the sixth year in this liaison seems very vague, despite the hints that, after some twenty years, the delaying of some first-time Highers presentations to sixth year might again be encouraged.

How do the analytical problems of difficulty, selection and motivation bear on such proposals? To take motivation first: it is clear that the present system does not foster a problem of motivation in the post-compulsory period that is remotely comparable with the problems to be faced during the period of compulsion. Only in one sense is there a problem: post-compulsory schooling is not sufficiently attractive to persuade a majority to stay on. Indeed, as chapter 5 has shown, the fifth year is probably attractive to fewer post-compulsory students than is commonly inferred from the numbers that are often quoted. But the very fact that students are largely self-selected (albeit with varying degrees of encouragement from parents and teachers) and are a minority of their age peers, virtually removes the problem of motivation in any other sense. Having chosen to do a fifth year, most volunteers in our study did not truant; most completed the year, and most afterwards thought it worthwhile, including even a bare majority of those who did not add to their fourth-year qualifications. Only in sixth year, and among students who are already certain that they have the qualifications they need, does a problem of motivation arguably arise, and then only on a small scale. The students in our sample may have felt pressurised, and dissatisfied in other ways with their Highers courses but, if they did, any discontent was trivial relative to the rewards of qualification. Thus we find the Inspectorate somewhat despairingly discussing "*the* objectives of Highers *courses*" in terms of teachers' and pupils' objectives in pursuing the certification which may result from the assessment of these courses (chapter 7, my emphasis).

Fundamental to the consensus for reform in third and fourth year has been the wide public recognition of the problem of motivation at that stage. Reform in the fifth year could well find that there is too little of a problem of motivation in the post-compulsory period, rather than too much, especially if schools continue to contribute to the education and training of only a minority, and an academically able minority, of 16-17 year olds. Evidently enough, however, just as it was the universal conscription of 15-16 year olds in fourth year that produced the problem of motivation in the 1970s, so any conscription of 16-17 year olds may be expected to produce similar problems, even if the conscription is less than universal and even if it is not all absorbed by the schools.

It is important therefore to be clear about the significance for student motivation of any intrinsically educational arguments for post-compulsory reform. The fate of the CSYS shows that courses based on a developed educational philosophy can be highly attractive but fail to motivate students to take them. Possibly the continuing dominance of the Higher demonstrates the converse. Everyone naturally wants courses that are "educationally valid", and courses that are intrinsically attractive to students, but neither attribute guarantees that students would choose them in preference to courses whose qualifying status was more robust. The main curricular innovations of the last 20 years – "Brunton" courses, CSYS and the Certificate of Secondary Education (CSE) – have all been targetted in Scotland at groups of pupils who lacked the cause, or the opportunity, or the ability, to improve their SCE qualifications. But, where qualifications have been at stake, innovation has been timid.

The case for quasi-vocational courses in the education of 16-18 year olds rests partly on the argument that the present Highers course is too difficult for many students to "get much out of it". This is partly a comment on the cognitive complexity and esoteric nature that are sometimes attributed to its subject matter (views which we have not discussed) and partly a comment on the level of difficulty at which the certificate examinations are set. How we judge the latter question in turn depends on the perspective we adopt. If we choose that of students who are concerned to improve the value of their qualifications relative to their fellows, then the question of what they get is purely empirical. Instead we have assessed the phenomenon of difficulty here mainly in terms of the more traditional view that the predominant legitimate outcome of the Highers course is entry to higher education, and entry by means of a qualification that has not a relative, but a fixed, value in that it has procured entry. We have set this qualification on the low side, at three Highers passes. Nevertheless the argument for an easier fifth-year examination (or for a longer course, or both) is supported *prima facie* by the experience of the sample. A majority had not reached this standard by the end of fifth year; a majority had not carried the five Highers courses that are presupposed by the traditional concept of breadth (expressed in terms of the spread of subjects); and, indeed, a majority in fifth year had not carried five subjects, at whatever level.

Again, however, it is important to be clear about the relationship between difficulty in this sense and the educational case for a certificate that is vocationally oriented in the way that the Action Plan proposes. There is in fact no necessary relationship at all. Much will depend on how the vocational elements, whether in the form of the SCVS or of developments from this, are married to the Higher. At one extreme the union might be very tenuous: that is, students could be required to choose after fourth year, and no doubt in the light of their performance in the O-grade examination or its successor, whether to do a mainly Highers course leading to qualifications for higher education, or a mainly pre-vocational course leading somewhere else. Such differentiation would not require formal selection along the lines of the 12-plus qualifying examination. However, the effects of a guided choice might well approximate those of formal selection, especially if the economics of provision dictated that the choice of subjects was also a choice between institutions, between schools providing mainly Highers courses and colleges providing mainly SCVS and other courses.

Using the fourth-year examination, such a differentiation could be effected in a manner that was unfair to about one fifth of volunteers for fifth year (or considerably less if we did not think it unfair to continue some students on academic courses at which they would not succeed). Arguably some of the unfairness could subsequently be ameliorated through the flexibility that is claimed for credit accumulation by module.

If there were such a degree of curricular, and maybe also institutional, differentiation at 16, then the average level of difficulty of SCVS or similar courses could be set quite low; and it would probably require to be set quite low if college students' motivation were to be maintained by their having a reasonable prospect of achieving examination success, and also if more 17 year olds were to be motivated to undertake full-time post-compulsory education. But it is doubtful whether such conditions would allow certified vocational elements to establish themselves in the schools as credible alternative qualifications to the fifth-year Higher, especially if students selected themselves into vocational courses not on the basis of their potential to do well in them, but on the basis of their lack of potential to succeed at a course that qualified them for higher education, as judged by fourth-year public examination performance.

At the other extreme, modularisation could mean that school students were free to combine less vocational and more vocational elements in a full union of more or less any permutation of number and level. If these combinations were random with respect to fourth-year public examination performance, then one could envisage that a qualification like the SCVS might soon rank with the Higher in public esteem. A problem here, however, is that this would almost certainly mean that the level of difficulty required for success in the SCVS would also tend to rise to that of the Higher. If it did not, or if the difficulty of the Higher were reduced, the fifth year would perform less of a differentiating function (Figure 7.1), and selectors for valued positions would have difficulty in distinguishing between applicants. All this might or might not matter, but it would require that the intrinsic attractions of both SCVS and Highers courses were high, for a lower level of extrinsic value would be entailed. It would also probably mean that the sixth year was more often devoted to improving the number and quality of qualifications than it is at present.

A more probable scenario lies somewhere between these two extreme eventualities, a scenario which one constructs from the present role of the O-grade in post-compulsory schooling and from the short history of the Munn and Dunning proposals for change in third and fourth year.

A virtue of the original Munn and Dunning strategy for change was its recognition of the systemic nature of certification and of the consequent need for change at the highest level of difficulty if change at the lowest level were to be successful. Hence one has the proposals for internal curricular and assessment elements at all three course levels and for overlaps between levels, the latter being intended to allow pupils to find their own level of difficulty and thereby to obviate the need for early decisions on differentiation. Such is the hold of established examination practices, however, that much of this is to be lost in implementation, and the likelihood is that schools will over-present pupils in the external examinations at the Credit and General levels rather than deny to them prematurely the opportunity to do well. In these circumstances Foundation-level courses will find it doubly difficult to develop an educational identity that commands public understanding and respect, partly because they contain elements of internal assessment that have been judged alien to the two higher levels, and partly because they will tend belatedly to recruit pupils who have found work at a higher level too difficult.

It is not hard to envisage something similar happening in fifth year to a quasi-vocational qualification like the SCVS. At least for the immediate future the Higher will remain an external examination whereas there are likely to be internal elements in the SCVS. Moreover, the ways in which students currently find the number and duration of Highers courses appropriate to their abilities also have implications for the status and coherence of the SCVS. It is a reasonable inference that teacher and student alike have regard to the fourth-year O-grade performance in setting the course load for fifth-year students. However, only a minority of students in our study started the fifth year with a firm intention to leave school at the end of it. A slight majority did indeed leave school at the end of fifth year, but about half of them had decided on this only during the fifth year. The possibility of a sixth year argues against foreclosing on Highers options too early in the fifth year, for most sixth-year students augment their Highers qualifications. Evidence on the effects of the preliminary examination in fifth year also suggests that teachers and school students would prefer to err on the side of starting Highers courses at too ambitious a level, and to allow students to test themselves against the asking standard before foreclosing decisions on the number of Higher courses, or on staying on at school.

The resultant indeterminacy at the beginning of fifth year means that fifth-year vocational courses in the schools, like fourth-year Foundation courses, will tend to recruit late and low, performing a function similar to that of the fifth-year O-grade by allowing students to carry five examination subjects without having to carry five Highers.

The role of a certificate like the SCVS in fifth year is a matter not only of possibilities, however, but also of decisions, decisions that ultimately have to do with whether and for how long post-compulsory schooling should offer an effective choice between "academic" and quasi-vocational courses. Are schools for example to continue to provide courses in fifth year for the O-grade (or for its successor examination)? This is more than just a question about O-grades. The fifth-year O-grade is one route up to a Higher pass in the same subject in sixth year; and one route back from a fifth-year Higher which is proving too difficult, but which might be resumed in sixth year. If the sixth year is to continue to allow students to augment their Highers awards, the O-grade or its successor must surely continue to have a place in fifth year; and if the O-grade is to continue to offer a relatively easy introduction to a new subject in sixth year, then it hardly seems possible to deny it to the fifth.

Moreover, we arrive at the same conclusion if we look forward to the fifth year from the fourth. If at least the Credit level of the new fourth-year examination is not also available in fifth year, and if it is to be the Credit level that leads to the Higher, then decisions in third year about levels for the fourth-year examination will for many pupils effectively be decisions about whether they are to be allowed to qualify for higher education, or to take Highers. It is doubtful whether teachers would want this responsibility and likely that they would err on the side of starting third-year pupils on courses that might prove too difficult for them. Perhaps such students would subsequently turn to quasi-vocational courses with relief, but it is doubtful whether such a process of selection would help maintain esteem for SCVS courses in fifth year. The alternative would be selection decisions in third and fourth year that moved the secondary system back towards the pre-1965 situation of differentiation between Highers pupils and those destined for Brunton courses.

From these considerations one may argue that attempts to augment the quasi-vocational component of the education of 16-18 year olds require further decisions on two related questions: the retention in the first post-compulsory year of the fourth-year examination; and the retention in the second post-compulsory year of the fifth-year examination. If these possibilities are removed, two main options remain: either students must be formally tracked into two distinct queues for two distinct types of certificate at the end of fourth year (and informally tracked somewhat earlier); or all differentiation between tracks must be dissolved. If these examinations are retained, some differentiation of students can be postponed to the first post-compulsory year, by allowing students to find their own place in the academic queue early in fifth year, and allowing them also to postpone decisions on the duration of their academic courses and therefore of their difficulty. In effect, present arrangements in the first post-compulsory year already offer possibilities for the evasion of formal selection along the lines that Munn and Dunning had hoped to achieve for third and fourth year through their largely abortive proposals for overlapping syllabuses. However, one wonders what the first year of a post-compulsory curriculum will look like when it offers, for the sake of argument, courses for the Higher, for Credit and General, and for the SCVS. One guesses that new vocational elements would be accepted into the family of subjects studied by the best-qualified 40 per cent only as poor relations; and it is unlikely, therefore, that any distinctly vocational certificate that emerged would enjoy parity of esteem.

One guesses also that a thriftily minded educational administration would not long tolerate such a diversity of courses in school and college alike. Institutional differentiation of provision would occur, driven partly by the local level of demand for post-compulsory academic education. Where demand was low all provision after 16 might conceivably be made in colleges, especially in larger centres of population. In the inner city and the outer council estate one might well return to the pre-1965 four-year school. And how vigorously and how economically would colleges related to these schools provide post-compulsory academic courses? Where, on the other hand, demand for such courses was high, they clearly would be provided by some agency; and teachers could plausibly argue that they should be provided by schools offering a sixth year in addition to a fifth. But would such schools be allowed also to offer a range of vocational courses, unless the schools were the only institutions serving remote areas? And what range of academic courses would the local colleges in more populous areas want to offer unless they were explicitly (and improbably) encouraged to compete with local schools for well qualified 16 year olds?

Present reforms in third and fourth year can only work if the pressures towards early differentiation are kept as low as possible and the fourth-year examination is not used to signal the subsequent direction of students down clearly distinct tracks. This means that the fifth year is likely to remain a stage at which a major differentiation of students occurs. At present this differentiation is conducted against a criterion of general academic performance. But if school provision is differentiated from college provision in the ways suggested, neighbourhood and social-class factors will become more closely associated with the direction students take at 16. Decisions about the structure of post-compulsory certification will have a causal bearing on such eventualities.

Whatever the social context of the choice at 16, the continuation of student differentiation at 16-17 years bodes well neither for a quasi-vocational fifth year nor for proposals to preserve in fifth year the best of CSYS philosophy and practice from the sixth. A major reason why the CSYS has failed to establish itself more widely in post-compulsory schooling has been the concern to protect the qualifying status of the Higher. But only if internal elements are built into all fifth-year courses, and not simply into the quasi-vocational elements, are they likely to "take" at all.

This brings the argument back (if we may scramble metaphors) to the dissolution of the tracks and to the marriage of the modules. One danger in present thinking, as reflected in the Action Plan, is that "modules" provide too facile an answer to the immense structural impediments to the reform of the post-compulsory curriculum. Describing as they do the elements of a course that may be assembled in a multiplicity of ways, "modules" seem magically to dispose of the problems of difficulty, selection and motivation. In the abstract they do, just as "overlapping syllabuses" disposed of the problem in Munn and Dunning's original prescriptions. "Modules" and "overlapping syllabuses" have the same logical and rhetorical function in their respective prescriptions. In practice (and in theory), however, modules will not randomly connect one with another; nor will they be randomly or universally provided for all students; nor will they have an uncontested entry to the field of the curriculum unless, that is, decisions on a quasi-vocational curriculum are taken as part of a wider set of decisions on the reform of existing post-compulsory certification. Munn and Dunning saw this. But the subsequent fate of their proposals indicates the improbability of a reform in fifth year that has not proved possible in fourth year. Moreover, selection for higher education is a further function that must be considered at the post-compulsory stage, and higher education has hitherto been unsympathetic to schools' control of curriculum and assessment.

The marriage of the modules would therefore seem to require that the SED contain the influence on post-compulsory courses of selection for higher education. If it can do this, it will be better placed to manage the problems of difficulty, selection and motivation; to offer courses that are extrinsically attractive as well as intrinsically; and thereby to resist encroachments by the Manpower Services Commission (MSC) into the courses provided for the majority of post-compulsory students. Will this mean, therefore, that the SED will encourage, or at least be happy to tolerate, the early selection of a small minority of school students to prepare for entry to higher education, and especially to university (moving the vertical line of differentiation to the right, as it were, in Figure 8.5)? If differentiation moves in this direction, the SED will be able to manage more effectively courses provided for the remainder of the age group. Alternatively, will the SED again be obliged by the community to maintain a single ladder of academic opportunity for as many students as possible, only to find that its scope for management, and therefore its scope for resistance to the MSC, is thereby reduced? A fine irony it would be if the very ideology of egalitarianism, which has sustained Scotland's claims to educational autonomy for so long, were to be taken so seriously by the community at large as to threaten the continuation of separate control.

Chapter 9

School attainment and the labour market

David Raffe

Introduction: school leavers in the labour market

Of all the young people who left school in 1979/80, a large majority went in search of a job. At the time of the survey, in May 1981, 76 per cent of the sample members (79 per cent of males and 72 per cent of females) were in the labour market. In view of the strong influence which further and higher education (and especially the universities) exert over secondary education, it is salutary to remember that most of its pupils are destined for the world of employment or unemployment. Moreover, most pupils in compulsory schooling, and a good number who stay on into post-compulsory schooling, are motivated to a large extent by vocational ambitions. They try to get good examination results, and often they stay on at school, in the belief that these will help them when they subsequently look for a job. This chapter asks how far this presumed connection between schooling and employment is justified by the evidence. It examines the association between Scottish Certificate of Education (SCE) qualifications and employment, distinguishing between the O-grades that are gained during the compulsory stage of schooling and the qualifications (both O-grades and Highers) that are gained in post-compulsory schooling. It also asks whether staying on into post-compulsory schooling is in itself – apart from any additional qualifications gained – of benefit to young people when they seek employment. It therefore addresses two questions of motivation that affect the labour-market-oriented school pupil: do I need to work hard and get good qualifications? and should I stay on for an extra year or two at school? First, however, the labour-market experiences of the sample as a whole are briefly described.

The 1980 school leavers had left school at least ten months before the survey in May 1981; the Christmas leavers had been out of school for well over a year by that time. The current destinations of those in the labour market are shown in Table 9.1.[1]

TABLE 9.1

**Destinations of school leavers in the labour market in May 1981
(percentage of leavers)**

	Males	Females
Employment:		
professional and related supporting management	0.4	0.3
professional and related in education, welfare and health	0.3	6.4
literary, artistic and sports	0.6	0.4
professional and related in science, engineering, technology	2.4	0.8
managerial	0.9	0.1
clerical and related	4.6	26.0
selling	2.8	9.8
security and protective services	3.2	0.1
catering, cleaning, hairdressing and other personal services	2.5	9.5
farming, fishing and related	4.3	0.4
materials processing, making and repairing (excluding metal and electrical)	9.1	7.1
processing, making, repairing and related (metal and electrical)	18.0	0.6
painting, repetitive assembling, product inspecting, packaging and related	3.0	2.4
construction, mining and related n.e.s.	4.4	0.0
transport operating, materials moving and storing and related	4.7	0.2
miscellaneous	1.0	0.2
inadequately described and not stated	2.8	1.9
Total employment	65.0	66.2
Unemployment	17.6	17.2
Special programmes	17.4	16.7
Total	100.0	100.1
Unweighted n	(1995)	(1971)

The jobs entered by males and females were very different. Indeed, the actual differences between the sexes were even greater than the table would suggest, since many of the categories (such as clerical and related) contain a diverse range of occupations, which in turn are divided into predominantly male and predominantly female jobs. Despite the very different occupational destinations of males and females, their overall rates of employment were similar. In May 1981, 66 per cent of males and 67 per cent of females were in "permanent" jobs. Most had found their jobs during the summer recruitment season (or earlier, in the case of the Christmas 1979 leavers); the rates of employment in the sample had risen only slightly since October 1980, when 62 per cent of males and 61 per cent of females had been in jobs.[2]

TABLE 9.2

Percentage employed by (a) SCE attainment and (b) year of leaving school: school leavers in the labour market in October 1980 and May 1981

	October 1980		May 1981	
	Males	**Females**	**Males**	**Females**
(a) SCE attainment				
Highers	75	82	80	88
5 or more O-grades (A–C)	84	76	89	82
3–4 O-grades (A–C)	75	70	80	82
1–2 O-grades (A–C)	65	56	70	68
D or E awards only	57	56	59	59
No SCE awards	49	48	51	50
(b) Year of leaving school				
Sixth year	72	79	78	83
Fifth year	72	73	73	79
Fourth year	58	52	61	57

School attainment and the probability of employment

Table 9.2 shows how rates of employment, in both October and May, varied according to school leavers' SCE qualifications and year of leaving school. Their job chances were strongly linked to qualifications. Only half of the unqualified school leavers were employed in May, compared with up to nine in ten of the higher qualification groups. However, the link between qualifications and employment differed slightly between the sexes. Among females, the highest rate of employment was among those who left school with Highers passes; the most successful males, on the other hand, were those with five or more O-grades at A-C, who did substantially better than Highers-qualified leavers. Table 9.2b shows that those who had stayed on beyond fourth year had better chances of employment. Once again, the pattern differed between the sexes, with the year of leaving more strongly related to employment among females than among males.

The table therefore suggests that the labour-market value of educational attainment may differ between the sexes. That said, the strong impression to be gained from the table is that the higher the level of school leavers' attainment, the greater their chances of employment; and this seems to have been the case whether attainment is measured in terms of qualifications (with some reservations concerning Highers) or of staying on beyond fourth year. However, the association between attainment and employment is not sufficient evidence of a causal relationship. School leavers with high levels of attainment tended also to have other advantages, such as a favourable family background or a home in an area of relatively low unemployment; their better employment chances may have reflected these advantages rather than the effects of attainment itself.

Even if their higher attainment was partly responsible for their better employment prospects, it does not follow that different types of attainment were equally important. We can distinguish three separate dimensions of school attainment, O-grades, Highers, and staying on into post-compulsory schooling. These three dimensions were strongly correlated; stayers-on had much higher O-grade attainment than the early leavers, and only stayers-on could take Highers. So an association between any one dimension of attainment and employment may merely reflect the effect of the other dimensions. Table 9.2 does not identify the separate influences on employment of these different, but correlated, dimensions of school attainment.

Below I describe an attempt to estimate the separate effects of O-grades, Highers and staying on into post-compulsory schooling on the probability of employment after school, controlling for the effects of the local unemployment rate and home background.[3] The analysis is restricted to those who were eligible to leave by the end of their fourth year; it is also restricted to those who actually left school in the summer term (whether of their fourth, fifth or sixth year), in order to standardise the length of time spent in the labour market. Since it deals with employment the analysis is necessarily restricted to those who entered the labour market. For each sex, separate analyses are carried out to predict the probability of employment in October 1980 and in May 1981 respectively.

The method used is standard multiple regression. This shows the difference in employment chances associated with each predictor variable (such as staying on) once allowance has been made for the effects of other variables. The regression is therefore an attempt to estimate the separate effect of each predictor variable on employment chances. This approach can never *prove* the causal influence of any one variable, since it is always possible that another variable, not included in the analysis, might have accounted for its effect. We return to this problem later in the chapter. The best the researcher can do is to allow for as many as possible of the likely influences on employment by including them in the analysis. The predictor variables used in the regression analysis are: O-grades at A-C, O-grades at D or E, Highers passes, staying on, the current local unemployment rate, whether the respondent's father was employed at the time of the survey, and the social-class category of the occupation currently, or most recently, held by the father. The effect of the age at which a young person entered the labour market is considered to be inseparable from the effect of staying on at school, so no separate age variable is included. Two different approaches to the analysis are followed.

The first approach attempts to estimate the separate effects of O-grades, Highers and staying on, conceived as distinct dimensions of attainment. It therefore distinguishes between the separate effect of staying on as such and the effect of any additional qualifications that are gained as a result. The results of this approach are shown in detail in Table 9A (models 1 & 3) in the addendum which follows this chapter, and summarised in Table 9.3. This shows the change in employment chances associated with each predictor variable. Employment chances are described in terms of percentage points (100 per cent representing the certainty of employment, and 0 per cent representing the certainty of unemployment). Thus, each extra O-grade award at A-C was associated with an increase of five percentage points in a male's probability of employment in October. (Two awards at A-C were therefore associated with an increase of ten percentage points in the probability of employment, and so on.) A minus sign indicates that the predictor was associated with lower chances of employment. Some of the predictor variables had no statistically significant association with employment once the effects of the other variables are allowed for; that is, there is a probability of more than one in twenty that there was no association at all and the association shown among the sample is the result of chance. The "effects" of these variables are shown in brackets.

Each O-grade award added five percentage points to a male's probability of employment in October, and nearly six percentage points in May; for females the effect was smaller but still substantial, between three and four percentage points. Perhaps more remarkably, O-grade awards at D or E,

---

TABLE 9.3

Percentage point increase in chances of employment in October 1980 or May 1981 associated with ...

	October 1980		May 1981	
	Males	Females	Males	Females
... each O-grade award at A–C	5.0	3.3	5.8	3.9
... each O-grade award at D or E	4.2	(–0.1)	3.7	2.0
... each Highers pass	(2.1)	(1.0)	(1.4)	(–1.1)
... staying on (leaving from S5 or S6 rather than S4)	–13.3	(4.5)	–16.3	(6.9)
... each percentage point increase in the current local unemployment rate	–3.3	–2.9	–2.2	–2.3
...father being employed in May 1981	9.2	10.0	12.1	9.3
... father's (current or most recent) job non-manual	8.4	9.1	10.4	(3.8)
... father's job skilled manual	(2.8)	(–2.9)	(2.3)	(–3.2)

Notes: A decrease in employment chances is represented by a minus sign. Bracketed estimates are not significantly different from zero.

commonly regarded as "fails", each added four percentage points to a male's probability of employment in October and nearly as much in May. This suggests that O-grade attempts were nearly as important as the results. (In practice, the more O-grades an individual attempted, the better his or her average result was likely to be.) D and E awards had no significant effect on females' employment in October, but added percentage points (just significant) to their chances of employment in May.

O-grades, therefore, were strongly associated with employment chances, especially of males. Highers, by contrast, had little influence on employment. Each Highers pass added about two percentage points to a young male's probability of employment in October, and a single percentage point for a young female. By May 1981 the estimated effect was smaller for males and actually negative for females. None of these estimates is significantly different from zero. Whatever the value of Highers as educational currency, their value in the labour market was slight, at least as far as being employed rather than unemployed was concerned.

Perhaps the most dramatic conclusion of Table 9.3 is its estimate of the effect associated with staying on into post-compulsory schooling. Among males this effect was powerfully negative. A male with given background, local conditions and SCE attainments on leaving school was considerably less likely to be employed either in October or in May if he had left from fifth or sixth year rather than fourth year. In October this disadvantage amounted to 13 percentage points; by May the disadvantage had actually increased, to 16 percentage points. Among females, staying on was positively associated with employment chances at both dates, but the effect was not statistically significant.

This finding challenges, for males, a widespread assumption about post-compulsory schooling – that merely staying on at school increases a young person's chances of subsequent employment. Of course, many of those who stayed on gained extra O-grades, or Highers passes; the positive effects of these qualifications must be weighed in the balance against the negative effects of staying on. An alternative approach to the regression analysis compares the employment chances of stayers-on and early leavers, allowing for the effects of background, local unemployment rates, and SCE qualifications achieved by the end of fourth year only. In this approach all Highers and O-grades obtained after fourth year, that is *after* the decision to stay on, are included as part of the effect of staying on. This approach is designed to model the options available to a typical 16 year old wondering whether to stay on at school beyond fourth year. The choice is between leaving now, with the O-grades currently held, or staying on, which in turn carries the possibility of gaining further qualifications. As might be expected, this approach shows staying on in a more favourable light than the first approach summarised in Table 9.3. (Full details are given in Table 9A in the addendum at the end of this chapter.) Among females, the effect of staying on was both positive and significant – more than eight percentage points both in October and May. Comparing this result with the (non-significant) effect in Table 9.3 suggests that staying on had a positive effect on girls' chances of employment but that this was largely due to the extra qualifications (more specifically the O-grades) that the stayers-on obtained. Among males, however, the effect of staying on was still negative, and statistically significant, in the second regression approach, even though the effects were slightly smaller than in Table 9.3. Staying on reduced males' chances of employment in October by nearly nine percentage points, and in May by more than eleven percentage points. For reasons explained in the addendum the significance of the October effect may be questioned but the

May effect is well established. Both effects were negative despite the fact that the positive effects of any extra qualifications are included with the effect of staying on in this approach. It follows that for the typical male the negative effect of staying on at school substantially outweighed, at least with respect to employment in May, the positive effects of the extra qualifications he obtained.

The local unemployment rate had a very large influence on school leavers' chances of employment. In October, each percentage point variation in local unemployment rates was associated with a three percentage point variation in the (un)employment chances of school leavers. Since local unemployment rates in October ranged from 4.2 per cent to 18.5 per cent, this shows that local conditions had an enormous effect on the variation in school leavers' employment chances across the country. Some of this had worn off by May (when the effect was a little over two percentage points) but the importance of local labour-market conditions was still considerable. Fathers' employment was strongly and significantly associated with the employment chances of their children, and the effect was about as strong for daughters as for sons. Having a father in a non-manual occupation also influenced unemployment chances, although the effect had worn off among females by May. Both of these variables are likely to reflect more diffuse social influences, as well as the specific effects of father's employment or occupational status.

Interpreting the results

The analysis described above has attempted to identify the separate and independent effects on employment chances of three different dimensions of school attainment: O-grade attainment, Highers passes and staying on into post-compulsory schooling. The analysis has been designed, not only to distinguish the separate effects of these different (but correlated) dimensions of attainment, but also to distinguish them from the effects of other factors, such as home background and the local unemployment rate, which may also influence employment chances. The analysis has concluded: first, that O-grades had a strong and positive influence on the probability of being employed at either time point; second, that Highers passes had a negligible influence; third, that staying on at school actually reduced males' chances of employment after school (at least at the second time-point measured) despite the extra qualifications they might have gained after staying on; and fourth, that staying on improved females' chances of subsequent employment, but largely only because of the extra qualifications that they gained.

These conclusions have serious implications for secondary schools, so it is useful at this stage to note their limitations.

In the first place, the analysis is restricted to labour-market entrants. The analysis says nothing about the value of Highers or of staying on at school for entrance to further or higher education, or of the indirect occupational value they may have had if further or higher education in turn increased employment chances. Moreover, many of the stayers-on who actually entered the labour market after school may have stayed on the off-chance of gaining a place in higher education. In the event they were not successful; but their chances could not have been predicted with certainty and their decision to stay on at school may well have been reasonable.

Second, the analysis covers only the first year in the labour market. It is possible that over a longer period of time the relative fortunes of Highers-qualified leavers and others who had stayed on at school improved, perhaps with a belated lowering of aspirations, or perhaps as they became eligible for some of the jobs which have minimum age restrictions.[4] Moreover, the analysis has looked only at chances of employment rather than unemployment; it has not looked at the type or quality or duration of the job obtained. Staying on may have been a wise decision for young people wishing to enter particular jobs which preferred to recruit older school leavers, or which demanded Highers passes.

These are important limitations. Nevertheless most young people did enter the labour market after leaving school, and most of them did aspire to a permanent job; and the analysis suggests that O-grades had a positive influence on the fulfilment of this aspiration, that Highers had a negligible influence and that staying on had a negative influence among males. However, surveys can never positively prove the existence of cause and effect. Even when attempts are made to control for other variables – in this case, home background and local unemployment rates – the conclusions are still open to the objection that other, unidentified or unmeasured factors might account for the associations. Might such objections be valid in this case? Below, each dimension of school attainment is considered in turn.

O-grades. Here the objection might be that employers cared little about O-grades as such, but selected young employees mainly on other criteria which in turn happened to be correlated with O-grade attainment. These other criteria might have included attitudes, personality and a willingness to work - personal characteristics of which we have no reliable measures in the surveys and for which we were not able to control in Table 9.3. These personal characteristics tended in turn to be correlated with O-grade attainment (not surprisingly, since they tended to influence motivation and performance at school as well as at work). Perhaps the association between 0-grades and employment was not a causal one at all, but merely reflected the importance of personal characteristics?

TABLE 9.4

"In your view, what do employers look for when school leavers apply to them for jobs? – Employers want school leavers who ..."

	Percentage of school leavers who tick item as "important"		Percentage of school leavers who tick item as "most important"	
	Males	**Females**	**Males**	**Females**
... talk well at an interview	68	72	4	3
... are smart and well dressed	75	89	5	8
... have good exam results	58	58	15	12
... have the right attitude to the job	91	90	57	57
... are good at English or arithmetic	31	30	2	1
... are good at other subjects	21	13	*	*
... are respectful	78	81	8	8
No "most important" item	–	–	9	10
Total (school leavers in labour market)			100	99
Unweighted n			(1995)	(1971)

Notes: * = <0.5

There is some evidence to support this interpretation. Surveys of employers, both in Scotland and England, consistently find that they attach greatest importance to personal characteristics such as personality, motivation and attitudes to employment among their young recruits; school qualifications are judged to be less important (MSC, 1978; Hunt and Small, 1981; Ashton *et al.*, 1982). The perceptions of young people themselves tend to support these findings. Sample members were asked to say which characteristics employers looked for in school leavers; Table 9.4 lists their answers. A majority thought that good exam results were important – and those who themselves had good qualifications were especially likely to think so. More than nine out of ten school leavers, however, thought that having the right attitude to the job was important; and large numbers also mentioned being smart and well dressed, being respectful and talking well at an interview. The most telling judgement is shown in the two right-hand columns of the table, which show that a majority of young people identified having the right attitude to the job as the one thing which employers wanted most.

There can be little doubt that employers attach considerable importance to attitudes and other non-academic characteristics. However, it does not follow that qualifications have no direct influence on young people's job chances.

In the first place, all of the surveys of employers cited above agree that employers do use qualifications as criteria in the occupational selection of young people; only the extent of their use is in doubt. Moreover, these surveys also show that qualifications are used most at the stage of pre-selecting or screening job applicants, in order to reduce a long list to a manageable number who can be considered in more detail (Lee and Wrench, 1983; Ashton *et al.*, 1982). Young people tend to be unaware of the importance of qualifications at this stage.

Second, employers in turn have inadequate information on young people's personal characteristics. They tend to place little reliance on reports from schools (Markall and Finn, 1981, p.40); they must depend instead on the fleeting impressions gained from a brief interview. Such impressions are unreliable – with the effect that a youngster who is rejected by one employer as having unfavourable personal characteristics may be employed by another who forms a very different judgement. Over a large number of cases, therefore, the effects of employers' decisions based upon unreliable assessments of personal characteristics may largely cancel each other out; qualifications, by contrast, are not subject to rival interpretations.

Finally, and perhaps most importantly, there is clear evidence that even employers who are primarily concerned with the personal characteristics of their young recruits frequently use qualifications as evidence of these characteristics (Ashton *et al.*, p.55). Qualifications not only reflect academic skills; they also reflect qualities of motivation, perseverance and a conformity to the discipline of work at school. Given the lack of alternative information which employers have on young job applicants, it is not surprising that qualifications should be a major criterion in their selection of young people.

There are therefore good reasons for believing that O-grade attainment has a direct and strong influence on an individual's chances of employment; although it is possible that the actual effects of O-grades are somewhat smaller than indicated in Table 9.3, because of the failure to control for all relevant personal characteristics.

Highers passes. The situation with Highers is rather different. In Table 9.3 Highers were found to have no significant effect on employment. If the argument applied to O-grades is also to be applied to Highers – that unmeasured personal characteristics artificially inflated the observed association between Highers and employment – the implication is that the true effect of Highers, independent of these characteristics, was actually negative. This is implausible; in which case it seems likely that the failure to control for all such personal characteristics made little difference to the observed effect of Highers in Table 9.3.[5] It is difficult to see how allowing for other unmeasured factors might affect the conclusion that Highers passes had at most a small effect on employment; although the earlier point should be reiterated, that the present analysis concerns only the probability of employment rather than unemployment and says nothing about the effect of Highers passes on the type of job entered.

Staying on. The analysis indicates that staying on had a positive effect on employment among females (but only on account of the additional qualifications gained) and a negative effect (at least in May 1981) among males. Are these associations of cause and effect? Two possible objections must be considered.

First, it is possible that in part the direction of cause and effect should be reversed: that some of the stayers-on remained at school precisely *because* they could not find jobs, and that when they eventually left school the same labour-market handicaps that prevented them from finding a job at the first attempt frustrated their second attempt to find work. However, if it were true that the stayers-on were, for social, educational or geographical reasons, less employable in the first place, then the effect of these handicaps would to some extent be controlled for by the variables used in the analysis; the argument is only valid to the extent that these variables do not adequately measure the ways in which the stayers-on were initially less employable than the early leavers. In any case, the objection is implausible because the stayers-on were, on average, much *more* employable than the early leavers with respect to their fourth-year qualifications, family background and local labour-market conditions. For example, the stayers-on already had an average of 4.3 O-grades (at A-C) by the end of fourth year, compared to the early leavers who had an average of only 1.2.

A second and more serious objection is that the analysis makes no allowance for increased aspirations among the stayers-on (see, for example, Ryrie, 1983). The stayers-on may have been more selective concerning the types of jobs they would accept and consequently more likely to remain unemployed for a period while waiting for an acceptable job to turn up. The data contain no measures of occupational aspirations, so there is no direct way to test this interpretation. However, theories of occupational development typically regard the process as one of continuous adjustment between aspiration and reality (Super, 1953); in the same vein, in labour economics search theories predict that aspirations tend to fall over time if an individual repeatedly fails to find an acceptable job (Hunter and Mulvey, 1981, p.280). If the early job aspirations of stayers-on were unrealistic they would therefore be lowered, and the negative effect on employment chances would wear off over time. Yet the negative effect of staying on on the employment chances of males actually *increased* over time, between October 1980 and May 1981. The negative effect of staying on on males' employment chances is therefore unlikely to have been merely a consequence of unrealistic aspirations.

The implications for schooling

The analyses in this chapter provide strong evidence that O-grade attainment had a strong positive effect on post-school employment chances, that the effect of Highers was negligible and that the effect of staying on into post-compulsory schooling was negative for males. Such conclusions must have serious implications for schooling.

As far as compulsory schooling is concerned, the analysis appears to confirm the widespread view that the O-grade is the source of much of the extrinsic value of schooling: that the O-grade is a currency which in the labour market is converted into employment, and that it therefore serves as a main instrument of motivation and social control within secondary schools. However, there are two reservations regarding this argument. First, the labour-market value of O-grades appears to have been greater for males than for females. Second, the motivating power of the O-grade depends on the extent to which it is perceived by pupils to be strongly linked to employment chances; Table 9.4 casts some doubt on the strength of these perceptions, and there is the further consideration that in a time of high unemployment many pupils may feel that there is little point in bothering about O-grades, for if there are no jobs anyway what help can it be to have qualifications? In fact, this reasoning is false (Raffe, 1983a); unemployment has risen among all qualification groups, but the relative advantage of those with O-grades is as great as ever.

How would the relation of fourth-year certification to employment be affected by the introduction of the reforms of certification and assessment proposed in the Munn and Dunning Reports? The evidence suggests that employers generally use O-grades, not as evidence of specific achievements or competences, but as a guide to an individual's general ability as well as to some of the personal characteristics discussed earlier in this chapter

(Gray *et al.*, 1983, chapter 7). It follows that, especially in a fiercely competitive labour market, an employer is likely to be more interestéd in a youngster's relative position in the hierarchy of qualifications than in evidence of attainment expressed in absolute (or criterion-referenced) terms. The differentials that presently exist among individuals with varying levels of O-grade attainment (or with none) will in future be repeated among young people with Credit, General and Foundation awards of the new certificate. Reforms of the curriculum will make little difference to this general pattern except insofar as they affect the ranking of individuals in the overall qualifications hierarchy.

Among the 1981 sample even the lowest level of O-grade qualifications made a significant difference to chances of employment. Even a D or E award at O-grade added nearly four percentage points to a male's chances of employment after leaving school. The implication is not only that Credit awards will have a relative value in the labour market; General awards will also have value (although less than Credit), and even Foundation awards will be worth working for if a significant residue of school leavers remained completedly uncertificated, since Foundation awards will at least convey a competitive advantage relative to this group. The major limitation, however, of any reform of certification (or curriculum) in compulsory schooling is that reforms which create intrinsic value cannot create extrinsic value in the labour market. The number of jobs to be competed for is more or less fixed; in managing a secondary-education system the trick is to devise a system of certificates so that as many pupils as possible have a chance of maintaining or enhancing their competitive labour-market position through compliance with that system.

However, the significance of D or E awards suggests, at least for males, that O-grade *attempts* are nearly as important in the labour market as O-grade results. This in turn suggests that, under the post-Dunning arrangements, being placed on a Credit-level course may be nearly as valuable in labour-market terms as gaining Credit awards. This may increase the pressure from pupils and their parents for pupils to be placed on Credit-level courses even if their previous attainments indicate that a General-level award is more likely to be within their reach.

For post-compulsory schooling, however, the implications are more serious. The Higher is revealed as a currency of negligible value in the labour market – although it may well be of value to those wishing to enter particular *types* of jobs. Moreover, staying on into post-compulsory schooling is in itself likely to be a wrong move for a male whose main objective is to secure permanent employment after leaving school. These findings might be disturbing for two reasons: for what they imply for the future educational choices of 16 year olds; and for what they reveal about the content of post-compulsory schooling.

Traditionally post-compulsory schooling in Scotland has attracted young people with a fairly narrow range of academic interests and abilities. This pattern has been reflected in the prevailing assumption that academic performance during compulsory schooling should be the main criterion for determining whether a young person should stay on (Ryrie, 1981). Nevertheless, growing numbers have stayed on in recent years in response to rising unemployment (see chapter 5); and there have been moves to provide courses for the vocationally oriented 16 year olds who stay on either to enhance their future chances of employment or for the more negative reason that they could not find a job (SED, 1983a, 1983b). The findings of this chapter cast doubt upon the success of these courses in terms of employment.

Possibly the new courses will be able to recruit some pupils because of the inertia of the system: because it is easier to stay on in the same school rather than face the unknown worlds of further education or employment, and because much of the advice available within the school will favour continued schooling. In part this must be regarded as a failure of careers guidance – especially if it fails to distinguish between the undoubted advantages of gaining good qualifications during compulsory schooling and the more questionable occupational benefits of staying on. Many young people (and teachers) appear to confuse these two dimensions of educational attainment. Moreover, even if the new post-compulsory courses were successful in recruiting students, this would not affect the fundamental criticism, that they would not improve their (male) students' chances of employment.

Against this it might be argued that the findings in this chapter merely reflect the vocational inutility of a largely unreformed "academic" model of post-compulsory schooling, and that the new courses, explicitly designed to be vocationally relevant, will have much greater value in the labour market. This indeed is the thrust of much recent policy development: to diversify the curriculum by introducing vocationally oriented courses alongside more academically oriented courses, and thereby to enhance the employability of students.

The underlying assumption on which this policy depends is that the employment chances of students completing a course of education (or training) depend primarily upon the content and quality of that education. This assumption is widespread in current discussions of the 16-plus age group, but it is substantially false. Students' chances of finding employment after completing a course of education or training depend largely upon the structure of the labour market, and upon two aspects of this in particular.

First, their chances depend upon employers' recruitment practices, and in particular upon the amount of information available to employers about potential recruits. Employers use O-grades as criteria for selection because they lack alternative reliable information on job applicants; they use them as evidence both of general ability and of the non-academic characteristics in which they are interested. Highers add little to this information and are not greatly used, except for specific occupations which recruit from a higher ability range; indeed it is possible that attempting Highers, and staying on at school, might be perceived negatively by employers as evidence of excessive aspirations and of a likely reluctance to fit in to the relatively unattractive jobs on offer. The value of specifically vocational qualifications gained in post-compulsory schooling is therefore uncertain. On the one hand, they may be perceived by employers as evidence of positive attitudes, of an initial commitment to the labour market; on the other hand, they may be perceived as inferior by employers whose principal interest is in an individual's overall position in the qualifications hierarchy (CPRS, 1980, pp.4-5).

The second, and probably more important, aspect of labour-market structure is the persistence of age restrictions in the labour market. Some employers might feel that 16 year olds are easier to train than older school leavers, or prefer them because their wages are lower. In particular, most apprenticeships are difficult to enter for young people who have passed their 17th birthday (Ashton *et al.*, 1982; Jolly *et al.*, 1980). These restrictions mainly affect jobs typically entered by males: hence the finding that staying on at school reduces the chances of employment of males but not females.

The moral is that the associations between the three dimensions of school attainment (0-grades, Highers and staying on) and employment have little to do with the content of schooling and a lot to do with the structure of the labour market. Yet the association between attainment and employment in its turn has serious implications for schooling, especially for post-compulsory schooling, in view of the introduction of the Youth Training Scheme, discussed in the next chapter. It forms part of the structural context which constrains the content and performance of schooling. Yet nearly all the discussion about the future of schooling has ignored the structure, and focused instead on its content. It has proposed curricular changes, to bring about greater vocational relevance: yet this alone will not prevent post-compulsory schooling from being an unattractive option, in labour-market terms, for many male 16 year olds. Reforms of the content of secondary education may be desirable, but they cannot be fully effective if no account is taken of these structural constraints. Whatever the case for educational reform, the evidence of this chapter points to the need for reform of the labour market itself; it highlights the irrationality of a labour market which rewards qualifications but which penalises one of the principle means for achieving them.

Addendum to chapter 9

The multiple regressions reported in chapter 9 are shown in Table 9A. The dependent variable is a dummy which takes a value of one if the respondent was employed at the relevant date and a value of zero if he or she was not employed. Each coefficient therefore represents the change in the probability of employment associated with a unit change in the corresponding independent variable. The variables are listed in Figure 9A. Eight equations are shown, corresponding to the permutations of two sexes, two time points and two approaches.

FIGURE 9A

Variables used in the multiple regressions shown in Table 9A

TOTOAC	number of O-grades at A–C gained before leaving school
S4OAC	number of O-grades at A–C gained by end of fourth year
TOTODE	number of O-grades at D or E gained before leaving school
S4ODE	number of O-grades at D or E gained by end of fourth year
HIGHERS	number of Highers passes gained before leaving school
STAYON	whether stayed on voluntarily beyond fourth year (O=no 1=yes)
UNEMPOCT	percentage unemployment rate in travel-to-work area in October1980
UNEMPMAY	percentage unemployment rate in travel-to-work area in May 1981
DADJOB	whether father reported as employed (O=no 1=yes; O includes unemployed, retired, disabled, deceased and not known to respondent)
DADNM	whether father's (present or last) occupation is non-manual (O=no 1=yes)
DADSKM	whether father's (present or last) occupation is skilled manual (O=no 1=yes)

TABLE 9A

Multiple regressions

| Independent variable | Predicting employment in October 1980 | | | | Predicting employment in May 1981 | | | |
| | Model (1) | | Model (2) | | Model (3) | | Model (4) | |
	Males	Females	Males	Females	Males	Females	Males	Females
TOTOAC	.050*	.033*			.058*	.039*		
	(.006)	(.007)			(.006)	(.007)		
S4OAC			.053*	.037*			.059*	.038*
			(.006)	(.007)			(.006)	(.006)
TOTODE	.042*	−.001			.037*	.020*		
	(.009)	(.010)			(.008)	(.010)		
S4ODE			.039*	.000			.037*	.024*
			(.008)	(.009)			(.008)	(.009)
HIGHERS	.021	.010			.014	−.011		
	(.017)	(.017)			(.017)	(.016)		
STAYON	−.133*	.045	−.087*	.081*	−.163*	.069	−.114*	.085*
	(.045)	(.042)	(.036)	(.035)	(.043)	(.040)	(.035)	(.033)
UNEMPOCT	−.033*	−.029*	−.033*	−.030*				
	(.003)	(.004)	(.003)	(.004)				
UNEMPMAY					−.022*	−.023*	−.022*	−.023*
					(.003)	(.003)	(.003)	(.003)
DADJOB	.092*	.100*	.092*	.099*	.121*	.093*	.121*	.092*
	(.029)	(.031)	(.029)	(.031)	(.028)	(.030)	(.028)	(.030)
DADNM	.084*	.091*	.083*	.092*	.104*	.038	.104*	.038
	(.034)	(.037)	(.034)	(.038)	(.033)	(.036)	(.033)	(.036)
DADSKM	.028	−.029	.028	−.031	.023	−.032	.023	−.032
	(.028)	(.029)	(.028)	(.029)	(.027)	(.028)	(.027)	(.028)
Constant	.759	.747	.758	.745	.693	.773	.693	.774
R^2	.166	.154	.167	.156	.168	.145	.168	.145
n	(1416)	(1331)	(1416)	(1331)	(1416)	(1331)	(1416)	(1331)

Notes: See Figure 9A for definition of the independent variables, and the text for further details of the analysis. Standard errors are shown in brackets; coefficients marked with an asterisk are significant at the five per cent level on a two-tailed test.

The first approach, summarised in Table 9.3, is shown in models 1 and 3 in Table 9A. This estimates separate coefficients for O-grades, Highers and staying on; the staying-on variable therefore represents the "separate" effect of having stayed on at school, over and above any effect of extra qualifications obtained. In the second approach SCE qualifications are represented only by the O-grades the respondents had obtained by the end of fourth year; the staying-on variable therefore represents the "overall" effect of staying on, defined to include any effect of the extra qualifications obtained.

The technique of multiple regression is normally considered appropriate for the analysis of dependent variables measured on an interval scale rather than of dichotomies such as being employed or not employed (Pindyck and Rubinfeld, 1976). Consequently the R-squares of around 0.16, which might be considered low in an analysis that used interval variables, are fairly high for the type of data used. The models are therefore re-estimated using logit analysis, a technique for predicting dichotomous variables. For this analysis some of the variables are re-specified in aggregated form. O-grade attainment is represented by a single six-category variable (respectively: no award, D or E awards only, one or two A-Cs, three or four A-Cs, five or six A-Cs and seven or more A-Cs). Highers attainment is represented by a dichotomous variable (any Highers passes, no Highers pass) as is the local unemployment rate (less than 14 per cent, 14 per cent or more). DADJOB, DADNM and DADSKM are represented by a single four-category variable (non-manual employed, skilled manual employed, other employed, not employed). With respect to employment in May 1981 (models 3 and 4) the logit analyses agree with the regression analyses concerning the direction and significance of all the effects. With respect to employment in October 1980 (models 1 and 2) the logit analyses differ from the regressions in two respects. First, they show a significant positive effect of Highers for females in model 1, but not in any other model. Second, the effect of staying on among males in models 1 and 2 is significant (in a two-tailed test) at the ten per cent level but not at the chosen level of five per cent. It seems likely that collapsing the categories of the other variables (especially the O-grade and unemployment rate variables) weakens their value as "control" variables and that this explains the failure of STAYON to reach significance for males in models 1 and 2. Nevertheless one must conclude that the logit analyses leave as not proven the assertion that staying on had a negative effect on males' employment chances in October, even though it seems likely that there was such an effect. The logit analyses support the findings of the regression analyses that staying on (both the "separate" and the "overall" effects) reduced males' employment chances in May. They also reveal that in models 2 and 4 the effect of the interaction between O-grade attainment and staying on was not significant; in other words, the effect of staying on did not vary significantly among pupils with different levels of fourth-year O-grade attainment.

Chapter 10

YOP and the future of YTS

David Raffe

Both in October 1980 and in May 1981 about half of the 1980 school leavers who were still looking for work were on the Youth Opportunities Programme (YOP); and nearly all those who had not found a job by May 1981 had been on a YOP scheme at some time since school. YOP explicitly aimed at a comprehensive coverage of school leavers, its main target group. Under the "Easter undertaking" the Manpower Services Commission (MSC) was committed to offering a suitable place on the programme to every 1980 school leaver who had not found a job by Easter 1981. Only three per cent of the summer 1980 school leavers were continuously unemployed, with no YOP experience, up to May 1981, and we do not know if they had been offered a "suitable place". YOP provided unemployed youngsters with periods of work preparation or work experience, ranging in length from two weeks to one year. The majority of YOP places were on Work Experience on Employers' Premises (WEEP) schemes. These usually lasted for six months and involved work experience in a place of normal employment, sometimes accompanied by off-the-job training or further education. YOP provided young people with something more bearable than the dole queue, but it also aimed to help young people into jobs, by breaking the vicious circle of "no experience – no job – no experience" and by giving young people general skills that would make them more attractive to employers.

YOP began in April 1978, and in its first year appeared to be fairly successful. Of the first main influx of YOP trainees, who joined the programme in September and October 1978, three quarters found jobs, or entered further education or training, when their schemes ended (MSC, 1982b, p.7). This good beginning was not sustained, however; of those who entered between June 1980 and July 1981, only 31 per cent entered employment after their schemes, and a further 11 per cent entered further education or training, usually on another YOP scheme (Bedeman and Courtenay, 1982).

The fall in employment among YOP trainees reflected the general rise in unemployment, which more than doubled over the period, rather than any apparent deterioration of YOP. Nevertheless the increase in unemployment gave rise to growing dissatisfaction with YOP. Even if it was unfair to blame YOP for the rise in youth unemployment, many felt that the new situation called for a redefinition of the programme's objectives and a quality improvement in its provision of training and education. Such proposals were contained in reports published in 1981 by Youthaid (1981) and by the House of Commons Committee on Scottish Affairs (1981); the same year witnessed demonstrations by YOP trainees and attempts to unionise. However, also in 1981, the MSC (1981a, 1981b) proposed a New Training Initiative (NTI), one component of which was a move towards comprehensive provision of training or education or vocational preparation for all young people under 18. In December the government announced that a new Youth Training Scheme (YTS) would replace YOP from September 1983 (DE, 1981); the government's plans were modified, and made more widely acceptable, following the MSC's (1982a) Youth Task Group Report of April 1982.

The Youth Training Scheme aims to provide opportunities for all 16 year olds who wish for them and at least for unemployed 17 year olds. The scheme offers a year's integrated work experience, training and education; at least three months of the year must be spent in off-the-job training or education. The Youth Task Group listed the variety of skills which the scheme should develop, and identified the need for adequate induction, assessment, guidance and counselling. In most of these respects YTS aims to take the best practice from the best YOP schemes and apply it more widely; where YTS differs most radically from YOP is in its coverage. YTS is not restricted to the unemployed, and firms are encouraged to bring the first year of their normal youth-training arrangements within the scheme. YOP was regarded as additional to ordinary employment and training, and in theory it was not allowed to substitute for them; YTS, by contrast, is intended to be an integral feature of employers' regular training, recruitment and employment practices.

In this chapter we consider three questions which educationists are likely to ask about YTS. How popular will the new scheme be with young people? What effects will it have on the employment chances of young people? And what effect will YTS have on the quality, quantity and distribution of vocational preparation for 16 and 17 year olds?

At the time of writing (summer 1983) YTS is only in its pilot stage; and in any case the first year or two of the new programme are likely to be atypical, as the MSC, local authorities and employers rush to meet the extremely ambitious deadlines, and as young people, teachers and careers officers come to terms with the new spectrum of opportunities. Any prediction about the long-term impact of YTS is bound to be speculative. However, the recent experience of YOP offers some clues as to the future prospects for YTS. There are substantial continuities between YOP and YTS – one programme has, after all, grown out of the other – and from a study of YOP one can draw more general conclusions that may be applicable to YTS. This chapter examines the experience of YOP among 1980 school leavers, looking in particular at their attitudes towards the programme and at its impact on their subsequent employment chances.

Young people's attitudes to YOP

Altogether 28 per cent of the 1980 summer-term leavers had taken part in a YOP scheme by May 1981. Among labour-market entrants the proportion was 37 per cent. More leavers entered YOP in Strathclyde than in the rest of Scotland (45 per cent compared with 28 per cent of labour-market entrants); and fewer leavers with O-grades (A-C) or Highers entered YOP (27 per cent) than their less qualified peers (49 per cent). The proportions among males and females were similar (36 per cent and 37 per cent). In nearly all respects the distribution of YOP trainees reflected the distribution of unemployment; there was a slight under-representation of Highers-qualified males and unqualified females among YOP trainees, but in general the programme was successful at meeting the demand. Few school leavers had remained with neither a job nor a YOP placement since leaving school.

Most of those who entered YOP did so during the summer or early autumn. August, September, July and October were (in that order) the peak months for entry to YOP. About two thirds (69 per cent) had left their first YOP scheme by May 1981, although several had already entered a second scheme.

Table 10.1 reports the attitudes of young people in the labour market towards special schemes for unemployed young people – of which YOP was by far the most important. The responses must be interpreted with some caution. Not only are the figures provisional (they are based on different questionnaire versions from those used in most of this book) but the nature of the questions allows for some ambiguity. The young people were asked to tick "yes" or "no" for each of the three items in Table 10.1, but some of the items were left blank, possibly indicating a lack of knowledge or a lack of opinion concerning the relevant aspect of YOP. (Fewer than two per cent left all three items blank.) These blank answers have been included in the 100 per cent base in Table 10.1, which may therefore underestimate the extent of positive attitudes among those who felt able to offer an opinion.

TABLE 10.1

"Young people who are unemployed can go on special schemes of work experience or training. Do you think schemes like this…"

	School leavers with no experience of YOP		School leavers formerly on YOP		School leavers still on YOP		All school leavers in labour market	
	Males	Females	Males	Females	Males	Females	Males	Females
… help unemployed young people to find jobs?	46	47	44	50	48	47	46	48
… give young people interesting things to do?	58	63	53	55	58	59	57	61
… are a useful way to get training?	64	75	59	70	66	80	63	75
Unweighted n	(1296)	(1294)	(417)	(412)	(308)	(307)	(2021)	(2013)

Notes: The estimates are based on unweighted data.
Only school leavers in the labour market are included.

Overall, most young people could find something positive to say about schemes. More than eight out of ten males and nearly nine out of ten females ticked "yes" for at least one of the items in Table 10.1. At the same time, young people could distinguish between different criteria for evaluating schemes. Rather less than half thought they helped unemployed young people to find jobs; more than half thought they gave young people interesting things to do; and nearly two thirds of males and three quarters of females thought that schemes were a useful way to get training. The proportion with favourable attitudes on training is surprisingly high. In 1981 only 22 per cent of work-experience trainees on YOP received any off-the-job training (Greaves *et al.*, 1982, p.9); and the alleged low quality and frequent absence of education and training on YOP was the main butt of contemporary critics of the programme (Raffe, 1984). Possibly the young people valued the on-the-job training received through work experience; or perhaps their opinions shown in Table 10.1 reflect the lack of training opportunities elsewhere. At any rate, it seems that young people were more likely to be dissatisfied with the poor employment propects after YOP than with the quality or availability of training. Since YTS is designed to improve training rather than (directly) to improve employment prospects, young people may not respond much more positively to YTS than to YOP. It is important to note that the judgements of young people did not coincide with those of the (adult-led) youth and training lobbies, who reserved their strongest criticisms for the quality of education and training provision on YOP, and who helped to provide the impetus for the replacement of YOP by YTS.

Table 10.1 also shows that attitudes to special schemes were broadly similar whether or not young people had had experience of YOP – except that those who had left YOP had rather less favourable attitudes with respect to interest and training. The attitudes expressed by our sample appear to reflect the prevailing opinions among young people, whether or not these were based on personal experience.

The attitudes of the Scottish school leavers were broadly similar to those reported in the MSC's own survey, which covered all of Britain but was restricted to YOP entrants (Bedeman and Harvey, 1981). The MSC's sample were rather more optimistic about employment prospects (69 per cent felt that YOP helped a lot or a little) but this may reflect the changing circumstances over time, as the MSC survey was based on earlier (1978/79) entrants to YOP. The MSC sample had similar views on training: 69 per cent agreed that their scheme had helped them get training to do a particular job.

Table 10.1 is based on structured questions which offered fixed-choice responses. Such questions provide easily quantifiable data but they cannot do justice to the range of perceptions and attitudes which young people may hold concerning YOP. Some school leavers were therefore asked to give their opinions on YOP in a less constrained context, on the back page of the questionnaire. The following account is necessarily selective and impressionistic. Although based on a perusal of a large number of questionnaires, it does not pretend to be representative of the views of young people, but it does identify themes common to many of the favourable and unfavourable comments on YOP. All the comments quoted below were made by young people who had never started an O-grade course at school.

The initial prompt to the young people ended thus: "What do you think of the government's special schemes for unemployed young people? Do they help young people to find jobs? Do they help them in other ways?" Sample members were thus invited to distinguish between employment and other benefits of YOP, and they seemed well able to do this. Indeed, many of the young people who responded were able to identify positive and negative aspects of the programme. For example:

> I think the schemes for unemployed are quite good. It gives us something to do rather than collect dole money and sit around. Schemes do not help young people find a job but it help us make new friends and experience of working. Also it is better to work for your money than be handed it for doing nothing.

Some favourable comments appeared to reflect very low expectations:

> It is a good thing, as it keeps you occupied, and if you enjoy it it is even better.

Other young people considered the schemes valuable as an opportunity for new kinds of learning and for personal development. One wrote:

> There should be more government schemes. I think it is a very good idea it trains you in different subjects and lets you know what working life is all about. It does help them find permanent jobs most of the time and it also gives you more confidence in yourself instead of staying on the dole for months.

Another wrote:

> The special schemes are a good thing because they help you to learn about things that you may not have had any idea about. They don't help you to find jobs. If you go on one when you are 16 years old like I did for a year then you wont get started as full-time, they told me I was too young and thats why I did not get started. They do help in other ways they help (young people) to understand about what they are doing when they are working, and they help them to learn more about the things they like.

Young people's criticisms of the programme tended to focus on one of three things. First, several young people commented on the low level of the allowance (£23.50 in 1981) especially since it had to cover additional expenditures that would not be incurred by someone who remained unemployed:

> I think goverment's special training scheme is a waste of time, for a start the wages are rubbish, by the time you pay your dig money, then you've got bus fare, dinner money and money to keep you going all week, it's just not worth it. Plus you are not promised a job at the end and you keep on getting messed about. It could help some people find a job because they have experience but the only problem is finding the job. I don't think it helps them in any others ways.

Young people were particularly resentful of the disparity between the YOP allowance and the earnings of regular employees who may have been doing identical jobs:

> I don't think government scheme are any good the employers only take you on because they don't pay you then when your Course is finished your really lucky if they want to keep you on. I also don't think its fair as you do the same amount of work as everyone else and only get £23.50 while they walk out with a lot more for doing the same thing as you, these employers would be better employing you as a slave for the money the give.

Another young person commented:

> The government's scheme are a waste of time. Most people
> do the 6 month training and after that the employer pays
> them off and they get another government scheme worker.
> They don't help at all, it just a way to get cheap labour.
> When I was on one I did just as much work and sometimes
> more as the rest of the staff and I was only coming out with
> half their wages or even less. When you have done one
> scheme you are lucky to get another one, I was told I would
> have to wait 6 months before they would even think of
> giving me another but I would not take it its just cheap
> labour. I am still trying very hard to get a job.

The government justified the relatively low level of the allowance on the grounds that it was a training allowance rather than a reward for productive labour. Many of the young people most critical of the allowance argued, by implication, that since they were performing as much productive labour as ordinary employees they should receive the same remuneration. If young people come to regard YTS as a training scheme, on which any work experience is planned for the trainee's benefit rather than for the employer's, then they may accept an allowance at levels similar to YOP as fair. If, on the other hand, they perceive YTS primarily as a source of "cheap labour" for employers, then resentment over the level of the allowance will continue.

Thus dissatisfaction with the allowance was closely linked to the perception that employers exploited YOP trainees. This feeling was explicit in both of the last two comments that were quoted; others made the same point more forcefully:

> I think the Gov. Schemes are Cheap Labour. They work
> you to the bone and when your time is up they give you the
> elbow and get another load in and do the same again and
> again. They don't help to get jobs the only job your most
> likely to get is another Gov. Scheme. I don't they help one
> bit they may help some of us but very few. Its the biggest
> con in history if you ask me. I am doing one just now and
> if they offer me another one they can take a jump. Working
> the same hours as full time staff and getting a handful of
> buttons at the end of the week. Its unreal thats all I can say.
> PS. I hope this information helps those who are leaving
> school just to let them know whats in store for them.

Another young person wrote:

> The governments schemes are cheap labour, a company
> would sack some of their experienced work force and take
> on the jobless on these courses (who) would do the same
> work and be paid by the government.

The third point of criticism was simply that the schemes failed to help
young people to find employment:

> I would just like to say I think the government special
> schemes for unemployed young people are just a pure con,
> in my view they don't help a lot to get young people jobs.
> The scheme I am on for instance I know I am not getting
> kept on but the only reason I stay in it is I don't want to
> hang about streets and get into trouble.

Implicit in this comment, and in the comments of many young people,
is the assumption that the main way YOP could help youngsters find jobs
was through being kept on by the sponsors at the end of the scheme.

The theme of the effect – or lack of effect – of YOP on young people's
employment chances runs through nearly all the comments quoted above.
In part this is in direct response to the questions which solicited the
comments in the questionnaire (see above). Nevertheless, it seems that the
young people in the survey would have forgiven YOP for a lot of things had
it offered them a better prospect of employment at the end. Most of those
who commented on the low allowance or the alleged exploitation of YOP
trainees also commented on YOP's failure to find them jobs; success in this
respect, they implied, might have made YOP's other failures tolerable. At
the end of the first three years of the programme young people's
dissatisfaction with the programme appeared to have grown.[1] During that
period, two main things had happened to explain that change: the real value
of the allowance had fallen by 20 per cent, and the proportion of YOP
graduates finding jobs had fallen by an even larger amount. There was no
evidence of a decline in the quality of education or training provided on
YOP. Indeed the MSC repeatedly told the public of its efforts to make
quality improvements.

All this has important implications for YTS. For the ways in which YTS
is planned to differ from YOP do not correspond to the main criticisms
which young people made of the old programme. The value of the YTS
allowance is the same as the YOP allowance, and it seems likely to continue
to decline, in real terms, over the next few years. (For the YTS allowance
to have had the same real value as the initial YOP allowance, it would need
to have been set at £34 in September 1983.) And accusations of exploitation

and "cheap labour" are likely to persist under YTS, fairly or not, since YTS (unlike YOP) is integrated into a firm's normal recruitment and training practices, and YTS trainees are therefore regarded as part of a firm's normal workforce. The major improvement which YTS promises is in the quality and quantity of training and vocational preparation; yet this is the very area where young people (unlike their adult spokesmen) appeared to show least evidence of dissatisfaction with YOP.

The main criterion by which young people are likely to judge YTS is whether or not it helps them to find jobs. Despite the emphasis on training as the declared purpose of YTS, the strong political support for the scheme owed a lot to the expectation that it was an improved measure to deal with youth unemployment; and most young people entering YTS hope that it will help them towards a permanent job. Fairly or otherwise, this is how the scheme will be judged, by its clients as well as its political backers. How will it measure up in their eyes? Once again we seek evidence from the experience of YOP.

The effects of YOP on young people's employment chances

Figure 10.1 shows the paths followed by summer-term leavers who had entered YOP. More than two thirds had left their first scheme by the time of the survey, around May 1981. Of these, about one in six (16 per cent of males and 18 per cent of females) found jobs with the sponsors of their schemes. This is almost as many as the number who found jobs elsewhere on leaving their schemes, who comprised 19 per cent of all leaving YOP schemes and 23 per cent of those who did not get jobs with their sponsors. Most of those who found jobs on leaving their schemes were still employed at the time of the survey around May 1981, which for the average YOP-leaver was about four months later. Conversely, few of those who did not enter jobs straight after their schemes had found jobs by May.

Altogether, only 36 per cent of males and 37 per cent of females found jobs on leaving their schemes, although by May 41 per cent of the females were employed. Nearly half of those who left YOP for employment were offered jobs by their sponsors. This particular route to permanent employment appears to have benefited females more than males; females were more likely to obtain a job with the sponsor, and if they did they were more likely to remain in it, although neither difference is statistically significant.

It would be wrong to measure the impact of YOP in terms only of the numbers finding jobs afterwards. The reason for the declining employment rate of YOP trainees is to be found in the declining level of employment in the economy as a whole. It is still possible that young people were in a better position as a result of YOP, even if their probability of employment

FIGURE 10.1
Employment chances after YOP: summer-term leavers, who had started a YOP scheme

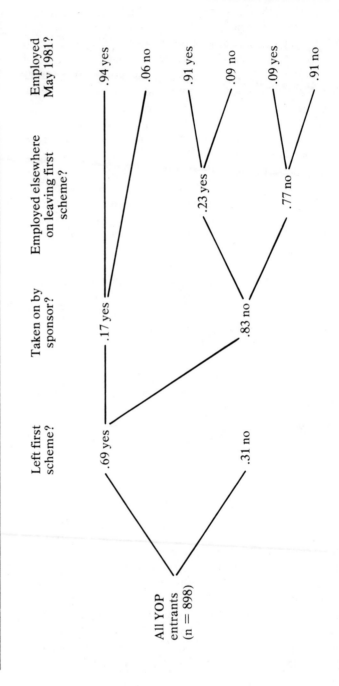

was low in absolute terms. Table 10.2 suggests that for females at least this may have been the case. The table describes summer-term leavers who had not found jobs by October 1980, and it shows their destinations by May 1981. Only a minority (about one quarter of the males and one third of the females) had found jobs by May; these young people had failed to find jobs during the summer recruitment season, and were suffering from the lack of demand from employers during the winter months (see Main and Raffe, 1983b). Females were somewhat more likely than males to find employment by May; moreover, this advantage appears to have been connected with YOP, since 41 per cent of females who were on YOP in October found jobs by May compared with only 26 per cent of females who were unemployed but not on YOP in October. Among males, the fortunes of those respectively on YOP and not on YOP in October were similar – 28 per cent of the former and 26 per cent of the latter had found jobs by May.[2]

TABLE 10.2

Destinations in May 1981 of summer-term leavers who were not employed in October 1980, by YOP in October 1980 (percentages)

	Employed	Unemployed	YOP	Total	Unweighted n
Males					
Not on YOP	26	37	38	101	(260)
YOP	28	25	47	100	(294)
All	27	31	42	100	(554)
Females					
Not on YOP	26	35	39	100	(270)
YOP	41	22	37	100	(301)
All	34	29	38	101	(571)

Notes: The table includes only young people in the labour market at both dates.

This association between YOP and subsequent employment among females is not, of course, sufficient evidence of a causal effect. YOP trainees were not selected at random from unemployed young people; they may already have been more advantaged and employable than other unemployed youngsters, and therefore more likely in any case to find a job by May. To test for the independent effect of YOP on subsequent employment, a multiple regression was conducted using the same predictor variables as in Figure 9A in the previous chapter. These controlled for the effects of various kinds of school attainment, the local unemployment rate, class and parental background; being on YOP in October was represented by an additional dummy variable. The analysis was restricted to the group covered by Table 10.2, that is summer-term leavers who entered the labour market but had not found permanent jobs by October 1980. Among males, only O-grade awards at A-C and father's social class had a significant effect on employment in May 1981. Being on YOP in October was estimated to add five percentage points to a male's chances of employment in May, but the effect was not statistically significant. Among females, by contrast, YOP had substantial and significant effects, adding an estimated 14 percentage points to the chances of employment in May. (The other significant variables for females were staying on, O-grades at A-C and the local unemployment rate.) The regression analysis therefore supports the impression gained from Table 10.2, that being on YOP in October had a sizeable effect on a female's chances of employment in May. The effect among males was smaller and not proven, although a similar analysis based on larger sample numbers shows this effect to be significant (Main, 1983).

The validity of these findings is supported by additional evidence from two sources. First, a logit analysis of the same data confirmed the findings of the regression – logit being in some respects more appropriate for the type of data used (see also Main, 1983). Second, comparable analyses based on less qualified 1978 leavers two years earlier produced remarkably similar findings (Main and Raffe, 1983a): the effect of YOP on females' employment chances was estimated at a significant 14 percentage points, whereas among boys the effect was estimated at six percentage points and was not statistically significant. The relative advantage of YOP trainees remained stable between 1978 and 1980, even though absolute employment rates declined. The claim that YOP helped girls to find jobs must nevertheless be interpreted with caution, for most of those who were unemployed but not on YOP in October themselves entered YOP at some time in the succeeding months – except of course for those who found jobs instead. There is no suitable comparison group of young people who never had an opportunity to go on YOP. Strictly speaking, Table 10.2 and the associated regression and logit analyses estimate the effect of being on YOP *in October 1980* on employment *in May 1981*; had the analysis used different time points the conclusions might have been different.[3]

So far the discussion has covered only the effects of YOP on individuals' chances of employment. Estimates of the effect on total levels of youth employment are much harder to produce. It is probable, however, that any such effect was relatively small and that it was offset by the substitution of some YOP places for permanent jobs. YOP may have had a more significant effect on the distribution of those jobs that were available to young people. From the start YOP was concerned with the distributive aspects of youth employment and unemployment, and aimed in particular to give more attention to females and to the less qualified than previous manpower policies for young people had done (Raffe, 1983b).

Table 10.3 shows the jobs held by those 1980 school leavers who were employed at the time of the survey around May 1981. It distinguishes school leavers who entered their jobs without having first gone on a YOP scheme from those who had first been on YOP. The table also distinguishes males and females and lower and higher qualification groups, the latter having at least one Higher or O-grade award at A-C.

The first four columns show how far sex and qualifications were criteria for distributing jobs among young people. Males were far more likely to work in security and protective-service occupations, farming and fishing, materials processing (metal and electrical), construction and mining or transport operating, materials moving and storing. Females were far more likely to work in clerical, selling or personal-service jobs. Higher-qualified youngsters of either sex were more likely to be senior white-collar or clerical workers, and less likely to be personal-service workers, materials processors (other than metal and electrical), assemblers or construction or transport workers. Among males the materials-processing workers were clearly stratified, those working on metal and electrical goods being mainly higher-qualified and the others mainly lower-qualified. Selling jobs mainly attracted the lower-qualified females.

The right-hand side of Table 10.3 shows the occupations of young people who had found employment after first going on a YOP scheme. The figures are based on relatively small sample numbers and detailed comparisons should be treated with caution. Nevertheless perhaps the most striking conclusion to be drawn is that the jobs of former YOP trainees were generally very similar to those of comparable young people who had not been on YOP. There are a number of small differences – rather more former YOP trainees were in selling jobs, for example – but no dramatic difference. The table appears to refute the claim that YOP only led young people into inferior jobs. Overall, former YOP trainees were more likely than other young people to be employed (if at all) in less desirable jobs; but this was largely due to their lower average qualification levels. YOP trainees who subsequently found jobs tended to enter similar jobs to their peers of the same sex and qualification level who found jobs without first going on YOP.

The corollary of this is that YOP did not have any major effect on the

TABLE 10.3
Occupation by SCE qualification level, sex and previous experience of YOP: percentage of school leavers in employment in May 1981

| | School leavers with no experience of YOP | | | | Former YOP trainees | | | |
| | Males | | Females | | Males | | Females | |
	Low qual.	High qual.	Low qual.	High qual.	Low qual.	High qual.	Low qual.	High qual.
Managerial, professional and related	2	11	2	20	2	8	2	8
Clerical and related	2	11	18	53	0	8	20	59
Selling	4	4	21	9	9	6	33	12
Security and protective services	7	5	0	*	0	7	0	0
Catering, cleaning, hairdressing and other personal services	6	2	26	10	8	2	14	8
Farming, fishing and related	10	5	*	1	8	9	0	2
Materials processing, making and and repairing (excluding metal and electrical)	22	11	24	3	10	16	22	7
Processing, making, repairing and related (metal and electrical)	15	39	1	1	26	24	2	1
Painting, repetitive assembling, product inspecting, packaging and related	7	3	6	2	10	5	6	4
Construction, mining and related	12	5	0	0	4	7	0	0
Transport operating, materials moving and storing and related	12	4	*	*	14	8	0	0
Miscellaneous	1	1	1	0	9	2	1	0
Total	100	101	99	99	100	102	100	101
Unweighted n	(293)	(809)	(265)	(833)	(82)	(126)	(99)	(134)

Notes: Low qualification = D or E awards only or no SCEs. High qualification = Highers or A – C awards at O-grade. 89 cases with missing information on occupation are excluded. * = Less than 0.5 per cent.

distribution of jobs by sex and qualification levels. Once again the small sample numbers permit conclusions only of a fairly general nature, but the differences among the four columns on the right-hand side of the table are not unlike the corresponding differences on the left-hand side. There are one or two possible exceptions (such as materials-processing jobs among males) but these may be due merely to sampling fluctuations.

Table 10.3 suggests that YOP had little effect on the distribution of occupations among those young people who found employment. The table does not, of course, take account of the majority of YOP trainees who did not find employment. Did YOP have any effect on the relative chances of different groups of young people finding any job?

TABLE 10.4

Employment chances after YOP, by SCE qualification level: summer-term leavers, excluding Highers leavers, who had left a YOP scheme

	Percentage who were kept on by sponsor of YOP scheme	Percentage of remainder who were employed elsewhere
O–grades (A – C)	17	35
D or E awards only or no SCEs	17	17

Table 10.4 suggests that at least in this respect YOP may have had some redistributive effect. It is based on Figure 10.1, and shows the relative chances of higher- and lower-qualified YOP trainees of each sex being employed by the scheme sponsor or, if not employed by the sponsor, of finding a job elsewhere on leaving the scheme. Among those who were not taken on by the sponsor the chances of finding a job were, as might be expected from chapter 9, linked to qualifications, with the higher-qualified group about twice as likely to find a job. The chances of being taken on by the scheme sponsor, however, were not significantly associated with qualifications.[4] YOP enabled employers who sponsored WEEP schemes to submit their trainees, in effect, to a six-month screening period; and employers who used YOP as a recruiting ground for young people had less need to rely on educational qualifications as a criterion for selection, since they could observe the young people directly. Employers who sponsor mode A schemes of YTS – the nearest equivalent to WEEP – will keep on

some 40 per cent of their trainees for permanent employment after their YTS schemes. If those young people are not pre-selected before entering YTS, the employers may similarly use the YTS year as an even longer screening period. They may come to rely far less on educational qualifications as a criterion for selection than has been the case in earlier years. Overall, however, the likely redistributive impact of YTS should not be exaggerated. Qualifications are likely to remain the principal criterion for selecting young people to mode A schemes in the first place; and many employers select their future permanent employees in advance, on entry to YTS.

Discussion

Content and context. One general theme runs through much of the discussion of YOP and employment. This is that young people's chances of finding permanent jobs are more strongly influenced by the context of the education or training they receive than by its content. By context I refer in particular to the extent to which the young people are made visible to a potential employer, either because the training gives them access to an information network which embraces potential employers, or because the employers provide the training. Thus the YOP schemes with the best rates of employment were those where trainees gained a reference that would be trusted by other employers; or where scheme staff gave them an introduction to employers' information networks (Knasel *et al.*, 1982); or, especially, whose sponsors recruited from among their YOP trainees. Nearly half of the YOP trainees who found jobs at the end of their schemes were taken on by their sponsors. Most of these were on WEEP schemes, and this largely explains why trainees on WEEP schemes have had higher rates of subsequent employment than trainees on other YOP schemes (Bedeman and Harvey, 1981, p.42). Yet WEEP schemes were generally agreed to be of lower average quality than other schemes, especially in view of the small proportion of WEEP trainees receiving any off-the-job training or education. Content was less important than context.

The attractiveness of YTS to young people. Earlier in this chapter we asked three questions about the future prospects for YTS. The first concerned the popularity of YTS with young people. YTS is designed to improve upon YOP, principally by providing better quality education and training, and more of it. This follows a crescendo of criticism from the education and training interests and from adult spokesmen for young people, all demanding improved provision. But young people themselves seemed to be relatively satisfied with the training on YOP. The main criteria by which they will judge the new scheme are the real value of the allowance, their perceptions of whether or not the scheme exploits their labour, and, above all, whether or not it gets them jobs.

Thus young people will judge YTS by its context more than by its content. Their willingness to enter the scheme will depend on the extent to which it monopolises the routes leading from school to desirable jobs. This depends not only on YTS offering good prospects of subsequent employment but also on alternative opportunities ceasing to be available to school leavers. This in turn requires that YTS incorporate existing traineeships and apprenticeships, notwithstanding the opposition of some unions, and that young people be excluded from large areas of the adult labour market in which they have traditionally competed. If these conditions are not satisfied, those better-qualified school leavers still able to find employment might prefer the certainty of a job to the very uncertain prospects of a YTS traineeship, even if the latter offered superior training. No doubt some schemes on YTS might offer good prospects and attract the more employable school leavers; but the majority of YTS schemes would be regarded as low-status provision for the unemployed, catering for the more disadvantaged school leavers and holding them only for as long as they could not find a job elsewhere. Such a scheme might still attract large numbers of young people, but in the long run it would be vulnerable to any future fall in unemployment. It would remain handicapped by its origins in a low-status, unemployment-based programme (YOP) rather than in a higher-status, employment-based institution such as apprenticeship.

The intention here is not to argue that this rather gloomy scenario will be realised; such predictions are premature. The point is simply that the future of YTS, and its ability to avoid this kind of future, depends largely on its context rather than its content, that is, on its future relation to patterns of occupational selection.

YTS and youth unemployment. The second question concerned the effects of YTS on youth employment. Quality improvements in YTS (or YOP) are unlikely on their own to produce a substantial increase in youth employment. Youth unemployment is the result of a complex interaction of cyclical and structural factors; there is little evidence that it is caused by a deficiency of skills among young people, or that increased skill training can have a substantial effect on employment levels (see Raffe, 1983c). Nevertheless YTS may lead employers to change their recruitment and employment practices, and this may affect the *context* of opportunities for young people. For example, YTS may encourage employers to direct more of their training towards young people, and to keep a larger proportion than before in employment after YTS. It may have a marginal effect on the distribution of employment. Thus the main impact of YTS on the level and distribution of youth employment may come about as a result, not of the content of YTS, but of its unintended effects on what we have called context.

Towards a better system of vocational preparation? The distinction between content and context helps us to answer the third question, which asked about the effect of YTS on the quality, quantity and distribution of vocational preparation for young people. It seems likely that this effect will be significant and positive; nevertheless a flaw in the system of provision must be noted. Many people have hailed the Youth Training Scheme, with its substantial public funding, as a partial reversal of the government's policy of "privatising" training which led it to close down two thirds of the Industry Training Boards. Nevertheless although current education and training policy depends upon public finance it still rests on at least two assumptions associated with the free-market principle. The first is that employers will tend to select young people who have undergone the highest-quality vocational preparation; the second is that young people, given choice, will tend to choose the opportunity which offers the highest-quality vocational preparation. This chapter has cast doubt on both assumptions.

Employers tend to be more concerned with the calibre and ability of young people than with the quality of their education or training; and for as long as courses of general vocational preparation continue to have low status and attract lower-ability students, employers are unlikely to discriminate in their favour. Moreover, given employers' desire to avoid risks in recruitment, and their substantial ignorance of the abilities and other characteristics of young people seeking jobs, they may restrict recruitment to members of their own information networks such as those with whom they have direct contact through training schemes, or others (such as relatives of employees) about whom they have information or some assurance of good work.

The signals emitted by this free market, in other words, are not those that would encourage 16 year olds to choose the best or most appropriate vocational preparation on offer. Young people's main concern is for jobs, not quality of vocational preparation; and the consequence of employers' recruitment practices is that the two do not necessarily coincide. Young people's choices are further distorted by the uneven availability of allowances or bursaries for the different post-16 options (see House of Commons Committee on Scottish Affairs, 1981, para.55).

Policies for the education and training of 16 year olds promise to improve the content of provision; but it is the context, the position of courses within the structure of educational and occupational selection, that now needs reforming. Until this happens young people's decisions and their routes through this structure will remain largely unrelated to the educational or occupational value of the content of provision. The irony of YTS is that it may have a significant impact on the context of vocational preparation because of its links with employment and recruitment. But these links, and the resulting change of context, were planned to facilitate the delivery of the scheme on a limited budget, rather than to make it more attractive to young people or to offer a coherent pattern of opportunities and incentives for young people. Any impact of YTS in this area, whether positive or negative, will be in this sense accidental.

Chapter 11

The content and context of educational reform

The schooling of the 1980 leavers

In this book we have followed the careers from age 14 to about 18 of a particular group of young people, those who left school in Scotland in 1979/80. In this concluding chapter we briefly summarise our findings, and discuss the implications of our study for the outcomes of current and prospective policy initiatives.

The 1980 leavers had passed through a secondary school system that was defined in terms of stages, closely but not precisely linked to age. The third and fourth years comprised the first stage in which differentiation among school pupils was both pervasive and formalised. Pupils formed a hierarchy, which corresponded to schools' assessments of their ability, but which also correlated with social class and parental education. Pupils' positions in this hierarchy (together with their sex) shaped decisions about the balance of the curriculum they were taught, the level at which subjects were studied, and whether subjects would be dropped before O-grade. Perhaps surprisingly, pupils at all levels of the hierarchy were taught using a similar mix of methods. Both the fact and the significance of differentiation were clearly recognised by pupils, whose evaluations of the fourth-year experience were strongly coloured by their positions in the hierarchy; but they were realistic in their perceptions of what schools could provide, and even the least successful appreciated the school as a social context, an experience to be shared with friends.

Those near the top of the hierarchy were likely to stay on at school beyond 16, principally in order to gain further qualifications. Those lower down the hierarchy tended to leave, citing the various attractions of work and life outside school as the reason. Altogether, about four in ten stayed on. This decision to stay on at 16 was not always a simple decision about starting a fifth year. A majority of the 1980 leavers who had stayed on beyond 16 did so, not to start a fifth-year course, but to complete a course that they had already begun. The fifth year attracted fewer voluntary entrants than is commonly supposed, as was evidenced by the behaviour of those whose first opportunity to leave came at the end of fourth year. The proportion starting a fifth year has increased steadily since 1978, but this reflects rising unemployment and an increase in the proportion who have had to stay on, probably more than the appeal of the fifth year itself.

The "volunteers" who stayed on were a relatively homogeneous group, selected or self-selected in terms of their earlier attainment. Nevertheless, most found the fifth year difficult. In planning their fifth-year courses they had to balance what was known about the fourth-year O-grade assessment of their ability against their teachers' and their own high aspirations; they also had to consider their fifth-year courses in the light of a possible sixth year. The resolution of these pressures was seen in the wide range of courses followed in fifth year, and in the tendency to aim at a relatively high level and move downwards during the year. The concept of the "new fifth year", among the 1980 leavers at least, proved to be little more than the old fifth year writ large. (This may have changed more recently.) Nearly one half of the fifth-year volunteers stayed on into the sixth year, which was typically dominated by the pursuit of further qualifications. Students were uncertain whether their fifth-year qualifications were adequate to meet the variable entry requirements for higher education; this tended to restrict the numbers taking the Certificate of Sixth Year Studies (CSYS), a course embodying a more liberal conception of the purposes of the sixth year, although this course retained a significant minority following in the east of Scotland.

Staying on at school, and the certificates it made available to young people, were obvious necessities for those wishing to enter higher education. Among those who entered the labour market, and who comprised the majority of school leavers, the value of staying on at school was more doubtful. Boys appeared to damage their chances of finding a job if they stayed on, and girls only improved their chances as a result of the extra O-grades they obtained. O-grades, even at bands D or E, substantially improved school leavers' chances of employment; Highers passes, on the other hand, made very little difference in terms of the probability of securing a job. Most school leavers who did not find jobs entered the Youth Opportunities Programme (YOP), which seems to have given a modest but positive boost to their chances of finding employment. At the time of the survey YOP had been widely criticised for its low quality of education and training, and plans were being laid for a new, higher-quality Youth Training Scheme (YTS). However, in 1981 school leavers were relatively satisfied with the training on YOP; they were more critical of the small allowance and poor employment prospects, features which YTS is less likely to improve.

The Scottish education system has not stood still since these young people left school in 1980, and several major policy initiatives are either in progress or soon to be implemented. The Munn/Dunning reforms, YTS and the Scottish Education Department's (SED) Action Plan for 16-18s may appear, when taken together, to promise a decisive break with the past. On the other hand past change in Scottish education has been incremental rather than radical in nature (Gray *et al.*, 1983). In the rest of this chapter we consider the future prospects for Scottish schooling in the light of these initiatives, but first we must identify some major constraints on change. We do this in terms of the concepts of content and context.

Content and context

There is a tendency among some commentators to dismiss the concept of individual choice within the education system and to present all behaviour as subject to external control, whether this is achieved through internalised norms or through more overt forms of coercion. This view, we believe, is mistaken and misleading. By ignoring the scope for individual choice within education systems, and the extent to which individuals make decisions which are reasonable for them, this view neglects a principal source of structural constraint on change.

The school system offers opportunities for choice at several stages of the school career. During compulsory secondary schooling the main choices formally offered to pupils are through the subject-options system at the beginning of third year. The scope for pupil choice is restricted here, especially with respect to the level at which courses are taken. However, there is a second and possibly more important area of choice available to pupils during compulsory schooling, although it is not formally recognised as such by the school system. This is the choice of whether or not to take courses seriously, to attend regularly, and to comply whole-heartedly with the academic and behavioural demands of the school. Further choices open up at 16, when pupils may enter the labour market or the Youth Training Scheme, go on to further education, or stay on at school; and if they stay on they are likely to face a widening range of choices especially between academic and vocational courses. Those who complete fifth year must choose whether or not to start a sixth; and the best qualified leavers can choose whether or not to apply to higher education. Young people, therefore, face several types of choices as they progress through the school system. What is important for our present argument is that all the policy initiatives we have discussed in this book aim to influence young people's decisions with respect to one or more of these types of choices.

In our analyses we have seen that young people, when faced with these choices, often make decisions that are highly predictable, given knowledge of such circumstances as their attainment, social background and local conditions. However, this does not mean that they have no real choice: the minority who go against the general pattern are proof that the scope for choice exists. Nor is the predictability of most decisions necessarily evidence of a lack of deliberation or rationality or free will. Rather we would argue that this predictability reflects the tendency for most young people to make decisions that respect and follow the (predictable) logic of the situations in which they find themselves.

Young people may share norms and perceptions which help to define these situations and suggest appropriate courses of action; they may be influenced by advice, shared values and assumptions, and other pressures from family, peer group and school; their decision-making may sometimes be confused, and at other times their behaviour may be the result of non-decisions, taken by default. It is also true that some young people make decisions which they (or others) later judge to be "wrong". Nevertheless the conclusion that flows, overwhelmingly, from the discussion in this book is that young people are not passive and unreasoning puppets, manipulated by convention or coercion. However muddled the processes which lead to their decisions may sometimes appear to be, the resulting behaviours do tend to observe and to follow the logic of their situation; and we must understand this situation if we are to understand the present or future behaviour of young people in an education system.

It is this situation and this logic that we refer to as "context". To a large extent it is constituted by the structure of selection and differentiation within the education system and by its relation to differentiation within the labour market and within society as a whole. Young people's educational decisions tend to be forward-looking; they are influenced not only by the more immediate, intrinsic considerations (such as liking the subject or the teacher), but also by considerations of longer-term advantage. Their decisions therefore reflect judgements about the routes through the maze of educational and occupational selection which are most likely to lead young people to their eventual goals. These goals are often directly or indirectly vocational. Frequently in this book we have seen how at successive decision points young people are influenced by considerations to do with jobs and employment. Even when they choose between alternatives within education, such as third-year options or different kinds of post-compulsory education, they often choose on the basis of occupational criteria. These criteria may be specific, relating to particular occupational aspirations, or general, relating to the desire for a "good" or well paid (or sometimes for any) job. This is not to deny that young people are also influenced by those hierarchies of esteem that are largely internal to the education system; but the disinterested scholar, motivated solely by a love of learning, is a rare figure in Scottish education.

We would argue that young people's decisions are influenced less by the *content* of the available educational provision – its intrinsic educational quality or relevance – than by its *context* and in particular by the relation of provision to the structure of educational and occupational selection. However, as we have observed, current policy initiatives depend for their success upon their power to influence young people's decisions. These initiatives variously aim to improve motivation and behaviour during compulsory schooling, to increase overall participation within post-compulsory education, or to induce students – the "right" students – to enter particular types of courses. Their success depends upon the decisions of young people, which in turn are influenced by context. It follows that educational policies, even if they are primarily concerned with changing the content of education, must also take account of its context.

A recurring theme of this book is that many educational policies fail to achieve their objectives because, although they pay considerable attention to the content of educational provision, they take insufficient account of its context. This is not to say that problems arising from the context of educational provision are easily solved. Indeed the nature of these problems is such that a balance must always be struck between competing objectives; elsewhere these conflicts have been described in terms of the related problems of difficulty, selection and motivation (Gray *et al.*, 1983, pp.7-14; and chapter 8, above). Nor do we argue that policy-makers wholly ignore context; both the Munn/Dunning reforms and the Action Plan can be thought of as attempts to influence young people's decisions by re-shaping the context of their choices. However, as we suggest below, the view of context underlying these initiatives tends to be narrow in scope and inadequate for reconciling the conflicting purposes of policy and for overcoming powerful structural obstacles to change. Moreover, the process of development and the testing of initiatives encourages this bias towards content: it is standard practice to pilot the content of new courses, but it is almost impossible to pilot their context. The backgrounds and interests of educational innovators also predispose them to think in terms of content. The focus of teacher education is on the purpose and content of education, not on the ways in which existing school systems provide differentiated pathways through the educational structure and into the labour market. Unlike pupils and parents, educationists have mistrusted instrumental views of education (Morton-Williams and Finch, 1968); they have particularly mistrusted vocational instrumentalism as this is seen to threaten their largely child-centred view of education. Unfortunately, the tenable opinion that context *should* not be important often leads to a false judgement that context *is* not important and that it can be ignored.

The tendency of policy-makers to think in terms of "modal groups" (see chapter 1) illustrates a narrow view of context and neglects the extent to which pupils and students, sometimes guided by their teachers, act in the light of wider considerations of context. The O-grade was designed for 30 per cent of pupils; but more than twice as many eventually took it. The CSYS was expected to attract intending university entrants and others who had acquired the qualifications necessary to their plans by the end of fifth year; but large numbers of them either left school after fifth year or devoted their sixth year to improving their Highers record. Throughout this book – in the Munn and Dunning reforms, in the official interpretation of staying-on rates, and above all in the bewildering tangle of opportunities at 16-plus – we have seen examples of a close and often admirable attention to the details of content thwarted by inadequate or inappropriate attention to the context.

Fourteen to sixteen

Several factors determine the context of educational choices made before the age of 16. Schooling is compulsory; the range of options is therefore restricted, and no option offers any immediate pecuniary advantage to the student. Decision points are related almost entirely to stage, rather than age. Although stage and age may be out of step for many pupils, this has little bearing on the nature or the outcomes of the choices at 14. Decisions made at 14, however, are influenced by their anticipated consequences for selection at 16 or later; the earlier decisions are therefore influenced by the logic of anticipated future ones. When selectors (especially employers) choose among students who have taken different options within a hierarchically differentiated curriculum, they tend to select those who have taken the options with the highest status in the hierarchy, rather than those who have taken the options whose content they judge most suitable. Employers tend to ask not "how relevant is the curriculum that this student has just mastered?" but "how good was this student in order to enter this course?" (For evidence of this see CPRS, 1980, pp.4-5 and Gray *et al.*, 1983, chapter 7.) This means that selection decisions at one stage in a young person's career (*eg* at 16) may be based directly or indirectly on selection decisions at an earlier stage (at 14); the earlier decisions must anticipate this effect. We call this anticipatory self-selection.

In the last two years of compulsory schooling a number of pupils plan their courses on the assumption that they will stay on for a fifth year; others assume they will leave at 16 and may therefore view choices in a shorter-term vocational perspective. Despite this, up to the age of 16 the hierarchy of educational differentiation tends to be unambiguous and unique. By and large the kinds of choices and attainments which are optimal do not depend on the ambitions of the pupil. In concrete terms this means that good attainment in public examinations at 16, and a diet of the more academic subjects, is of probable future benefit whether a pupil wishes to continue with full-time education after 16 or whether he or she wishes to leave at 16 and look for a job. This means, for example, that there is little in the context of education as it is presently organised to force a choice between academic and vocational streams at 14; on extrinsic grounds, most pupils would be advised to remain in the academic one if they can.

The fact that education up to the age of 16 is characterised by a unique hierarchy of attainment and advantage is critical for the future of the Munn and Dunning reforms. The strategy is based upon the promise of "prizes for everyone". The logic of this strategy is only viable if there are many different competitions and if each pupil is capable of success in at least one of them. Such an approach is consistent with the notion advanced by a number of commentators that comprehensive education should attempt to develop, and reward, competence in a much wider range of fields than the cognitive or academic skills that it currently esteems (Gatherer, 1980; Ryrie, 1981; Hargreaves, 1982). However, for this approach to work, each area of competition must be perceived as both valid and worthwhile; but this is unlikely. For the present context of 14-16 education indicates that one type of competition, one dimension of attainment, is of overwhelming importance on the criteria that count with most pupils; and the Munn and Dunning plans do not attempt to eliminate this aspect of context. They seek, instead, to extend it and systematise it by relating the difficulty of courses more closely to ability. Two considerations help to explain the limitations of the Munn and Dunning proposals. First, as we have noted above, the structural logic of educational context means that policy-makers cannot fully realise all policy objectives simultaneously, but must find a compromise among them. Second, the terms of reference of the two reports restricted them to reforming only those aspects of context that were internal to the third and fourth years of secondary schooling. Patterns of subsequent selection, in post-compulsory education and in the labour market, were outside this remit.

To the extent that the problems which Munn and Dunning sought to redress were created by the context of education rather than by its content we therefore see little reason to expect the new reforms to solve them. For example, we anticipate strong pressures from pupils and parents for over-presentation at Credit level, just as there were strong pressures for over-presentation at O-grade. We anticipate similar pressures at the borderline between Foundation and General. This trend is likely to be accentuated by the evidence that D or E awards at O-grade, though widely regarded as "fail" grades, nevertheless significantly influence employment chances: a finding which almost certainly means that O-grade presentations and not only results can be important. In the post-Dunning situation this suggests that merely attempting a Credit (rather than a General) or a General (rather than a Foundation) will have occupational value: more encouragement to over-presentation. Further encouragement will be provided by the knowledge that after starting courses in many subjects it may be possible to transfer downwards but only exceptionally to move up to a higher level of course.

In similar vein we doubt if the mere extension of certification to include pupils on the new Foundation courses can totally remove their low motivation and feelings of exclusion from the moral community of the school. Such pupils will be well aware that their prizes are of little more than nominal value, the wooden spoons of the Scottish educational race. Yet our scepticism is itself qualified. The introduction of Foundation awards will at least give pupils something to work for; a Foundation certificate will presumably be better than no certificate. Equally important, the performance of schools will now be publicly certifiable at all ability levels; the extension of certification might reduce the pressure on schools to concentrate limited resources on the abler (and formerly certificate) pupils at the expense of the others. This of course depends on whether the three Dunning levels are perceived as of equal importance within the educational community and among pupils and parents.

We also doubt whether the Munn and Dunning reforms can abolish the status hierarchy of subjects, not least because this hierarchy is deeply embedded in the context of 14-16 education as a result both of subsequent occupational and educational selection and of the values and organisation of the secondary schools themselves. Indeed the persistence of this hierarchy is evident in the more recent Munn and Dunning proposals discussed earlier in this book. Some critics have alleged that "(t)he proposed curriculum is no more than a crude device for differentiating pupils on the single dimension of ability in the 'cognitive intellectual' subjects" (Drever et al., 1983, p.4). This drift in the policy process – the subversion of Munn by Dunning – is evidence less of an ideologically based conspiracy than of coming to terms with a context of selection based on such a hierarchy.

More generally, throughout the Munn and Dunning debate one can detect a conflict between the anti-hierarchical tradition which seeks to develop the "whole child", and the more practically oriented approach which tends to accept the hierarchical assumptions that it finds embedded in present practice but seeks to make their application more efficient and fair. Every major change in the organisation of secondary schooling could be related to these two perspectives. Thus, on the one hand, moves to lengthen the period of compulsory schooling, a campaign which has had a wide consensus of support throughout this century, could be seen as an attempt to extend the time spent in the protected environment of the school in which children could be free to develop their general education unfettered by the demands of the labour market. From the more pragmatic and achievement-oriented perspective, on the other hand, it could be said that one of the most important features of the latest stage of that long campaign, the RSLA decision of 1972, was that it guaranteed for (almost) all pupils the opportunity to compete for public accreditation within the period of compulsory schooling. Aspects of the Munn/Dunning programme which most clearly reflect the anti-hierarchical tradition – for example the attempt to broaden the curriculum of all pupils and to introduce more flexible school-based assessment into all examination courses – were under threat from the outset. As the Munn and Dunning proposals have made the transition from general philosophy to specific practical proposals, it is the hierarchical view, reinforced by the context of education, which has gained the upper hand.

Sixteen to eighteen

After the age of 16, the context for educational choices changes in at least six important ways. First, schooling is no longer compulsory; young people can leave school, occasionally to enter full-time further education or more often to try their luck in the labour market. We have argued that for educational policies to be successful they must induce pupils to make appropriate choices; and that before the age of 16 one of the "choices" that matters most is whether or not to comply with the demands of the school. (For many pupils the problem is perceived as a *lack* of choice, but this does not affect the logic of our argument.) After 16, however, motivation is a less critical problem, and the central concern of policy becomes how to attract the "right" young people to enter the "right" courses in the first place. In practice, policy is often devoted to attracting any young people to enter any courses, in other words, to maintain a high rate of participation in education or vocational preparation. A key and variable aspect of context is the state of the labour market. The relative attractiveness of full-time education after 16 depends in part on the probability that a young school leaver will find a job.

Second, the decision to leave or stay on at school is made in relation both to stage and to age. Only one half of all pupils have their first opportunity to leave school at the end of fourth year, the "modal" end of compulsory secondary schooling. Nearly a half of all pupils faces this decision not at the end of a stage of education, but part-way through it (usually in December). Staying on for a further five or so months would enable many of them to complete their current courses and gain further qualifications. The relative costs and benefits of staying on beyond 16 are much more favourable for these pupils than for those who would need to stay on for a full year in order to complete a course; consequently their staying-on rates are significantly higher. The importance of this particular structural effect has been almost totally overlooked in recent discussions about the decision at 16. As a result some misleading conclusions have been drawn from the observed patterns. For example, the fact that relatively high proportions of Scottish pupils stay on beyond 16 (compared with England) is often cited as evidence that pupils approve of the Scottish fifth year and the provision of an exit point at 17. Yet when we looked at those for whom the decision to stay on beyond 16 actually coincided with entry to fifth year we found a much lower staying-on rate, a third of girls and only a quarter of boys, and one comparable to that south of the border.

The third way in which the context of educational choice at 16-plus differs from that in earlier years also involves greater complexity. Up to 16 the hierarchy of curriculum and attainment is unique; after 16 there is a tendency for students' optimal paths to diverge according to whether they have the desire and the ability to enter higher education, or whether they wish to enter the labour market at an earlier stage. For males, at least, 16 is the point of divergence, largely as a result of age restrictions in the labour market. If a male stays on at school he keeps open his chances of higher education; but if he then fails to secure the necessary qualifications, or changes his plans, staying on may have harmed his occupational chances. For many students there seem to be two favoured tracks through education: one which ends at 16, and one which carries on through higher education and ends at 21 or 22. A student who aspires to the latter track but fails to last the course may fall between two stools and suffer disadvantage. This divergence appears to affect males more than females; it is possible that for girls the same effect occurs *via* the differentiation of optimal curricular tracks, rather than different ages of entry to the labour market, but we have not tested this possibility. Moreover, our analysis has not covered the occupational chances of the small but growing proportion of school leavers who enter full-time further education at 16. It is possible that they are following an intermediate route of occupational value equal to either of the other favoured tracks. The divergence of optimal tracks, to the extent that it exists, does not mean that anticipatory self-selection ceases to occur after 16, but it affects the way that it operates. For there are status hierarchies within each of the tracks; and once a student has joined one or another of the tracks there are still pressures to take the highest-status courses, since future selectors will tend to choose students from these courses even if they are not the highest-quality or most relevant courses in terms of content.

The fourth distinctive feature of the context of educational choice at 16-plus is that students make decisions, having been differentiated formally and publicly through the O-grade examination at 16. Their choices can be informed by more concrete information about their own attainments than was previously available.

Fifth, there are immediate monetary advantages to some of the options. Typically this makes remaining at school the least attractive option, and entering employment the most attractive.

Finally, some of the options give young people privileged access to sources of future rewards. This was the case with young people on YOP schemes whose sponsors recruited directly from their YOP trainees. There is nothing new about this type of contextual influence; it is seen whenever people choose schools or colleges on the basis of the employment advantages which the old-school tie and the old-boy network can convey.

These aspects of context provide the framework within which policy for the 16-18 age group must operate, although policy has occasionally attempted to change the context of young people's decisions and at other times it has inadvertently done so. There are currently three main policy initiatives affecting the 16-18s – or, rather, two initatives and a third area in which some kind of explicit or implicit policy change is expected. The two initiatives already declared are the Manpower Services Commission's (MSC) Youth Training Scheme and the SED's Action Plan for 16-18s. The area where an initiative is anticipated is the sixth year; since the structures of fifth and sixth years are interdependent, this means that the future shape of all post-compulsory schooling, especially for the intending higher-education entrant, is in question. Through oblique hints rather than by a direct challenge, the Inspectorate has even thrown into question the future position of the "holy of holies" of Scottish education, the Higher-grade certificate.

The very fact that we can identify three policy initiatives is significant. Critics on both sides of the border have lamented the absence of a unified policy for the 16-18 age group (Maclure, 1982; Gatherer, 1982). The separate existence of YTS – part of the MSC's New Training Initiative – and the Action Plan reflects both departmental and national rivalries. Although the Action Plan was presented as complementary to YTS it was also an attempt by the SED to retain its influence over the areas of education and training invaded by the MSC and to impose its own definition of the form that new provision should take. The separate development of policy for "academic" provision in post-compulsory schooling is a direct reflection of context: through their role as selectors the universities have considerable influence over this area of schooling and they seem likely to resist attempts to integrate it with the rest of 16-18 provision.

The CSYS provides a classic illustration of the dominance of context over content. Our evidence shows considerable approval among young people of the content of the sixth year; the problem lies in the context, which impels a majority of sixth-year students to take Highers to make certain of their qualifications for entrance to higher education. To make the CSYS a more popular option requires an improvement in context rather than in content. This too involves difficult choices for policy-makers. One possible solution would be to give formal qualifying status to CSYS; but this would disrupt patterns of entry to higher education, especially in the west, and might thereby reduce opportunity. It might also damage the value of the CSYS itself if pedagogical reforms were swamped by the rush for better grades. Another proposed solution would base selection for higher education solely on fifth-year attainment, leaving the sixth year free for CSYS. However, *taking* CSYS courses might still need to be made a requirement for entry if many students were not to by-pass the sixth year entirely. Perhaps more seriously, such a change would go against the spirit of the Action Plan, which aims to increase second (and third and fourth) chances for educational mobility.

The essential problem facing CSYS is thus one not of content but of context and, in particular, of its role in relation to educational selection. The same is true for all policy issues affecting the 16-18 age group; the central issue is the same, concerning as it does the timing and the liberality of selection to high-status tracks. The problem is how to defer final selection for as long as possible without allowing the high-status tracks to dominate the content of provision for nearly all students?

On paper the MSC's Youth Training Scheme and the SED's Action Plan have similar objectives. Both aim to increase participation rates among the 16-plus age group and to develop vocational preparaion of a more general (rather than occupationally specific) nature. A higher participation rate is assumed to benefit both individual and society; the argument is supported by comparisons with European countries, with the implication that their higher participation rates contribute to their superior economic performance (MSC, 1981a). In practice a more immediate reason for seeking high participation is youth unemployment; this has left a gap in the career patterns of many young people which education is asked to fill. It would be hard otherwise to justify the policy emphasis on the age group which has just completed 11 years of compulsory education and which is arguably in least need of immediate additional provision. There is moreover a powerful (but misplaced) tendency to regard the participation rate as a vote of confidence in the system, and therefore to want to raise it; nor is it surprising that people whose professional identities are as educators or trainers should seek educational or training solutions to current problems.

The overall participation rate is an unsatisfactory target of policy, since the nature, quality and purpose of provision vary widely. A second objective of policy has been to change the quality and the nature of provision. Formally, both the MSC and the SED appear to be pursuing similar goals. The MSC policy assumes that occupational demands, the uncertainty of any individual's employment destination, and the need to satisfy young people's own expectations and aspirations, call for a form of vocational preparation that can "meet the needs of a variety of industries, firms and occupations" and also benefit the young people as well as the economy (MSC, 1982a, para. 2.5). The SED similarly proposes "a more general approach, less specifically occupation-oriented and including both training and education" for "the majority of the 16-18 age group" (SED, 1983b, para. 3.11). However, there are differences in practice. Although the content of YTS varies widely, the balance is geared towards training rather than education. Many YTS trainees receive no college education, and managing agents have substantial discretion over the content of courses. Work experience is the main feature of most schemes, filling three quarters of the time. The Action Plan, by contrast, defines the principle of a broadly based vocational preparation in terms of an educational input rather than merely general training. It argues that industry should have less influence in such provision since industry defines its needs in vocationally specific rather than general terms. Through the Action Plan the SED is reasserting its influence in an area which MSC is threatening to take over, and between the lines of the document one finds arguments from the old education/training debate and the conflicts of philosophy and interest that this has embraced.

So the practical expression of policy objectives is obscured by the latent conflict between the SED and the MSC; it is further obscured by other conflicts of interest, between the different bodies involved in YTS, between schools and colleges, and between different subject groupings. In practice therefore, the uptake, content and quality of post-16 provision have been left in large part to a kind of free market, in which students' choices are assumed to be governed by considerations of both educational and occupational value. YTS and the Action Plan, as well as the more dispersed efforts of individual schools and colleges, can be seen as the products of struggles for competitive advantage within this market framework.

However, our analysis of context suggests that the market is distorted, in the sense that students' choices tend not to be optimal in either educational or occupational terms. Students' choices are influenced instead by considerations of the status of courses (through what we have termed anticipatory self-selection), by anticipated age restrictions, by relative monetary advantages and by other factors which determine the extrinsic attractions of different options.

The future success of YTS depends on its ability to attract young people and to motivate them to learn; in particular it must attract some of the better qualified and more employable youngsters, and not be seen as a dumping ground for labour-market failures. It must therefore be seen as something different from YOP, as a positive source of learning and employment opportunities. However, from the evidence of chapter 10 it is clear that young people's attitudes to YTS will not be transformed by the improved education or training that it manages to offer. Instead, these attitudes will depend primarily on its ability to offer them the prospect of a good job.

It follows that the success of YTS depends less on its content than on its context, that is, on its position in future patterns of occupational selection. Here the future is hard to predict. While YTS is likely to have a significant effect on the context of labour-market selection, this effect was not deliberately designed as such but is a by-product of attempts to achieve a relatively cost-effective structure for the provision of training. In other words, the context of YTS is a largely unanticipated consequence of efforts to realise its content. The future context of YTS, and its ability to offer good employment prospects to young people, depends on the extent to which it monopolises apprenticeships and other career routes for young people, which in turn depends on trade union policy and on the financial advantages and disadvantages perceived by employers. It also depends on the relative preferences of employers for YTS graduates and for 17 and 18 year olds leaving school or college. YTS may displace some of the jobs currently available for older teenagers; on the other hand, if YTS only recruits less qualified school leavers in the first place its graduates may be stigmatised by potential future employers. The context of YTS also depends, crucially, on the extent to which segregation between the adult and youth labour markets increases; otherwise many young people will by-pass the scheme and enter jobs also available to adults.

To illustrate these points we can imagine two possible models for the development of YTS. In the first "high-status" model YTS becomes the most sought-after option for 16 year olds who do not aspire to higher education and is preferred to continued schooling or full-time non-advanced further education. It monopolises the most attractive routes to employment, and even if trainees are not recruited by their YTS employers they still have better chances of subsequent employment than young people who have not been on the scheme. The allowance and other conditions of YTS traineeships are adequate to discourage better qualified school leavers from seeking work elsewhere. Young people are optimistic about the scheme; it is not regarded as a second choice for those who cannot find employment. Most young people remain on the scheme for the full year.

The second model is rather different. A small minority of YTS places lead automatically, with no further selection, to permanent jobs. Apart from these, the most desirable opportunities for young people remain outside the scheme, including many apprenticeships and traineeships and a wide range of jobs which are not age-specific. The employment chances of YTS graduates are poor in both absolute and relative terms. School leavers who can find jobs prefer to accept the relative security of employment to the uncertain prospects following a YTS traineeship; 16 year olds who cannot find jobs tend to stay on at school or enter a full-time FE course. The real value of the allowance continues to decline; the schemes are widely regarded as exploitative. The scheme attracts only those less qualified and less employable school leavers who cannot find jobs elsewhere (except for the small elite of trainees who are guaranteed permanent jobs in advance). YTS trainees leave the scheme as soon as they can find a real job. The process is self-reinforcing; because YTS only attracts the less qualified school leavers, employers consider its graduates inferior to older school leavers, to students from more traditional FE courses, or to youngsters with a record of real employment. Anticipatory self-selection further discourages entrants. The long-term future of YTS is in doubt; since it is effectively only a scheme for the unemployed, the scheme will collapse if future unemployment levels fall. Moreover, the main curricular innovation of YTS – the development of a more broadly based form of vocational preparation – will have failed, for the more traditional forms of academic education and vocationally-specific training will continue to attract young people, especially the better qualified.

The conditions have not yet been fully met for either of these models; we do not attempt to predict the future here. Our point is rather to show that despite the important implications for the future *content* of vocational preparation, whether the development of YTS follows one model or the other depends very largely on its *context*. When 16 year olds choose among school, further education and YTS, and among the different opportunities within each, their choice will depend on very much more than the quality or intrinsic relevance of the education and training on offer.

The Action Plan is an attempt to deal with some of these problems by providing a co-ordinated modular structure of courses which permit greater flexibility. It makes it easier for young people to "move sideways", and change their specific area of study, since many general modules will serve as a common base, capable of linking with different specialist ones. The Action Plan also offers students a variety of more or less distant targets depending on how long, and how many modules, they wish to study.

There is no doubt that the Action Plan offers a significant step forward in educational terms, a way to increase the options available to individuals and to maintain the coherence of disparate educational and training initiatives. Perhaps the most promising feature of the Action Plan is that it facilitates the mixing of different kinds of learning, namely academic education and specific and general vocational preparation. If such mixing becomes widespread the status boundaries between these three types of post-compulsory provision will be eroded, and the emergence of a new tripartite structure of post-compulsory schooling will be prevented. However, the effectiveness of the Action Plan may be limited if it is unable to reform key features in the context. In the first place it fails to remove the divergence of tracks at 16 – indeed under present plans it may accentuate this by placing all post-16 provision under either the SEB (academic) or the new SCOTVEC (vocational). The power of the universities over the Highers examination, and their distaste for many of the innovations proposed by the Action Plan, makes it unlikely that this divergence can easily be resolved. An important but uncertain consideration here is the future role of the Dunning certificate in fifth (and indeed sixth) year. The role of the O-grade in post-compulsory schooling has been noted in chapters 7 and 8. If a Credit-level award becomes formally or effectively a prerequisite for attempting a Higher, then schools will face an awkward dilemma. If fifth-year students are not permitted to re-sit Credit-level examinations or to convert their General-level certificates to Credits, then the differentiation of pupils at 14 will be irreversible since it will determine which pupils can follow the academic track through to higher education. If, on the other hand, Dunning courses are available after fourth year, then four different qualifications will compete for the post-compulsory curriculum; the rationalisation implied by the Action Plan will be dissipated and the relative roles of Dunning courses and vocational modules will remain to be determined.

Even if the spirit of the Action Plan is fully implemented – if the modular structure embraces all post-16 courses, and no educational routes are finally closed to students on the basis of their earlier attainment, although some students may need to travel further than others – then the key structural problem, outlined above, will be faced more acutely than ever. If ultimate selection to high-status tracks is genuinely deferred, how will it be possible to avoid the kind of curricular drift that has been observed in relation to 14-16 schooling: the displacement of vocational education by the higher-status "academic" curriculum, and (in post-16 courses) the displacement of general vocational preparation by specific occupational training? The answer possibly lies in informed self-selection by students, perhaps in awareness of the divergence of favoured tracks at 16 that we outlined above; but it will also depend on whether the flexibility implied by the modular structure works in practice. Here the danger is that selectors, whether in further or higher education or employment, will be confused by the new modular certification system, and will try to read between the lines for evidence of attainment in the traditional terms with which they are familiar. This might, for example, lead them to place even more emphasis on the higher-status "academic" subjects, or on the more traditional vocational skills. In other words, if certificates lose their credibility as indicators of the "level" of a student's attainment, then selectors will place more emphasis on curricular differences as judged on traditional criteria. This would probably have an effect directly opposed to the intentions of the reformers.

The more general problem is that the Action Plan only attempts to reform patterns of selection and differentiation that are internal to schools and further education. In other words, it does not remove all the distorting influences on choices that we listed above. It may reform the patterns of selection within 16-18 education but it does not confront the more serious constraints imposed by patterns of selection to jobs or higher education. Indeed there is a danger that it might make matters worse if employers distrust, or are confused by, the modular certificates.

Our general argument is not that current efforts for reform are misdirected, or misplaced, but that they are in danger of being dissipated if no more rational system can be found for framing the choices of students. Current policy depends on the willingness of 16 year olds to make choices that are appropriate on both educational and occupational criteria. Yet our evidence suggests that there are too many other considerations that influence their decisions. Whether young people are choosing among school, college or YTS, or whether they are selecting from the different options that exist within each of these, there is no certainty that they will choose either the option that is most suited to their educational needs or the option that will best meet general social and economic requirements.

Appendix 1

The 1981 Scottish School Leavers Survey

Peter Burnhill

Introduction

For most analyses in this book the data have been drawn from the 1981 Scottish School Leavers Survey (SSLS). This was a sample survey of young people who left school in Scotland during the academic year 1979/80. It was conducted jointly by the Centre for Educational Sociology (CES) and the Scottish Education Department (SED), and forms part of a series of biennial surveys conducted by the CES and housed in machine-readable form in the Scottish Education Data Archive (SEDA).

The 1981 Scottish School Leavers Survey was a large-scale multi-purpose postal survey. The target sample corresponded to a 37 per cent nationally representative sample of 1979/80 school leavers in Scotland. Over 30,000 questionnaires were despatched by post to home addresses in April 1981, thus reaching respondents some nine or more months after their school-leaving dates. The survey data analysed in the chapters of *Fourteen to Eighteen* come from a random sub-sample of the 1981 SSLS data, equivalent in size to a nominal sampling fraction of about nine per cent. The achieved sample size of that sub-sample was 5550. (Details of response and coverage rates are given below.)

The design of the survey

Survey unit and target population. The principal units for the survey were the young people who left school during or at the end of the 1979/80 school session. The survey's target population was defined as all such leavers from Scottish schools not denoted as "special schools". (The 1640 leavers from special schools in Scotland were excluded from the target population.) In the analyses for *Fourteen to Eighteen* this target population was further restricted to the 86295 leavers from education authority schools (thus excluding 3882 leavers who left from the small number of independent and grant-aided schools).

231

Sample design. The survey data were collected in order that they might be analysed by teachers, administrators and others whose statistical sophistication might be limited, as well as for analysis by more experienced researchers. A high premium had therefore been placed upon the ease with which analyses could be performed. A "self-weighting" design was therefore employed.

A uniform sampling fraction was applied within each school: pupils from each school were selected in numbers proportionate to the number of leavers per school. The design was a *double-phase, proportionately stratified, systematically selected, replicated, (element) sampling scheme* in which each leaver had an equal probability of selection. (A justification for each feature of the design is not given here but is available in Burnhill, Lamb and Weston, 1982).

Sampling frame. There was no national list of school leavers which could be used for sampling purposes. Instead the Statistics Division of the SED had to compile one. It sent forms to all schools in Scotland in November 1979 and requested that information on name, address, date of birth and some summary detail on exam presentation and qualification level be supplied for pupils eligible to leave school from the session 1979/80 (*ie* born on or before 30 September 1964). The forms were designed in such a way that they could be completed by the pupils themselves and, in order to reduce workload, participation was limited to pupils whose date of birth was an odd number. This birth date sampling was carried out in each of 475 secondary schools in Scotland. Later, in October 1980, that is after the end of the 1979/80 session, the collected names of those eligible to leave were checked against the SED's qualified school leaver (QSL) returns in order to ascertain who had left school. (This could of course only be done for the pupils who had sat Scottish Certificate of Education (SCE) or General Certificate of Education (GCE) examinations: those who had not were presumed to have left, and corrections were made on the return of questionnaires at a later stage.)

Sampling. The second phase of the survey was conducted by the CES and involved the selection of sub-samples from the effective sampling frame, which had been compiled by the SED.

In the collection of names and addresses, useful items of background information were obtained which were known to be correlates of many of the survey variables. These were used in a proportionate stratification scheme of sample selection. The sample was stratified by sex, ten geographic areas and four levels of examination presentation. With 475 schools, explicit stratification by school was not feasible but some implicit stratification was achieved by sampling systematically within strata from a list of elements ordered by school. The effect of this stratification was to make the sample data more representative of the population (by reducing the sampling error) than would have been the case under simple random sampling. The gain over simple random sampling may be measured by the design effect, the ratio of the achieved sampling variance to the sampling variance under simple random sampling. For the sample data used in *Fourteen to Eighteen* the design effect was just under 0.6, meaning that the sample provided estimates which were as precise as those that would have been obtained from a simple random sample of five-thirds the size. (Strictly speaking the "effective" sample size was a little less than this, at 9000, because of the finite population correction factor.)

The sampling fraction decided upon was 37 per cent. This 37 per cent was spread evenly over 32 replicates. Each replicate was therefore equivalent to a separate sub-sample with a sampling fraction of approximately 1.15 per cent. The data used for the *Fourteen to Eighteen* analyses come from eight replicates and therefore correspond to a pooled sample with a nominal sampling fraction of nine per cent. (As reported below the achieved sample fell short of the target sample but the increase in sampling error from the non-response was more than compensated for by the design effect from the stratified sample design.)

Questionnaire design and content

The questions asked in the 1981 SSLS were broadly similar to those asked in previous CES surveys. The range of topics covered included the examined and non-examined school curriculum followed during the later years of secondary schooling; parts of the "hidden curriculum"; the process of leaving school; a record of post-school destination; and questions on family background. In order to improve both the level and quality of response, questionnaires of differing lengths and complexity were sent to leavers having different levels of school attainment.

There were four questionnaire levels in the 1981 survey, labelled A, B, C and D:

A 6 pages:	for leavers who in November 1979 had not intended to sit for SCE O-grade at school
B 7 pages:	for leavers who in November 1979 had intended to sit for SCE O-grade at school but who did not do so
C 11 pages:	for leavers who sat for SCE O-grade at school but who in November 1979 had not intended to sit Highers before leaving
D 15 pages:	for leavers who in November 1979 had already sat or intended to sit Highers at school

(For this purpose O-levels were equated with O-grades, and A-levels with Highers.)

Differences between levels A and B were limited to one page: the inclusion of this extra page in B ensured that leavers in this group were asked the same questions about curriculum and examinations in third and fourth year as those in groups C and D. (Group B constituted about ten per cent of the sample.) The additional information on the third- and fourth-year curriculum for this group strengthened the potential of the data to describe aspects of selection among 14 and 15 year olds in the age group as a whole.

At each level, core questions (for example, on examinations or family background) were asked of all leavers, and specific questions asked of random sub-samples who received different versions of the questionnaire. The same formal structure was applied to all levels. Across the whole of the 1981 survey there were eight versions, each version containing a mixture of core and version-specific questions. Across the eight replicates from the sub-sample analysed in *Fourteen to Eighteen* there were two versions, labelled versions 3 and 4.

Copies of the questionnaires are not included here but the interested reader is referred to Burnhill, Lamb and Weston (forthcoming).

Response and non-response to the survey

Non-response in the first phase. Efforts were made throughout the survey to identify and to remedy losses from the sample. Inevitably some non-response occurred. During the first phase of the sample design, the construction of the effective sampling frame, several forms of non-response were experienced.

> (i)   *School short-fall.* Initially three schools in the SED sample of secondary schools did not comply with the request for information on pupils eligible to leave school. This was remedied by direct contact between the CES and the school prior to the despatch of the survey.

> (ii)   *Pupil short-fall.* Some eligible pupils did not complete, or have completed for them, the SED form. It proved possible to remedy this short-fall for those pupils who attempted SCE or GCE; but it was not possible to identify the non-certificate leavers on whom we had no information.

> (iii)   *Non-co-operation.* On the SED form pupils were given the opportunity to opt out of the next phase of the

survey; those who opted out were not sent questionnaires in April 1981. This resulted in an average loss of 12 per cent across all pupils and ranged from about eight per cent among those intending to present for Highers (level D, above) to about 19 per cent among the non-certificate (level A, above). There was of course no remedy for this particular form of non-response.

The effective sampling frame was therefore incomplete in such a way that the sample was biased, against the inclusion of non-certificate leavers for example, even before the survey was conducted. An indication of the adjustments made in analyses for this bias is given below. A discussion of the social and statistical implications of such sampling-frame bias is given in Burnhill and McPherson (1983b).

Non-response in the second phase. Once the sub-samples had been drawn and the questionnaires despatched, different forms of non-response arose.

(i)   *Non-delivery (non-contact).* Some four to five per cent of the despatched questionnaires were returned as "undelivered". The proportion of non-contact varied with achievement level, initially reaching eight per cent among the non-certificate group. With the assistance of the members of the careers service, new addresses were obtained for over half of those whose questionnaires were undelivered. In all the attrition through non-contact was not serious.

(ii)   *Non-return.* About nine in ten (89.6 per cent) of the questionnaires presumed to have been delivered were returned. About 60 per cent were returned within two weeks. For the rest, a reminder procedure had to be invoked, involving (where necessary) two postcards and a second copy of the questionnaire. (Records were kept of the effect of each reminder on the rate of return.)

In summary, and for the survey as a whole, it is estimated that 96 per cent of the nominal target population were on the sampling frame, of whom 88 per cent agreed to co-operate in the survey; 84 per cent of the nominal target sample were therefore sent a questionnaire. The rate of contact was high (fewer than five per cent were eventually "undelivered"), as was the response rate to the questionnaire (at almost 90 per cent). The achieved sample therefore succeeded in covering about 72 per cent of the nominal target sample. As has been suggested above, rates of coverage differed across the four levels of school attainment for which different types of questionnaires (A,B,C,D) were designed, being lower among leavers with no qualifications (A, 56 per cent; B, 62 per cent) than among qualified leavers (C and D, 79 per cent). This lower coverage was only partly a result of difficulties which may have been experienced by non-certificate school leavers in completing their (short) questionnaire. The rate of response to the level A questionnaire was in fact 82 per cent.

Non-response occurs in nearly every survey and the response rates given here would generally be regarded as high, especially for postal surveys. By being rigorous in our investigation and reporting of sampling-frame deficiencies and therefore of overall coverage rates we have perhaps been more self-critical than many others would have been. A countervailing advantage of this, and of our having conducted nationally representative surveys, is the facility of being able to compare the distribution of the achieved sample with that pertaining in the population as a whole. By making comparison with population figures supplied by the SED on the distribution of the 1979/80 leavers by sex, highest qualification obtained on leaving and type of school (education authority maintained, grant-aided and independent), it is possible to reweight the achieved sample data. For the *Fourteen to Eighteen* analyses there were 28 weighting classes defined by sex and 14 levels of school qualification, the latter ranging from no qualifications, through the number of O-grades obtained, to the possession of six or more SCE Highers. The weighting procedure had the effect of giving greater weight in the analyses to the data obtained from, say, non-certificate boys (who would otherwise be under-represented in the data) and less to Highers girls (who would be over-represented), and of reducing the bias arising from the association of non-response with sex and school qualification. Unless otherwise stated the statistics reported in *Fourteen to Eighteen* have been produced through the reweighting procedure. The sample sizes reported are taken from the actual, or "unweighted", count in the sample.

Appendix 2

Glossary

Action Plan: document published by the SED in January 1983 proposing an integrated modular structure for all non-SCE courses for the 16-18 age group.

Brunton Report: SED report *From School to Further Education*, published in 1963, which proposed that courses for non-SCE pupils be designed around the "vocational impulse".

CCC (Consultative Committee on the Curriculum): permanent body responsible for reviewing the school curriculum in Scotland.

Christmas leavers: pupils with birthdates from October to February (inclusive), who first beome eligible to leave school at the end of the Christmas term.

CI (Central Institution): one of 14 colleges administered by central government offering mainly advanced and degree-level vocational courses.

Credit: see Dunning Report.

CSE (Certificate of Secondary Education): English examination designed for pupils between the 40th and 80th percentiles of the ability range. Never formally adopted by central government in Scotland, but taken up by some local authorities and individual schools in the late 1970s, using English examination boards.

CSYS (Certificate of Sixth Year Studies): qualification gained after a one-year course for sixth-year students. Introduced in 1968, especially to increase opportunities for independent study.

Dunning Report: SED report *Assessment for All*, published in 1977, proposed a system of assessment to cover all ability levels in S3 and S4, replacing O-grades with a new certificate to be attempted at Credit, General and Foundation levels.

237

Foundation: see Dunning Report.

General: see Dunning Report.

Highers: the Higher-grade certificate of the SCE, attempted by school pupils at 17 or 18.

MSC (Manpower Services Commission): British agency established in January 1974, responsible for running employment and training services on behalf of the government.

Mode A: the mode under which a majority of YTS places are provided. A managing agent, usually an employer, receives a lump sum from MSC for providing or sub-contracting all elements of the programme.

Mode B: the other YTS mode. Mode B1 is based mainly on community projects, training workshops or information technology centres; Mode B2 is mainly college-based.

Munn Report: SED/CCC report *The Structure of the Curriculum in the Third and Fourth Years of the Scottish Secondary School*, published in 1977, proposed a core-plus-options model.

O-grade: the Ordinary-grade certificate of the SCE, attempted by school pupils at 16 or later.

P1, P2,...P7: the first, second... seventh year of primary school.

Prelims (preliminary examinations): the trial or "mock" examination before O-grades or Highers. School-run, but to a common pattern and often common (commercially produced) papers.

RSLA: raising of the school-leaving age to 16 years in 1973.

S1, S2,...S6: the first, second... sixth year of secondary school.

SCE (Scottish Certificate of Education): see Highers, O-grade.

SCEEB (Scottish Certificate of Education Examination Board): body responsible for administering the SCE exam. Replaced by SEB in 1982.

SCOTBEC (Scottish Business Education Council): body responsible for administering business and commercial examinations mainly for further education students.

SCOTEC (Scottish Technical Education Council): body responsible for administering technical examinations, mainly for further education students.

SCOTVEC (Scottish Vocational Education Council): body to be formed from the merger of SCOTBEC and SCOTEC.

SCVS (Scottish Certificate of Vocational Studies): new post-16 certificate based on a vocationally oriented one-year course.

SEB (Scottish Examination Board): body which took over responsibility for SCE examinations from SCEEB in 1982.

SED (Scottish Education Department): department of central government responsible for all education in Scotland except universities.

UVP (Unified Vocational Preparation): schemes for providing unified education and training for young workers in jobs which normally offered no such provision (1976-1983).

WEEP (Work Experience on Employers' Premises): the largest component of YOP, providing young people with work experience (typically six months) with an ordinary employer. Fore-runner of Mode A YTS schemes.

YOP (Youth Opportunities Programme): MSC programme providing unemployed young people with schemes of work experience or work preparation (1978-1983).

YTS (Youth Training Scheme): MSC programme providing 16 year olds and unemployed 17 year olds with work experience and training. Replaced YOP and UVP in 1983.

Notes

Chapter 4

1   A small sample of pupils who had studied for the Certificate of Secondary Education (CSE) were asked about methods of study which were closely associated with the Mode 3 CSE approach. Just over half of them thought that their CSE course had helped them to find out things for themselves, and just under half considered the courses had helped them to work as members of a group or team.

Chapter 5

1   The term "voluntary schooling" is used with some misgivings. No connection with the system of Voluntary Schools is intended. And it is recognised that even during the period of "compulsory schooling", which characterises that provided for young people aged five to 16, truancy constitutes an act which may define those who attend school as volunteers. Clearly, the usage here is somewhat different.

2   Recently the uptake of full-time further education has greatly increased, but it still caters for less than ten per cent of 16 year olds. (This information, and that given in Figure 5.1a and 5.1b, was kindly supplied by Jack Arrundale of the Statistics Division, Scottish Education Department.)

3   The argument about the misfit between course provision and the statutory school-leaving age which will be advanced in this chapter also had relevance to earlier school organisation as is evidenced in a section of *Junior Secondary Education* (SED, 1955a, para.122) entitled "The Length of the Course".

4   An inquiry by the SED, based on reports from the headteachers of senior secondary schools in Scotland, revealed that of the 19,600 pupils who had embarked on the five-year senior-secondary course in 1949 only 6,600, or 33 per cent, had stayed on into the fifth year at school at the beginning of the session 1953/54 (SED, 1954). And in 1959 it was reported that of the 26,502 who had started five-year courses in public (meaning "maintained by public authorities") and grant-aided schools during 1953/54, 8,700 (again 33 per cent) had stayed on into fifth year and had been awarded the Scottish Leaving Certificate five years later in 1958 (SED, 1959). Of major relevance to the study of senior-secondary completion rates is *Sixteen Years On*, a report of a cohort born in 1936 (Maxwell, 1969).

5   The relevant SED Circulars are Circular 1058 (SED, 1980b) and Circular 956 (SED, 1976c), of which the latter contains details of school-leaving arrangements.

6   Interest in the three School-Leaving Age groups grew from discussions with David Raffe and Penelope Weston, and a debt is owed to them and to the members of a Scottish Education Data Archive (SEDA) course held in 1981 as part of the Centre for Educational Sociology's (CES) Collaborative Research Programme. A measure of their contribution may be had by consulting work by SEDA course members (1981) and Weston (1982b).

7   This differential with respect to sex in rates of participation in post-compulsory schooling may be seen as part of the greater tendency for young women to stay in the education system full-time. Young women are more likely to obtain at least one Higher, and among those who leave school without Highers, they are more likely to go on to full-time further education (Burnhill, 1983). A convergence in career intention has been noted among Highers-qualified young men and women leavers in a separate analysis of data from school-leaver surveys conducted by the CES (Burnhill and McPherson, 1983a). It is not clear what the implications of this convergence would be for the differential in staying-on rates. There is a growing literature of relevance on this topic including some which have made use of data from the Scottish School Leavers Surveys and which look at the process of selection in the third and fourth years (Bibby and Weston, 1980; Kelly, 1981). The implications of greater equality in subject selection are also unclear: a greater differential in staying-on rates perhaps?

8   For those who were not on certificate courses, there was hardly any advantage in staying on. There may now be particular disadvantage. For example, the current Department of Health and Social Security regulations (which were not in force in summer 1980) preclude summer leavers from claiming Supplementary Benefit until the following September. No such restriction is placed on the Christmas leavers.

9   These statistics were kindly supplied by Trevor Knight of the Statistics
    Division, Department of Education and Science. It might also be noted
    that during the school session 1979/80 in England and Wales 44.6 per
    cent of pupils at maintained schools left at the minimum school-leaving
    age. Thus in England and Wales 55.4 per cent stayed on for voluntary
    schooling, compared with 40.5 and 48.5 per cent for boys and girls in
    Scotland (the latter two figures being weighted averages of the
    percentages shown in bold type as part of Figure 5.2).
10 Of relevance here are the Statistical Bulletins published by the SED
    (SED, 1982b and 1982d). The assistance of David Braunholtz of the
    SED Statistics Division in providing the series of SED "voluntary"
    rates is gratefully acknowledged.
11 In Circular 956 (SED, 1976c) the date 31 May was deemed to be the
    summer school-leaving date with effect from 1977. There was a
    "transitional order" which prescribed 30 June as the leaving date for
    1976. It was estimated that 4,500 pupils, who had their sixteenth
    birthdays in late August and September and who had previously
    expected to remain at school until the following Christmas (1976),
    ceased to be of school age on 30 June 1976.

Chapter 6

1   The open-ended statements quoted here are edited extracts from a
    source book of written comments: see Hughes (1984). Interested
    readers may wish to subject the statements made here to a critical re-
    examination, and to test out their own (prior) hypotheses, through a
    more thorough content analysis of the material in that source book.
2   "Brew" is a slang term for the Social Security office. "Brew money"
    therefore describes the Supplementary Benefit paid to the young
    unemployed people.

Chapter 9

1   To facilitate comparison with Table 9.2, Table 9.1 is restricted to young
    people who were in the labour market both in October 1980 and in May
    1981.
2   For details of the process of absorption into employment or YOP see
    Main and Raffe (1983b).
3   No allowance is made for CSE qualifications in this analysis. CSE
    courses were only offered in schools in particular regions of Scotland,

and only in Lothian Region were they offered on a large scale by 1980 (see chapter 4). Moreover, pupils who took CSEs tended also to take O-grades in other subjects. Consequently the omission of CSEs is likely to have only a small effect on the outcome of the present analysis. The labour-market value of CSEs will be the subject of a future study.

4   It has not been possible, in this cross-sectional analysis, to distinguish the (lasting) effect of the age of entry to employment from the (temporary) effect of the respondent's age at the time when the criterion (employment/unemployment) was measured. Typically the analysis has compared the status of early leavers at around age 17 with the status of stayers-on at around age 18 or 19. It is conceivable, if very improbable, that unemployment among the early leavers rose by the time that they reached the ages of the stayers-on in this study.

5   This in turn suggests that the failure to control for all personal characteristics made little difference to the observed effect of O-grades in Table 9.3, although it is conceivable that the O-grade variables effectively "controlled for" the effects of personal characteristics in estimating the Highers effect. One should also note the possible effects of multicollinearity on the robustness of the estimates. However, one's confidence in the estimates is enhanced by their relative stability, both between October and May, and when using different methods of analysis (see addendum to chapter 9).

Chapter 10

1   Evidence for increased dissatisfaction with YOP is based on a comparison of open-ended comments in the 1979 and 1981 surveys, a comparison of responses to structured questions in a 1980 pilot survey and the 1981 survey, and on current press reports.

2   The table also shows that of those on YOP in October 47 per cent of males and 37 per cent of females were still on YOP in May. However, more than half of these were already on their second YOP scheme in May. They had already left their first YOP scheme, and it would therefore be wrong to infer from the table that about half the males who had left a YOP scheme between October and May, and about two thirds of the females, were employed in May. As Figure 10.1 showed, these estimates would be too optimistic.

3   See Main and Raffe (1983a), especially pp.2-3, for further discussion.

4   The chances of being kept on by the sponsor were also less strongly associated with the local unemployment rate than were the chances of finding employment elsewhere.

References

Ashton,D.N., Maguire,M.J. and Garland,V. (1982), *Youth in the Labour Market*, Research Paper no.34, London, Department of Employment.

Bedeman,T. and Courtenay,G. (1982), *One in Three: The Second National Survey of Young People on YOP*, Research and Development Series no.13, Sheffield, Manpower Services Commission.

Bedeman,T. and Harvey,J. (1981), *Young People on YOP: A National Survey of Entrants to the Youth Opportunities Programme*, Research and Development Series no.3, London, Manpower Services Commission.

Bibby,J. (with Weston,P.B.) (1980), 'Sex differentials in maths enrolments; sudden death or gradual decline?', *Collaborative Research Newsletter*, no.7, pp.3-10, CES.

Blackburn,R. (1979), 'Repeated and deferred presentation for Highers', *Collaborative Research Newsletter*, no.5, pp.61-74, CES.

Blaug,M. (1970), 'Raising the school age: bribery v compulsion', *Higher Education Review*, vol.3, no.1, pp.53-58.

Burnhill,P.M. (1981), 'Key table 2: examinations and social class', *Collaborative Research Newsletter*, no.8, pp.55-57, CES.

Burnhill,P.M. (1983), *Destinations of Young People Leaving School*, Statistical Bulletin no.2/E1/1983, Edinburgh, Scottish Education Department.

Burnhill,P.M., Lamb,J.M. and Weston,P.B. (1982), 'The National School Leavers Survey (NSLS) 1981: a preliminary account', unpublished paper, CES.

Burnhill,P.M., Lamb,J.M. and Weston,P.B. (forthcoming), *Collaborative Research Dictionary and Questionnaires 1981*, CES.

Burnhill,P.M. and McPherson,A.F. (1983a), 'Careers and gender: the expectations of able Scottish school leavers in 1971 and 1981', in

S.Acker and D.Warren Piper (eds), *Women and the Higher Education System*, London, Society for Research in Higher Education.

Burnhill,P.M. and McPherson,A.F. (1983b), 'The Scottish School Leavers Survey since 1966: socio-political and statistical considerations', paper read to the Social Statistics Section of the Royal Statistical Society, January.

Central Policy Review Staff (1980), *Education, Training and Industrial Performance*, London, HMSO.

Committee on Higher Education (1963), *Higher Education*, London, HMSO (the Robbins Report).

Consultative Committee on the Curriculum (1983), *An Education for Life and Work, Final Report of the Project Planning Committee of the Education for the Industrial Society Project*, Glasgow, Jordanhill College.

Department of Education and Science (1963), *Day Release, The Report of a Committee set up by the Minister of Education*, London, HMSO (the Henniker-Heaton Report).

Department of Education and Science (1983), *Projections of School Leavers to 1990/1 with an Estimate for 1995/6*, Statistical Bulletin no.6/83, London, HMSO.

Department of Employment (1981), *A New Training Initiative: A Programme for Action*, London, HMSO, Cmnd 8455.

Dickson,C. (1979), 'The state of modern languages', *Collaborative Research Newsletter*, no.5, pp.3-22, CES.

Drever,E. *et al.* (1983), *A Response to 'A Framework for Decision'*, Stirling, Department of Education, University of Stirling (mimeo).

Forsyth,J.P. and Dockrell,W.B. (1979), *Curriculum and Assessment: The Response to Munn and Dunning, A Pre-publication Summary*, Edinburgh, SCRE.

Further Education Curriculum Review and Development Unit (FEU) (1979), *A Basis for Choice: Report of a Study Group on Post-16 Pre-Employment Courses*, London, FEU (the Mansell Report).

Gatherer,W. (1980), 'Educating the 16s to 19s: choices and costs', in *Choice, Compulsion and Cost*, Edinburgh, HMSO.

Gatherer,W. (1982), 'The education of the 16-18 group', *Scottish Educational Review*, vol.14, no.2, pp.93-100.

Gow,L. and McPherson,A.F. (eds) (1980), *Tell Them From Me: Scottish School Leavers Write About School and Life Afterwards*, Aberdeen, Aberdeen University Press.

Gray,J. and McPherson,A.F. (1978), 'Piecemeal exam reform: some lessons from Sixth Year Studies', *Collaborative Research Newsletter*, no.3, pp.70-82, CES.

Gray,J., McPherson,A.F. and Raffe,D. (1983), *Reconstructions of Secondary Education: Theory Myth and Practice since the War*, London, Routledge & Kegan Paul.

Greaves,K., Gostyn,P. and Bonsall,C. (1982), *Off the Job Training on YOP: A Summary of Research Findings in Work Experience Schemes 1979-82*, Research and Development Series no.12, Sheffield, Manpower Services Commission.

Hargreaves,D.H. (1982), *The Challenge for the Comprehensive School: Culture, Curriculum and Community*, London, Routledge & Kegan Paul.

House of Commons Committee on Scottish Affairs (1981), *Youth Unemployment and Training*, vol.1, HC 96-I, London, HMSO.

Hughes,J.M. (ed.) (1984), *The Best Years? Reflections of School Leavers in the 1980s*, Aberdeen, Aberdeen University Press.

Hunt,J. and Small,P. (1981), *Employing Young People: A Study of Employers' Attitudes, Policies and Practices*, Edinburgh, SCRE.

Hunter,L.C. and Mulvey,C. (1981), *Economics of Wages and Labour*, Second Edition, London, Macmillan.

Hurman,A. (1978), *Charter for Choice: A Study of Options Schemes*, Monographs in Curriculum Studies no.3, Slough, NFER.

Jolly,J.,Creigh,S. and Mingay,A. (1980), *Age as a Factor in Employment*, Research Paper no.11, London, Department of Employment.

Jordanhill Unified Vocational Preparation Group (1982), *UVP: It Works! If You Do*, Glasgow, Jordanhill College.

Keeves,J.P. (1972), *Educational Environment and Student Achievement*, Stockholm, Almquist and Wiksell.

Kelly,A. (1976), 'A study of the comparability of external examinations in different subjects', *Research in Education*, vol.16, pp.37-63.

Kelly,A. (1981), 'Choosing or channelling?' in A.Kelly (ed.), *The Missing Half*, Manchester, Manchester University Press.

Knasel,E.G., Watts,A.G. and Kidd,J.M. (1982), *The Benefit of Experience: Individual Guidance and Support within the Youth Opportunities Programme*, Research and Development Series no.5, London, Manpower Services Commission.

Labour Party (1982), *16-19: Learning for Life, A Labour Party Discussion Document*, London.

Lee,G. and Wrench,J. (1983), *Skill Seekers: Black Youth, Apprenticeships and Disadvantage*, Studies in Research no.1, Leicester, National Youth Bureau.

Lothian Region Education Department (1982), *The Implications of Falling Rolls in Secondary Schools, Report of a Departmental Working Party*, Edinburgh.

McIntyre,D. (ed.) (1978), *A Critique of the Munn and Dunning Reports*, Stirling Educational Monographs no.4, Stirling, Department of Education, University of Stirling.

Maclure,S. (1982), 'The educational consequences of Mr Norman Tebbit', *Oxford Review of Education*, vol.8, no.2, pp.103-120.

McPherson,A.F. and Neave,G.R. (1976), *The Scottish Sixth: A Sociological Evaluation of Sixth Year Studies and the Changing Relationship between School and University in Scotland*, Slough, NFER.

Main,B.G.M. (1983), 'School-leaver unemployment and the Youth Opportunities Programme in Scotland', Discussion Paper Series, Edinburgh, Department of Economics, University of Edinburgh.

Main,B.G.M. and Raffe,D. (1983a), 'Determinants of employment and unemployment among school leavers: evidence from the 1979 survey of Scottish school leavers', *Scottish Journal of Political Economy*, vol.30, no.1, pp.1-17.

Main,B.G.M. and Raffe,D. (1983b), 'The "transition from school to work" in 1980/81: a dynamic account', *British Educational Research Journal*, vol.9, no.1, pp.57-70.

Manpower Services Commission (MSC) (1977), *Young People and Work*, London, MSC (the Holland Report).

Manpower Services Commission (1978), *Young People and Work: Manpower Studies no. 19781*, London, HMSO.

Manpower Services Commission (1981a), *A New Training Initiative: A Consultative Document*, London, MSC.

Manpower Services Commission (1981b), *A New Training Initiative: An Agenda for Action*, London, MSC.

Manpower Services Commission (1982a), *Youth Task Group Report*, London, MSC.

Manpower Services Commission (1982b), *Review of the Fourth Year of Special Programmes*, London, MSC.

Markall,G. and Finn,D. (1981), *Young People and the Labour Market: A Case Study*, Manchester, William Temple Foundation.

Maxwell, J. (1969), *Sixteen Years On: A Follow-Up of the 1947 Scottish Survey*, London, University of London Press for SCRE.

Morton-Williams,R. and Finch,S. (1968), *Young School Leavers: Schools Council Enquiry 1*, London, HMSO.

Office of Population Censuses and Surveys (1980), *Classification of Occupations*, London, HMSO.

Pascoe,I. (1979), 'Deferred presentation for Highers: a follow-up', *Collaborative Research Newsletter*, no.6, pp.61-68, CES.

Pickard,W. (1983), 'Prosaic but precise', *Times Educational Supplement*

(Scotland), 6 May.

Pindyck,R.S. and Rubinfeld,D.L. (1976), *Econometric Models and Economic Forecasts*, New York, McGraw-Hill.

Raffe,D. (1983a), 'Some recent trends in youth unemployment in Scotland', *Scottish Educational Review*, vol.15, no.1, pp.16-27.

Raffe,D. (1983b), 'Education and unemployment: does YOP make a difference (and will YTS)?' in D.Gleeson (ed.), *Youth Training and the Search for Work*, London, Routledge & Kegan Paul.

Raffe,D. (1983c), 'Can there be an effective youth unemployment policy?' in R.Fiddy (ed.), *In Place of Work: Policy and Provision for the Young Unemployed*, Lewes, Falmer.

Raffe,D. (1984), 'Youth unemployment and the MSC: 1977-1983', in D. McCrone (ed.), *Scottish Government Yearbook 1984*, Edinburgh, Unit for the Study of Government in Scotland, University of Edinburgh.

Rutter,M., Maughan,B., Mortimore,P. and Ouston,J. with Smith,A. (1979), *Fifteen Thousand Hours: Secondary Schools and their Effects on Children*, London, Open Books.

Ryrie,A.C. (1981), *Routes and Results*, Sevenoaks, Hodder & Stoughton for SCRE.

Ryrie,A.C. (1983), *On Leaving School: A Study of Schooling, Guidance and Opportunity*, Sevenoaks, Hodder & Stoughton for SCRE.

Ryrie,A.C., Furst,A. and Lauder,M. (1979), *Choices and Chances: A Study of Pupils' Subject Choices and Future Career Intentions*, Sevenoaks, Hodder & Stoughton for SCRE.

Scottish Education Department (SED) (1947), *Secondary Education, A Report of the Advisory Council of Education in Scotland*, Edinburgh, HMSO, Cmnd 7005.

Scottish Education Department (1954), *Early School Leaving in Scotland*, Edinburgh, HMSO.

Scottish Education Department (1955a), *Junior Secondary Education*, Edinburgh, HMSO.

Scottish Education Department (1955b), *Early Leaving from Senior Secondary Courses*, Edinburgh, SED (Circular 312).

Scottish Education Department (1959), *Report of the Working Party on the Curriculum of the Senior Secondary School: Introduction of the Ordinary Grade of the Scottish Leaving Certificate*, Edinburgh, HMSO.

Scottish Education Department (1960), *The Post-Fourth Year Examination Structure in Scotland: A Report of a Special Committee of the Advisory Council on Education in Scotland*, Edinburgh, HMSO, Cmnd 1068.

Scottish Education Department (1963), *From School to Further Education*,

Edinburgh, HMSO (the Brunton Report).

Scottish Education Department (1965), *Reorganisation of Secondary Education on Comprehensive Lines*, Edinburgh, HMSO (Circular 600).

Scottish Education Department (1967), *The Organisation of Courses Leading to the Scottish Certificate of Education*, Curriculum Paper no.2, Edinburgh, HMSO (the Ruthven Report).

Scottish Education Department (1968), *Modern Studies for School Leavers: Suggestions for Courses Other Than Those Leading to the Scottish Certificate of Education*, Curriculum Paper no.3, Edinburgh, HMSO.

Scottish Education Department (1969), *Science for General Education*, Curriculum Paper no.7, Edinburgh, HMSO.

Scottish Education Department (1970), *Community Service and Scottish Secondary Schools*, Curriculum Paper no.8, Edinburgh, HMSO.

Scottish Education Department (1971), *Raising the School Leaving Age*, Edinburgh, SED (Circular 813).

Scottish Education Department (1972), *Technical Education in Secondary Schools*, Curriculum Paper no.10, Edinburgh, HMSO.

Scottish Education Department (1976a), *The Social Subjects in Secondary Schools*, Curriculum Paper no.15, Edinburgh, HMSO.

Scottish Education Department (1976b), *The Raising of the School Leaving Age in Scotland, A Report by HM Inspectors of Schools*, Edinburgh, HMSO.

Scottish Education Department (1976c), *The Education (Scotland) Act 1976: School Leaving Arrangements*, Edinburgh, SED (Circular 956).

Scottish Education Department (1977a), *Assessment for All, Report of the Committee to Review Assessment in the Third and Fourth Years of Secondary Education in Scotland*, Edinburgh, HMSO (the Dunning Report).

Scottish Education Department (1977b), *The Structure of the Curriculum in the Third and Fourth Years of the Scottish Secondary School*, Edinburgh, HMSO (the Munn Report).

Scottish Education Department (1979a), *Curriculum and Assessment in the Third and Fourth Years of Secondary Education in Scotland, A Feasibility Study*, Edinburgh, HMSO.

Scottish Education Department (1979b), *Curriculum and Assessment in the Third and Fourth Years of Secondary Education in Scotland: Proposals for Action*, Edinburgh, SED.

Scottish Education Department (1980a), *The Munn and Dunning Reports: The Government's Development Programme*, Edinburgh, SED.

Scottish Education Department (1980b), *Education (Scotland) Act 1980*, Edinburgh, SED (Circular 1058).

Scottish Education Department (1982a), *The Munn and Dunning Reports: Framework for Decision, A Consultative Paper on the Government's Proposals for Implementation*, Edinburgh, SED.

Scottish Education Department (1982b), *School Leaver Projections*, Statistical Bulletin no.8/E3/1982, Edinburgh, SED.

Scottish Education Department (1982c), *Learning and Teaching in Scottish Secondary Schools: The Contribution of Educational Technology, A Report by HM Inspectors of Schools*, Edinburgh, HMSO.

Scottish Education Department (1982d), *Education Authority Schools in the 1970s*, Statistical Bulletin no.3/A3/1982, Edinburgh, HMSO.

Scottish Education Department (1983a), *Teaching and Learning in the Senior Stages of the Scottish Secondary Schools, A Report by HM Inspectors of Schools*, Edinburgh, HMSO.

Scottish Education Department (1983b), *16-18s in Scotland: An Action Plan*, Edinburgh, SED.

Scottish Education Department (1983c), *The Munn and Dunning Reports: Implementation of the Government's Proposals*, Edinburgh, SED (Circular 1093).

Scottish Education Department and Scottish Examination Board (1982), *Full-time Education After S4, A Statistical Study*, Dalkeith, SED and SEB.

Scottish Examination Board (SEB) (1983), *Joint Working-Party Report on English at Foundation, General and Credit Levels*, Dalkeith, SEB.

Scottish Universities Council on Entrance (SUCE) (1981), *Report for 1980-81*, St.Andrews, SUCE.

SEDA course members, reported by Weston,P.B. (1981), 'Fifth-year conscripts and curriculum planning', *Collaborative Research Newsletter*, no.8, pp.9-14, CES.

Spencer,E. (1983), *Writing Matters across the Curriculum*, Sevenoaks, Hodder & Stoughton for SCRE.

Strathclyde Regional Council (1981), *A Strategy for Post-Compulsory Education and Training, A Report of the Officer/Member Group on Further Education*, Glasgow.

Stubbs,M. and Delamont,S. (1976), *Explorations in Classroom Observation*, Chichester, John Wiley and Sons.

Super,D. (1953), 'A theory of vocational development', *American Psychologist*, vol.8, pp.185-190.

Taylor,J. (1978), 'How vital is the sixth year?' *Collaborative Research Newsletter*, no.4, pp.17-25, CES.

Thomas,R. and Wetherall,D. (1974), *Looking Forward to Work*, London, HMSO.

Times Educational Supplement (1983), 'Marked for life' by J.Cross,

17 June.

Times Educational Supplement (Scotland) (1983), 'The view from below', 10 June.

Waller,W. (1965), *The Sociology of Teaching*, New York, Wiley.

Weir,D. and Nolan,F. (1977), *Glad To Be Out? (A Study of School Leavers)*, Edinburgh, SCRE.

Weston,P.B. (1977), *A Framework for the Curriculum: A Study of Secondary Schooling*, Monographs in Curriculum Studies no.2, Slough, NFER.

Weston,P.B. (1979), *Negotiating the Curriculum: A Study in Secondary Schooling*, Monographs in Curriculum Studies no.4, Slough, NFER.

Weston,P.B. (1982a), 'Routes through school: a case for collaborative research', *Scottish Educational Review*, vol.14, no.2, pp.128-135.

Weston,P.B. (1982b), 'Key table 3: staying on to fifth year', *Collaborative Research Newsletter*, no.9, pp.6-7, CES.

Wishart,D. (1980), 'Scotland's schools', *Social Trends*, no.10, pp.52-60.

Youthaid (1981), *Quality or Collapse? Report of the Youthaid Review of the Youth Opportunities Programme*, London.

Index

ability, 21-22,, 30-32, 47, 237; *see also* differentiation; difficulty; mixed-ability classes; selection
accounting, 37
Action Plan, 237; *see also* Scottish Education Department Publications: (1983b)
Advanced grade, 6
Advanced-level, *see* General Certificate of Education: Advanced-level
Advisory Council on Education, 1947, *see* Scottish Education Department Publications: (1947)
aesthetic studies, 42-46, 48-49
age-banding, *see* banding
agricultural science, 29
A-level, *see* General Certificate of Education: Advanced-level
Allan,D., viii
allowances for young people, *see* Youth Opportunities Programme: allowances; Youth Training Scheme: allowances
anatomy and physiology, 29
anatomy, physiology and health, 29
applied studies, *see* neo-Munn schema; science 'B' (applied studies)
apprenticeships, 9, 211, 227-228

"areas of activity", 27-29, 39; *see also* "modes of activity"; Scottish Education Department Publications: (1977b)
arithmetic, 29, 36, 37, 39, 40-43, 183
Armstrong,P., viii
Arrundale, J., vii, viii, 240
art, 29, 37-41
art and design, 29
Ashton, D.N., with Maguire, M.J. and Garland,V., 183-184, 189
assessment, 4-5, 30, 56, 165
Assessment for All, *see* Scottish Education Department Publications: (1977a)
attainment, 34, 60, 63, 65, 67, 71, 94, 220; and employment, 12, 174-193; *see also* Higher(s) and employment; O-grade(s) and employment
attitudes, leavers': to courses, 12, 23, 161-162; to examinations, 12, 20, 58-59, 77, 129, 133-135, 140-142, 146-148; to school, 1, 12, 19, 58-78, 104-122, 140-142, 214; to staying on, 12, 93, 104-122, 133-134, 140-142, 146-148; to YOP, 12, 74, 195-203, 215, 243

NTI, *see New Training Initiative*

Office of Population Censuses and Surveys (OPCS) Publication: (1980) *Classification of Occupations*, 97, 98

O-grade(s), 2-4, 6, 16, 18-20, 31, 36, 39-41, 48, 50-51, 59-60, 62, 64, 66-67, 69, 85, 94-95, 100, 102, 109, 111, 119, 123-144, 173, 215, 219, 224, 229, 233, 236-238; and employment, 3, 55, 113, 116-118, 141, 174-193, 196, 206-209, 221

O-level, *see* General Certificate of Education: Ordinary-level

OPCS, *see* Office of Population Censuses and Surveys

Ordinary-grade, *see* O-grade(s)

Ouston, J., *see* Rutter, M., *et al.*

outdoor education, 29

over-presentation, 3, 47, 54-55, 97, 220-221

Oxford Certificate of Educational Achievement, 56

P1, P2,...P7, 238, *see also* primary schooling

parents, *see* family, influence of

Pascoe, I., 150

pass rates, 19, 36, 95, 131-132, 138-141, 154-159, 176

personal characteristics, and employment, 180-185

physical activity and leisure, 28; *see also* physical education

physical education, 29, 36-39, 43-49; *see also* physical activity and leisure

physics, 29, 31, 37, 39-40, 61-62

Pickard, W., 126

Pindyke, R.S. with Rubinfeld, D.L., 192

policy, 10, 12, 127-128, 144-145, 160, 188, 212, 216, 218-220, 224, 226, 230

post-compulsory schooling, 5-10, 12-13, 79-103, 123-143, 144-173, 180, 187-189, 222-230, 241; *see also* staying on

post-fourth-year schooling, *see* post-compulsory schooling

post-school destinations, 79-103, 174-193, 194-213, 233

preliminary examinations, 40, 48-51, 59, 134-135, 137, 142, 169, 238

prelims, *see* preliminary examinations

presentation rates, 3-4, 18, 36, 40-41, 48-51, 84, 134-137

primary schooling, 16, 91, 102

pupils' attitudes, *see* attitudes, leavers'

QSL, *see* qualified school leaver returns

qualifications, 145-148, 154-163; *see also* certification; examinations

qualified school leaver returns, 232

questionnaire, *see* Scottish School Leavers Surveys: 81 survey: questionnaire

Raab, C.D., viii

Raffe, D., 241; (1983a), 7, 184; (1983b), 205-206; (1983c), 211; (1984), 8, 198; with Gray, J. and McPherson, A.F., 3, 11, 23, 34, 90, 95, 104, 123-124, 148, 150, 164, 187, 216, 218-219; with Main, B.G.M., (1983a), 206, 243; (1983b), 205, 242

raising of the school-leaving age (RSLA), 3-4, 16, 18, 85, 91, 100, 102, 118-120, 127, 222, 238

Raising the School Leaving Age, *see* Scottish Education Department Publications: (1971)

The Raising of the School Leaving Age in Scotland, *see* Scottish Education Department Publications: (1976b)

Registrar-General, 97-98

religious and moral studies, 28-29, 43,